Byron

by

Michael Corrigan

This book is a work of fiction. Any resemblance to actual events or persons, living or dead, is entirely coincidental.

"Byron," by Michael Corrigan. ISBN 1-58939-763-0.

Published 2005 by Virtualbookworm.com Publishing Inc., P.O. Box 9949, College Station, TX 77842, US. ©2005, Michael Corrigan. All rights reserved. No part of this publication may be reproduced, stored in a retrieval system, or transmitted in any form or by any means, electronic, mechanical, recording or otherwise, without the prior written permission of Michael Corrigan.

Manufactured in the United States of America.

THE SNAKE

THE THREE INDIANS SAT ON THE RIVERBANK, drinking. The Snake River seemed like a painting of a copper-green river, but they knew about the deadly tides surging under the flat water. The moon was full and the horseshoe-shaped gravel road curving into the Fort Hall Reservation shone chalky in the moonlight. Horses and buffalo grazed or stood silently out on the prairie cut by the single road.

"Good wine," Edmo said.

"Excellent wine," said Hernandez. The third Indian named Hayball was silent, watching the dark swollen waters. They could hear insects in the golden grass and nesting birds. Occasionally, a distant coyote howled. They didn't like the sound of the coyote at night since it conjured Bannock Shoshone legends about death.

"No Water Babies, tonight," Hayball said. "They quiet."

"That's an old story," Edmo said. "Just no good."

"They eat you," Hayball said. "Then kill people and die theyselves."

"I believe in Water Babies," said Hernandez. "I seen 'em."

"Seen 'em? When?"

"Never mind when. I seen 'em. Long time ago, Injuns leave sick babies in the river to die. They live under the water, you go to drink—bam! You meal for Water Baby. They take your shape. You remember Teton? Water Baby done got him."

"I seen Teton yesterday," Edmo said.

The three men were squat and sedentary, dressed in jeans and Levi jackets. They passed the bottle back and forth, the river unusually quiet except for a low hissing. Few Indians came to the river bottoms at night, and not just because of the quicksand or the hidden current. Old people took the legends seriously, and even

1

young braves avoided the Snake River after dark.

"Water Babies won't bother us," Hayball said. "They only eat white people."

"They eat Injuns too," Hernandez insisted.

"We got bad white people invading again," said Edmo. "Dumping all their poison…as if the reservation isn't polluted enough with whites."

They continued to drink and talk about the avenging Indian spirits of a former century, how they roamed the land disguised in victim's bodies, killing fresh whites until they died themselves—withered mummies.

"Mummies? That's a white people story! A Tybo legend," Edmo argued.

"That's because they get old," Hayball said. "Old as Water Baby."

They sat, listening to the warm breathing darkness all around them. They knew the Indian police would not arrest them, but if anything happened, no one would come until morning. A plaque marking the original Fort Hall was a short distance away.

"Listen."

It was Edmo. There was a slight breeze through the meadow grass, and the sound of the river.

"I don't hear nothin'."

"A coyote?" said Hernandez.

They saw a white mist over the water, and their voices echoed down the river that flowed dark and swift, swirling beneath the undercut banks. They saw no reflections, even in the moonlight. Edmo pointed. "Look."

They saw something gleaming on the waters, floating with the current. Hernandez reached as it drifted in, bobbing and turning.

"It's a Water Baby," Hayball said.

"It's a can of somethin'," said Edmo. Hernandez took a silver canister out of the water. It was an urn for human ashes. "Hell," Edmo said. "White people throwing ashes in our river."

Hayball backed away. "Bad luck. Throw it back," he said.

"It's empty," Hernandez said, holding the urn. He laughed. "Maybe Water Babies ate the ashes, too."

"Careful, Injun," said Edmo.

They knew many drunks and hunters had slipped on the undercut banks and fell into the treacherous river. Even a good swimmer could be swept away and sucked under. Hernandez tossed the light-colored urn into the river, but he lost his balance and splashed into the dark water. Edmo and Hayball watched but Hernandez was gone in an instant, the current swiftly moving along the bank.

"Edmo, we got to git him!"

"Go ahead. *You* jump in."

"Where?"

"Anywhere."

The river flowed past them. "It's too late."

A coyote came up behind them and howled once, the sound tearing through them. They turned and saw the reflection of acid-green eyes and then an unusually large coyote shape approaching them.

The two men ran crashing into the thick brush, the loud echoing howl carried on the warm moist air, vibrant with the sound of insects and the rushing river itself. They ran into an open meadow past a herd of buffalo grazing nearby. Later, the Tribal police would find them walking dazed on the road at sun-up, and they would hear the story of another drowning. The body would float to the surface eventually.

A two-lane highway ran outside the Fort Hall Café; across the road was a grass-grown vacant lot. Inside, Teton sat at an orange counter drinking coffee and reading the police report. At a corner table, white construction workers ate breakfast. Known as the Game Warden, Teton was a big man and might have played Chief Bromden in *Cuckoo's Nest*. The drowning incident was common; despite the ban on alcohol, it had happened many times. Still, his large brown face expressed a timeless sorrow. Too often he felt like Priam in *The Iliad*, watching the destruction of his people.

BYRON

IT WAS A GOOD MORNING for Byron Duffy to resign.

When he returned from the meeting the previous evening at the English Department chairman's house, it seemed evident that budget cuts would eliminate the adjunct faculty, and Byron felt no need to fight it. David Sterling had informed him that graduate assistants were replacing all the MA teachers and even a few tenured faculty faced the ax. Perhaps since terrorist attacks, it was just a sign of the times. Sterling, impeccably dressed, was middle-aged but shockingly handsome; whenever Sterling spoke in his lilting voice, Byron often looked around for a director, a camera and crew, reflectors, and a video assist. Sterling's polished face had the glow of a soap actor. Byron had always considered himself the marginal "artist" type and even attended many artistic retreats to prove it, but here, in Idaho, he seemed to be the most normal of the faculty: Rex, plump with red hair resembled a well fed missionary but was extremely radical; Chan, a short muscular weight lifter turned English teacher and writer savagely played Beethoven on the piano and had a reputation for insulting students; Shanahan who sat alone, drinking, occasionally smiled at guests in an unnerving way, and of course, the ultimate enigma, Maria Jones—pretty and intelligent—always suggested a hidden agenda.

"Get your PhD, Byron," Sterling had said, slightly scolding. "That way, you could qualify for tenure. Eventually, I want to upgrade and build a great English Department on the prairie—with doctorates, of course."

By not fighting the system, Byron would get an excellent recommendation somewhere else. At thirty-five, with no desire to go to school and no immediate work in education, Byron had limited choices. The Idaho teaching job had been a surprise. He sat stalled in LA traffic one afternoon when the cell phone rang and he heard Sterling's sweet resonant voice offering him a job. Cars were stopped dead, radios and CD players competed, smog covered the sky, and the main artery of freeway ran across areas of cinder-block offices, buildings surrounded by barbed wire, fast food restaurants, abandoned warehouses with broken windows, neon motels and neighborhoods where gangs shot it out every night. A police helicopter hovered overhead. Byron had wondered for a brief moment if he wanted to give up his shot at writing screenplays for big money, and then he decided: Idaho would be a welcome break. How Sterling even knew his name came through Byron's chance meeting with a hitchhiking poet.

Leaving LA had not been easy.

"You're crazy," Byron's agent shouted over the phone. Ashley Roland was a Canadian working in Los Angeles. "You're leaving Los Angeles for some railroad town in Idaho? I hear the state is populated by inbred cracker racists."

"That's an exaggeration, and nothing's happening, here," Byron said, "and it's a *job*, Ashley."

"A job? So work a fast food joint. Wear a chicken suit. LA is where it's happening."

Byron did feel some regret. There were things one could miss: film premieres, the theatre, Malibu, the beach, and walking through Griffith Park.

"Let's meet at the Shamrock Bar. We need to talk."

"Okay."

The Shamrock bar had an Irish name though Iranians had bought the tavern and soon, Iranian music would replace live American folk and blues songs. One of the performers was a blond-haired, blue-eyed columnist named Michael Wells who was an accomplished guitarist. Occasionally Byron sat in on harmonica as they ran through Paul Simon, Jimmy Reed and Bob Dylan. Byron entered the smoky bar as Michael Wells ended a set, a love song about infidelity and lovers going to hell. Wells pointed at him.

"Byron! Let's go," he said.

"Go where?"

"I just found out Dylan is playing at a hotel ballroom in Burbank." He named the hotel. "Get your guitar. Let's sit in."

"I thought you didn't like Dylan."

"He can't sing for shit but he's a great writer," Wells said, glaring at him. He lit a cigarette. "I might get a good article out of jamming with Dylan. You want a drink?"

"Not now."

"Why not?" He puffed on the cigarette and glanced at young women sitting at the bar. "Boy, there's some fine underage pussy in this joint."

"Then maybe we should stick around. I'm supposed to meet Ashley."

"Forget Hollywood. For a serious artist, the film industry is anemic."

"Who said I was a serious artist? I'm leaving."

"Leaving where?"

"LA," Byron said, but Michael Wells didn't hear him as the jukebox kicked in.

"Listen," Wells said. "You need to work on your guitar technique. Loosen those fingers. Maybe use your little finger to anchor that right hand of yours."

"I'll keep that in mind." Byron glanced around the bar. "Where's Melanie?"

"She's divorcing me," he said.

"Good."

"It is good. I have nothing left but art, music, and staying drunk as possible. We live in LA."

"If you hate LA, why don't you leave?"

"The action is here," Wells told him.

They drank, Wells gulping a shot of whiskey, Byron nursing a 7 Up. Another folk singer got up on the stage. He was bearded and fat, and played a loud twelve-string.

"What a big sound," Wells said, "and it makes him even more boring. Let's go."

"I'm waiting for Ashley."

"You need another agent."

"She's also a friend. Maybe she can sell a screenplay."

"You're not a writer, Byron."

"And you are?"

"Of course. That's how I pay the rent. I got a novel coming out."

"You call that pretentious essay on art a novel?"

"Absolutely."

"What do you know about art?"

Wells suddenly laughed. "Everything," he said. "Get your guitar."

"Around you, I'm not a guitarist."

For a moment, Wells seemed genuinely appreciative. "Sure you are. Let's go."

"Maybe later."

It was then that Byron saw Ashley Roland enter. She was in her late twenties, sensuous and plump with dark eyes and hair and a pleasant, pretty face. Her 'O's' carried the sound of Canada. She sat down and ordered a beer. Michael Wells drank another shot.

"Ms. Roland. I got a screenplay you should check out."

"Sure." She turned to Byron. "Don't leave. You belong here."

"I don't think so."

"He belongs with me," Michael Wells said. "We're going to check out Dylan. He's playing in town—an open jam session."

Ashley shrugged. "So many older people like him. I mean, Dylan's okay, but he can't sing."

"Oh yes he can," Wells insisted. "You have to listen close, but he gets inside a song, like Sinatra."

"Really? You're an expert critic?"

"What I do for a living." Michael Wells put away his guitar. "Byron, you comin' or not?"

"No," Byron said.

"Okay then, I'm off."

Byron spoke up: "I'm pulling out, Michael. Leaving LA."

"You call me tomorrow, Byron. I got a short story I want you to hear."

Wells got up and left the bar. Ashley leaned back, listening to the plaintive resonant twelve-string. The singer had a rich voice.

"What do you see in that loud mouth, Wells?"

"I don't know. I like him. He is smart."

Ashley met his eyes and took one of his hands.

"I know LA is a rat race, but you're good and it's only a matter of time before you make some serious money. Why live in some small town in total obscurity?"

"I don't need money and fame to exist. I'm sick of gang shoot-outs, smog, traffic, trash, crime, the freeways, and shallow people. My last girlfriend dumped me. Complained I was too old." Ashley nodded to herself and then he added, "I will miss you, however."

"I'll miss you. You might be too old for LA," she said, bluntly. "My other clients are kids."

They listened to the music and split a pitcher of beer, talking together; later, Byron got up to leave. Outside the tavern, Ashley looked down the wide boulevard at the moving cars. A theatre on the corner showed old films.

"I was going to ask you a favor."

"What's that?"

"Marry me. I'm not legal."

"Do I get laid in the bargain?"

"Of course not," Ashley said. "We're just friends."

Byron hesitated. Then he gently kissed her.

"I have to go, friend."

But before he went home, he drove to Burbank and found the hotel. Inside, a bartender saw him and shook his head. "If you're here for that Dylan guy and his friends, they stopped coming. Too many freaks hanging around."

"Really? I can imagine."

Byron drove home. On his answering machine, he heard Wells explaining what had happened. "Dylan got spooked and left. I knew I shoulda gone earlier. Damn! Hey, call me, tomorrow. Leave a message."

A week later, Byron stopped in Baker to get gas. It was hot and the light was blinding on the highway and desert. He remembered Ashley's last call. She was leaving LA and going to London. He had left a note for Michael Wells, who recorded a message on his answering machine moments before Byron

8

departed Los Angeles.

"Byron, why the hell didn't you tell me earlier? I *love* road trips! But now I got a deadline. You keep in touch!"

A day later, a smoking factory shot flames near the highway when Byron pulled into Pocatello after sunset. Had he left one hell for another?

And now, his university job had ended. Once again, Byron drifted in a world of random events. In his cubicle, Byron remembered old voices and wondered what had happened to Ashley and Michael Wells. His thoughts were interrupted when he heard a rap on the door and saw Becky, an attractive sophomore with blonde frizzy hair and a slight drawl; a black panther tattoo crawled up her calf. She had an edge in class, and wrote an impressive paper comparing Jacobean tragedies to horror films. Under the initials B.J., she had circulated a chapbook of poems titled: *Behind the Barn: Two Dollar Blowjobs.*

"What can I do for you, Becky? What's the problem?"

"My boyfriend, Ted Bear. He's the problem."

"I don't write a love lorn column."

"It's not just about romance," Becky said, sitting down. "Have you heard of the Posse?"

"Of course. The Aryan Nation people. White Supremacists. Idaho takes a bad rap because of those people. They were driven out of Sandpoint."

"Maybe so. They took over Meridell Park where Ted lived with some burned-out hippies. Something is happening to him, and it scares me."

"Something is *always* happening to Ted," Byron said.

"This is different. Listen!"

Byron listened.

Becky spoke of Ted's anger at the Posse takeover of what had been a commune, and how he was roaming late at light, like a self-styled commando, shooting high-speed film and coming home at dawn. She had found a gun in his drawer, and Ted was ignoring his theatre vocation. Byron remembered Ted's college Hamlet, and was impressed. He had also heard of Ted's exploits on the river, sailing down the middle fork of the Salmon on a raft, Ted wearing nothing but street clothes and no life jacket. Byron recalled Ted's face, with the wispy thinning hair and penetrating eyes as he carried himself wrapped in a kind of gothic melodrama.

"What am I supposed to do about it?"

"Talk to him. I know you admire the civil rights activists."

"That was another lost decade," said Byron, looking into Becky's face. "They're all dead or sell real estate." After a pause, he said: "I don't want to confront racists with guns."

He could see Becky's disappointment. She had lost her normal sarcasm, and seemed already defeated.

"You're an artist—like Ted."

"Please."

"I don't know who else to talk to. I'm afraid something terrible will happen. Ted's a romantic. He likes to take his life in his hands. He thinks of himself as a kind of bad-ass revolutionary, even joined Citizens for Intelligent Anarchy."

"I know the breed," sighed Byron. "I *do* like the Che Guevera tee-shirt."

Byron did know the breed. Ted's legend had followed him to Idaho State University from the campus of Brigham Young where students told stories of Ted walking across the manicured campus, cigarette in mouth, eyes blazing with a new theory about the Theatre of Cruelty. Had he not impregnated the daughter of the school President? Perhaps most significant, Ted had demanded the Mormon Church excommunicate him, since he was an Existentialist anyway and doomed to wander in outer darkness. The church had refused his demand until the President's daughter got her abortion. There were stories of Ted breaking into the women's dorm to find the girl and say good-bye, then fleeing campus police. One version had Ted swimming a raging river in the winter to escape the law.

Byron leaned back in his chair, distracted by another reality.

"I'd like to help you, Becky, but right now, I got to find a job. We're all being let go."

They sat in the small, close office. Byron heard Maria Jones stirring in her chair next door. He finally leaned close to Becky who was nervously rocking, pumping one leg.

"Ted's talented, but he really needs to get out of this place."

"Thanks," Becky said. "Thanks a lot."

She left, carrying her books. Byron gazed at some student

papers with little enthusiasm to read or grade them. In the doorway he saw Maria's pleasant face, framed with straight brown hair.

"How does lunch sound?" she said.

"I'm getting fired. You're buying?"

"I'm buying."

"Then I'm having."

Maria always wore conservative suits, and her eyes lingered on him for a moment. They walked to Buddy's Pizza. Shanahan, an English professor, stared at the quad and bare trees.

"Those trees look so orderly," he said. "But it might be an illusion. Even a lie."

Shanahan had a small pinched face beneath short, bristly white hair.

"Is that right, Shanahan? Join us for lunch?"

"Oh no." The thin older teacher smiled and walked away, grinning at some secret joke. Maria and Byron walked on, the day bright but cold.

"He seems a bit strange, lately."

"I overheard your conversation with Becky," said Maria. "It's none of my business, but I'm curious to know what is happening with her. She hangs out with some marginal people."

"Define marginal."

"People who wear tattoos, ride motorcycles drunk, rape twelve year olds."

"Tattoos are in. Her boyfriend's a filmmaker. She's a good student," Byron said.

They sat in Buddy's pizza joint, filled with posters of half naked women and celebrated smiling football players advertising beer. Byron found a certain comfort in the fact the place never changed, and seemed to have the inevitable docile clientele, depending on the time of day. The bartender was a heavy-set man named Duncan, a promising football player in college until he flunked out. Right now, he was addressing Edmo, his favorite Indian.

"How ya doin', chief?"

"Not so good. Hernandez drowned in the Snake last August and they haven't found the body yet." Edmo stared at the surface of the bar.

"That's a tough one," Duncan said. "Beer? Glass—or maybe a pitcher?"

"Maybe a glass," Edmo said.

Duncan slid a full glass toward Edmo's big hand.

"That might light you up, Chief."

Edmo's dark eyes rested on Duncan's round soft body. "Hernandez be walkin' soon."

"Sounds scary," said Duncan.

At the table, Byron had a question. "Maria? Are you getting sacked?"

"No."

"Why not?"

"I don't know." She hesitated. "Not to pry into Becky's affairs, but I am always surprised when such students single out a teacher. Why you?"

"I guess I look like a burned-out hippy, myself." Byron smiled at Maria, struggling with a pastrami sandwich. "I was a writer for a while. Spent time in LA. You're not with the FBI, are you?"

Maria almost choked.

"Of course not." She laughed quietly. "Why would you think that? Am I asking too many questions?"

"No," Byron said. He noticed Maria studying him. "What's wrong?"

"You and Judson McGee have amassed quite a reputation as rogues."

"Says who?"

"Says everyone. I heard about Suzi, that twenty-year-old."

"That was last summer. Who told you about her?"

"I hear things."

"It's old news. Who gives a shit?"

He looked around the restaurant, filled with the lunch crowd. Two men were discussing bird dogs. "I made a big mistake and got involved with an attractive younger woman who dumped me, as I knew she would from experience. As for Judson, he saw his daughter off and doesn't know about the department bloodletting. I don't see myself getting a PhD, but I don't know if I can go back to LA or San Francisco, either. I hate being in limbo."

Maria had a way of observing him that made Byron a little

uncomfortable. She wiped her mouth and smiled, revealing perfect white teeth.

"I got a nice little house on the hill overlooking the town," she said. "Let's talk. I'd like to get to know you better, Mr. Duffy."

"How is it they're not firing you?"

"I have a two year contract."

"I thought we *all* had two year contracts with an option for a rehire."

"Who knows?"

A wrestling match was on television but no one watched. Voices echoed off the tile floor. Byron finished his meatball sandwich and stood up.

"Too bad all the latter day hippies got chased from Meridell Park. I could use a nubile hippy girl."

It was meant to be a joke but Maria frowned. "You're too old for hippy girls."

"Ain't that the truth?" said Byron. He knew there came a day for all men when the old smile and masculine charm didn't work and the women looked past or through them. "Thanks for lunch."

"Say hello to Judson," said Maria. "Let me know what happens with Mr. Bear. He is a talented young man, but a little crazy."

"Who isn't a little crazy?" He smiled. "I'll call you," Byron said.

Byron left Buddy's. He walked to his house, but felt too restless to read or take a nap. Judson had never learned to keep their place neat. He had started a novel, and the first page sat on the cluttered desk, buried with other papers. Byron was anxious for a real spring. The Idaho winter always seemed to hang on too long and Byron didn't ski.

———————

"What is the significance of the scene when Isaac has a chance to shoot the bear and doesn't? Midge?"

Midge stared at the thick anthology; her eyes seemed to empty. Byron continued.

"Why doesn't Sam Fathers shoot this bear they have named, for that matter? They've been hunting Old Ben for a lifetime. Joe?"

Byron looked around the class. For a moment, he felt as though he were addressing an oil painting. "That's not a rhetorical question," he said. "Let me refresh you about the scene. The young Isaac and Sam fathers, the half Indian, half black hunting guide and his mentor, come upon the legendary bear. A tiny dog called a fyce charges him. The boy catches the little pinwheeling dog and lands at the feet of the bear, close enough to see a tick on its leg. He doesn't shoot the animal they've been hunting every season. Sam, the son of a black slave and an Indian king, doesn't shoot either. Why?"

A young man in the back, with a round face and crew cut, finally lifted his hand.

"Who knows? Why is Faulkner so difficult? Man, all this…this *writing*. You know, cut to the chase."

"But he finally does cut to a very *big* chase. You think he writes too much?"

"Yeah. Jumps all over the place. Too many words."

"Originally, *The Bear* was a short story that Faulkner expanded. That one had *short* sentences, Jared."

"Maybe we should read it, instead."

"Maybe you could learn from Faulkner's use of active verbs and powerful nouns. Don't you want a challenge? Part four is difficult when he discusses slavery, but the hunting story is clear."

"To you, maybe."

Byron had always loved teaching the great American novelists and poets, but over a two year period, with student evaluations growing more hostile, Byron had felt a difference in his classes.

"Let me ask another question. When he talks to McCaslin, and his cousin asks him why he didn't shoot, Isaac can't answer. Maybe it's a question of freedom?" He looked around the class. "Anyone?"

The class remained silent.

"McCaslin then reads from Keats's 'Ode on a Grecian Urn'. He explains how the poem shows what the heart accepts as beauty becomes the truth. Love of justice. Love of liberty. Why does he then say that the land is cursed? Anyone?"

Outside the window, the sky was gray and overcast. Cindy, a heavy set young woman, raised her hand. "Is this gonna be on the test?"

"I will ask you questions about *The Bear*, yes, of course." He turned to Shack, his one black student. "Shack, why does McCaslin say America is cursed?"

Shack, wearing a comb in his thick hair, shrugged his large shoulders. "Got me, Dog. I don't know."

The class tittered. Byron pressed on.

"Slavery," he said. "McCaslin ties the bear's freedom to the tragedy of slavery. *The Bear* is not just a hunting story, but like all great literature, it is about something else, in this case—I believe, anyway—the stain and horror of American slavery."

Slouching in his chair, Shack nodded. "Okay. That's cool. Why doesn't he just write a story about slavery?"

"Good point. Faulkner wanted to discuss the loss of the wilderness personified by the old bear making his last stand, but he had confront the tragedy of slavery, as well. The land is cursed. The bear dies. The forest dies. Isaac gives up his southern birthright which turns out to be bankrupt, anyway."

"Why not just write an article for the newspaper?"

"Class, it's drama! Faulkner didn't want to write an essay." Byron looked intensely at the class. "Well? Is America cursed by slavery?"

No one answered. Finally, Shack said, "We just need to get on with it."

"And win more football games," added Jared. The class laughed again.

Byron had expected the usual complaints: Faulkner was always too difficult, Hemingway too simple, Fitzgerald too romantic, and Henry James was just a quaint old bore. What did his people do for a living besides sit in museums sipping tea? Did his male and female characters even *have* sex organs? Lately, Byron felt something more alarming than sophomore complaints.

"Did anyone love Faulkner's use of language? The way he evokes that wilderness and the wild men who hunt it?" The silence continued. "Are there *any* questions?"

"Why does he write those long sentences, some without

punctuation? If I do that, you'll flunk me."

"Right, Cissy. Good point. In Faulkner's case, it was a sense of rage, getting all that horror of slavery into one long sentence."

For a moment, Byron remembered Ted arguing in class that even Shakespeare was a white Euro-centric imperialist. Byron closed his eyes, feeling a sudden unexplained panic.

"Okay, class, for today's journal, write about the shoot-out at the Capitol. We'll finish *The Bear* tomorrow."

The class began writing. Jared raised his hand. "Dude? What shoot-out?"

For the third time, the class laughed.

"This past weekend, an angry congressman sneaked a gun into the senate and shot a rival dead. Then he was gunned down by Washington police. It's been on the news, Jared," Byron said. "A *lot*. Headlines, too."

"No kidding?"

Byron watched them write, fondly remembering Ted quoting Antonin Artaud's famous line, "All writing is pig shit." Byron preferred the mad Artaud's quote to this apathy. These students had been raised on fast moving music videos with rapid fire editing, so slow moving black and white films, even classics, were like dinosaurs: dead and archaic. Had classic books suffered the same fate?

Outside, he was stopped by Soumya, a dark-eyed, black-haired student who rarely spoke in class but wrote strong papers. She wore a short skirt even with the cold.

"I love *The Bear*," she said with a slight British flavor to her speech. "True, part four is difficult, but so what? Those people don't know anything but football."

"Glad you appreciated it."

"In India, we appreciate great literature."

He smiled at Soumya and noticed she returned his stare. It was a knowing look he recognized: sensuous and vulnerable. For a moment, he imagined them in bed, touching her firm small breasts, thinking to himself, *not with students. It's unethical.*

"The short novel is really about racism," Byron said.

Soumya nodded. "Yes, I got that. I really like your class."

"Thank you."

After an awkward pause, he said, "I better get going."

"Oh. Mr. Duffy?

"Yes?"

"Do you like Cricket?"

"Not really. Why would I? I'm a Yank."

"A group of Indian students are watching a cricket tournament, tonight, India against Pakistan. I hope we destroy them."

"I hear your two countries have some problems."

"The Pakis are pigs," Soumya said. "Well, come join us if you want an education in Cricket."

"I will." Byron gave Soumya slight wave and walked away.

Later that the evening, Byron took a call from Shanahan. The man's voice sounded hollow, barely audible.

"I have a lot of Negroes in my Milton class," he said. "I thought I would tell you."

"I don't understand. You have blacks taking Milton? And that means what?"

There was a pause on the other end.

"It means *you* people were right all along."

"*You* people?"

"Have you ever heard of the Wrecking Crew?"

"No. Who are they?"

"You'll find out. Good bye."

Byron heard the sudden click. He put down the receiver. The hollow sound of Shanahan's voice disturbed him. When the phone rang again, it was Becky calling from the Owl Club Bar near Meridell Park.

"What's up?"

"Ted's about to take on some Posse guys. Please come out here. I'm scared!"

"Call the police, Becky."

"They won't come out. They're afraid, too!"

Becky hung up. Byron had heard loud shouting in the background and country music played on the jukebox. Byron paced in the house for a moment, then called the police.

"We don't go out unless something happens, sir."

"I see," said Byron. "I suspect something *will* happen, officer."

"When a crime's been committed, call us."

Byron left for the Owl Club, a short drive south of town. It seemed absurd to Byron that he attempted this, knowing that anyone in the bar could attack him, or that he might find himself drawn into a fight not his. Perhaps it was the attitude of the police that drove him out to the redneck bar, formerly a place for poetry readings and folk music. Meridell Park sat in a grove of cottonwood trees, against a landscape of foothills. The roads were slick, and his car slid across the two-lane highway. A number of pick-ups were parked in front of the bar and even two motorcycles despite cold weather. Across from the bar was a new prison, gray and plain. A wooden owl perched on the roof of the tavern.

Byron parked his car and walked into the Owl. It was loud with voices, the smoke thick. He didn't hear the jukebox, nor did he see Becky. The bar was full of skinhead bikers and men wearing down jackets, baseball caps and heavy boots. There were a few ranch hands, and two men shot pool. The bartender was a heavy man with an old fashioned mustache. It took some time for Byron to adjust to the bar. Then Becky grabbed him, pulling him toward a corner where Ted Bear, wearing a leather vest, jeans and a broad-brimmed hat, sat on the jukebox; he had pulled the plug. Ted projected in a stage voice:

"I'm a hippy from that former commune up the road. My father was a Jew, my mother part black, and I will beat into whining anyone who denies one syllable of what I am saying."

"Get off the jukebox, asshole," a skinhead said, reaching for Ted who pushed the man back.

The tattooed biker's bald scalp gleamed in the light from the overhead lamp. Byron slipped in between the two men and turning, seized Ted by the throat.

"You owe me money, buddy. Outside!"

"Beat his ass," someone else said, plugging in the jukebox that drowned out all further conversation with screaming heavy metal guitar.

"Unhand me," shouted Ted, but Byron and Becky pulled him toward the door. Ted stopped, and Byron felt his strong grip. "English teacher, I'll bust you one!"

"Let's talk outside. Move!"

18

They stepped outside. Becky was angry and Ted glared at them, quick and light on his feet. A few men had followed them outside, their faces passive and dead. They watched in the cold as music came from inside the Owl. One of the men had a protruding chipped tooth.

"This is none of your business," said Ted. "They're going to plow my house under, tomorrow. You wanna join the fight, great. Otherwise, back off!"

"I *asked* him out here," argued Becky.

"For what? I can take care of myself!"

Ted walked some distance from the bar, then glanced up the dark road toward a yellow house on the hill, visible in the moonlight. He turned back to them as the sheriff's car pulled up, stopping abruptly. The sheriff got out; he was a large man with pale blue eyes, short blond hair, stocky build, his face appearing bloodless in the electric bar light. For an odd moment, Byron wondered if the sheriff came from central casting for an old film about rednecks and crackers.

"We got a problem, folks?"

"I was just taking these two students of mine to breakfast at Poppa Paul's," said Byron.

The sheriff observed Ted while addressing Byron. "You're a teacher?"

"I think so. Yes."

"My name's Sheriff Dale. A pleasure. I own the bar and all this land." He grinned at Ted. "Mr. Bear? I suggest you move on. The vibes ain't no good, here, understand?"

Ted approached the sheriff, but Becky stopped him. For a brief instance, Byron saw the predatory look in the sheriff's eyes.

"Let's go," Becky said.

"Let's meet at the all night truck stop," suggested Byron.

Ted walked toward Becky's car, slamming the door. Becky followed him, and they drove off. One of the men standing by the door spat. The sheriff shook his head and grinned at Byron.

"What do you teach?"

"English."

"I never was much good at English." He turned to his assistant. "I think we best be gone."

Sheriff Dale drove off. Byron stood on the cold road, listening to the country music inside the bar. Edmo stood outside the bar but didn't make eye contact. The house up the hill seemed deserted, the windows dark. Byron saw newly constructed barracks behind barbed wire, and a man in military fatigues stared at him with an empty gaze, passive yet somehow threatening. Then he turned to Edmo. "You're welcome here," he said. "I know the government took your land. We'll take it back."

"That's real good to hear," Edmo said.

The crowd dispersed as Byron walked to his car and drove to the all night truck stop. He was surprised to find them still inside. Ted was very happy, speaking with animation, as though he had somehow proved something. Becky sat next to him, sullen, still angry that Ted had risked getting beaten. Byron was curious.

"The sheriff seems to know you."

"He was the landlord at Meridell Park."

Ted began talking about what the park had been, though never really a park but rather a few houses and shacks in a grove of old cottonwoods that had fostered a quaint, out-of-date colony of artists and free thinkers. None of them had produced any art. There was a sauna, and nudity was the rule. No music past 1969 was allowed, and only psychedelic drugs were encouraged. The Beatles' *Sergeant Pepper* was played over and over for secret meanings. They cultivated an organic garden for vegetables, and eating meat was forbidden, even for the local dogs. They celebrated pagan holidays and lived in a time warp. A woman named Smoky ruled as a communal earth mother and witch. Then Dale bought the land and plowed under bungalows, cut down trees, and displaced the former residents. Land was cleared for a new prison.

"Everything has to end, Ted."

Ted glared at him.

"But look what follows. Dale is a member of the Posse. Those barracks are for racist commandos to take over the State."

Ted continued, caught up in his own tale, describing nightriders in white sheets terrorizing the country. Byron listened, intrigued but not concerned. Ted liked to pepper his speech with lines from Shakespeare, and knew how to throw his voice so that other patrons of the restaurant would turn and look.

"We've heard this," Becky drawled.

Becky smoked her cigarettes, watching Ted's excited face. Her drawl gave the impression of stupidity, when Byron knew from her writing that Becky had a keen mind. According to Ted, the Posse was making money on the side with an illegal toxic dump, and Dale had taken pains to control the city zoning.

"He's covering his ass from any prosecution."

"A toxic dump is still unhealthy," said Byron. "Citizens can protest."

"Protest!" Ted slammed his fist on the table, shaking the coffee cups. "Dennis, who owned the Owl Club in the old days, is at the bottom of the river."

"We don't know that for sure," said Becky.

"These people are not TV bad guys."

Becky kissed Ted, stroking his hair. "Go back to theatre. Do a play. Mellow *out*."

"Brecht is the only playwright I can do now. I can't do any theatre that is not about the apocalypse."

Becky pretended to snore. Byron watched Ted's face, wondering how much was due to his theatrical persona, and how much was reality. Sheriff Dale did seem like a television sheriff, even with a potbelly and mirrored sunglasses. Did he have an assistant with brain damage giggling in the back seat?

"Ted, you're living in the past," Becky said. "Those hippies were lame, passive, stupid!"

"So what?"

"You just wanted to get laid."

"The Posse is still dangerous. I hear they plan to take over the reservation and sell it to the Mafia."

Ted drank his coffee and confronted Byron with burning eyes. It was difficult to imagine the man at rest. Byron felt tired, but wanted to talk.

"Ted, the Posse is a fringe movement, the lunatic fringe. We will always have them. There are people who insist we never landed on the moon."

Ted seemed genuinely offended. "We didn't."

"And another thing. I was never heavy into the flower power generation, but Becky has a point. They *are* passive, they *are* naive in more dangerous modern times, and they don't contribute to the greater society."

"Why feed the corporate greed of straight America?"

"I spent a week on a commune in California visiting an old girlfriend named Rainbow. Rainbow didn't do drugs but she was an alcoholic, and had a lovely body owned by everyone at the commune."

"She was free," Ted said.

Becky snorted.

"We met in a bar in town the first night and Rainbow couldn't remember how to get to the camp. We had to call and have someone lead us there. The driver found Rainbow's behavior disturbing, even by hippy standards. The commune was run by a fat bald guy named Herb. He joked about how he never had a girlfriend until he started a porno company, and even starred in a few videos. He made a fortune and bought the land for the commune, and there were girls naked to the waist everywhere, and groovy guys stoned or meditating, 'sitting' as they called it, and there was a nice river running through the camp and children running around, some of them with bad teeth because of their honey diet. And after a week of wine, soaking up the sunshine on the beach, and Rainbow when she was sober, I snapped—and do you know why?"

Ted's eyes glared at him. "You sold out to consumer capitalism?"

"Ham and eggs," Byron said.

Both Becky and Ted did a second take, like a comic team in the movies.

"Ham and eggs?"

"The commune residents were super vegetarians. They didn't even eat eggs. One day I was standing in a stream and saw this beautiful naked woman named Kaylee wading toward me. She had complained her boyfriend meditated too much if I caught her drift and she wanted to walk downstream. Rainbow lay passed out in the shadows. I imagined making love to Kaylee when I saw a naked little girl on the bank. She was about three and taking a dump in the river. 'Poopy girl,' Kaylee said, laughing. Concerned the child might drown, not to mention hepatitis, I picked her up and found the mother stoned with two gentlemen on the beach, including Herb."

"So you snapped because of the kid?"

"No. I realized I needed something else. I was starving after a week of mush so I dressed and drove into town. There I had a glorious breakfast of ham and eggs. When I got back, the tribe surrounded the car and after I explained, they called me a carnivore. They demanded I repeat every moment of my crime against innocent animals, so I described cutting into and chewing that juicy pigmeat. They gasped in horror. The odd thing is that I felt they enjoyed the details, like puritanical voyeurs at a porno film. The next day I drove into town for a hamburger and fries and after hearing all the details of that vile tourist-filled corporate menace called McDonald's, they voted me out. I heard Rainbow didn't know I had left for two days. Later, she starred in one of Herb's films and became a born again Christian."

"What is the point of this long story?" demanded Ted. "Except you like meat?"

"I don't know."

"His point," Becky shouted, "is that those hippies *then* and these hippies *now* are lame, passive and stupid!"

Ted shrugged. "So what? They meant well. They were part of a counterculture. You got a better suggestion? This lunatic fringe is armed."

Byron hesitated, then asked a question: "Where do I fit in?"

"Good question," said Ted.

"We trust you," said Becky. "Shanahan is drunk at six in the morning, Judson's too critical, and I don't trust Maria. There is something creepy about her. I smell cop."

"Really? A cop? Ted?"

"What?"

"*Do* a Brecht play. Enlighten us."

Ted didn't answer, and seemed suddenly drained, sitting in the all night truck stop, a haven for smokers, a symbol of America with its late night customers: drifters going nowhere, truckers, sobering drunks, youths out on a roll, Indians, farmers, off duty police. The entire community would eventually be bolting a huge breakfast at 3:00 A.M.

"I have to shove off," Byron said. Ted had slipped on his broad-brimmed brown hat. "Oh, Ted. Have you ever heard of the Wrecking Crew?"

"Yes," said Ted. "Assassins! Maybe they planned hits on the Kennedys and King. Last I heard, they were disbanded. Fear of reprisals from the Jewish Defense League. But I am sure a few of the old guard are around." Ted stared at his face, seeming to hold his breath. "Why?"

"I was just wondering."

"Christ, Byron, don't you get caught up in this," said Becky. "Jesus."

Byron gently touched her hand on the table, dramatically cocking an eyebrow.

"I *am* caught up in this, thanks to you. Ted, stay away from the Owl Club."

"Tomorrow, Dale's gonna plow the house under. I'll be there."

"Why?"

"So I can remember and get revenge."

Byron thought of offering some alternative, but did not. He got up, paid and left. It was snowing, again, past the time for snow. When he got home, Judson McGee was not around, but the answering machine light was blinking. Ashley Roland had called from England to say hello and invite him to her wedding. Michael Wells's book on art had bombed. Byron played the message again, enjoying the rich Canadian sound of Ashley's voice. It would be good to see his former agent in London. For a moment, he thought of calling Michael Wells at the Los Angeles paper. He also thought of Maria.

Byron examined his face in the mirror, seeing a man past his prime for wooing women. After one divorce, brief LA romances and Suzi leaving, it seemed his time as a dashing rogue was over. Perhaps his shot at being a serious writer had passed. Yet he was able to look at his reflection and see something in the clear eyes, an open honesty and sense of irony that pleased him. He would've played the John Caradine part in John Ford westerns. Perhaps the mad preacher or the tall florid actor. Certainly, never the leading man. Byron lay down on his bed and stared at the ceiling. The coffee had wired him, and he knew it would be some time before he slept. Byron lay on his back, listening to the wind outside.

The phone rang, shrill in his ear. It was Maria.

"How did it go, Byron?"

He noticed how sensual her voice sounded, with a rough edge like a blues singer. The voice did not fit the wholesome face.

"How did what go?"

"Your talk with Ted."

"How did you know about that?"

"I know everything."

"It went fine. I'm tired. Talk to you, tomorrow, okay?"

"Okay. The road is too slick, tonight, anyway."

"What did you have in mind?"

"Nothing. Good night."

Byron hung up and closed his eyes, trying to sleep. It helped to listen to the wind; often he had listened to the rain falling on the roof while far from home, letting his mind drift.

He didn't want to think about Suzi. It always went badly to be involved with an impressionable young woman whose beauty would attract many rivals, whose friends would regard him as an odd older brother, and in a few years, her father. It was only a matter of time before it ended. As Byron went to sleep, Suzi's young beautiful face came back to him, mixed up with rushing white water and rafters risking death. He had come so close to death in the Salmon River that day, caught in the freezing hydraulic wash of the powerful watery surge, Judson thrusting an oar at him. He remembered a fire and his body furiously shaking and then the old bush pilot flying them out

Byron began dreaming.

In the cloudy mirror of the dresser facing his bed, he saw the naked images of Suzi and Maria, kissing and touching each other with a voluptuous abandon; they looked at him with sadness, reaching out as the mirror glass turned to water and their lovely but strong hands pushed him under.

He sat up in the bed, panting.

Across town, Maria also sat up, escaping from a recurring nightmare. A tall man in black, his face obscured, was trying to kill her. She couldn't remember if he had a weapon. Maria got up in the cold room and walked naked to the closet where she found a man's thick shirt and slipped it on, and then she walked barefoot into the front room and opened a drawer. A half empty pack of cigarettes lay near a .38 revolver. She took one out and walked to the window, enjoying the cool air on her naked thighs. Sitting by the window with her knees under her chin, she lit the cigarette and watched the dark empty street. The window glass was cold. The hot smoke helped to calm her nerves, even though she knew it could fire her nicotine addiction once again. It was quiet outside.

THE RIVER

THEIR LOVE AFFAIR HAD BEGUN with a near fatal river trip.

The river had seemed to them one endless river, or even two rivers, one called the Middle Fork of the Salmon with rapids that had been filmed and charted and seen by generations of river guides, and the other an unseen river with treacherous currents overturning rafts, sucking men down into whirlpools. Now they were sitting on a narrow stretch of beach beneath the rim of a canyon in Idaho, knowing they would have to go on the river again. Martine Coke Brown, their river guide, had dumped his raft. He glanced at Byron Duffy wringing out his clothes and at the others who stood quietly. None of them wore helmets.

"We never shoulda hit the water," Martine said. "It's just too high and too dangerous. We can't stay, either."

"Why not?" Byron asked.

Judson McGee answered Byron's question.

"We have to reach the next point to get out of here."

Byron noticed Suzi's face drawn by fatigue, hearing the edge in Judson's deep voice. Drenched, Martine ran a hand through his thick red hair and nodded at Judson.

"I'll go first," he said. "Judson, you take Byron."

Judson did not answer. Byron, shivering from the wet cold, stared at the river, remembering how it felt when he dumped into the white water, feeling the numbing shock of the powerful rapids. It would be nice to sit in his office reading Keats, but the Salmon River waited for them.

They pushed the two small rubber rafts into the river, jumping in as the current took them, first with little tentative tugs and touches, then gripping force as they shot into the rapids, Byron riding with Suzi and Judson as their raft seemed to skip across the crest of curling white water before dropping down with a splash and riding up another wave, shooting downstream, past rocks, over falls, following turns in the river. Judson steered from the back.

Byron stared in amazement as a group of half naked drunks without life jackets sailed by, waving to them, oblivious of the danger. Then Byron saw the big rock coming up fast which they surged past, only to drop off another falls; there was no warning. Byron heard Suzi scream, and he was shooting up, up into the wet air; for a moment, he heard Judson's curse, and saw their faces frozen in a moment in time before he crashed into the swift churning water. Byron was sucked under, his limbs going dead, even as Judson in the raft pushed an oar toward him. Byron went under again, turning in a swirl of bubbles, not knowing up from down, caught in a hydraulic wash. A flood of violin music seemed to fill his being, vibrating, beautiful.

Byron saw Suzi's naked body, then her radiant face. She was crying, waving good-bye, standing on an emerald wave.

He saw his Irish grandmother who raised him, now staring at him with glittering eyes. His dead father's handsome face hovered near him, imploring, concerned.

This is it, he thought, strangely calm.

He was not thinking anything when the rough hands pulled him from a gentle eddy only a few yards from the mainstream; it was as though Byron had stepped out of his body to watch as they prepared a fire, with Judson drinking from a bottle of whiskey, and Suzi shivering, watching Byron stretched out by the flames. Byron tasted the whiskey and gagged, shaking violently with cold, the warmed blood bringing sensations of pain to his extremities.

"The river god usually wants his quota of victims," Judson said. "I guess he doesn't need English teachers, today."

Byron's boyish face was bluish-white.

"The river gets warmer downstream."

Judson took another drink from the bottle being passed around. Byron drank more coffee, feeling a dead cold inside. Suzi held him, and her wet clothes set off another spasm of violent shaking. Byron looked up at Judson's round face, covered by a day's growth of beard, the hair cut in rough bangs, the eyes possessing an almost feminine prettiness for someone whose voice often startled strangers with its cutting masculine resonance.

"You were lucky," Judson said.

"Where is Martine?" said Byron. "He's the one who talked us into this river trip."

"Byron, listen—"

Byron saw the old man enter the camp. He was wearing old fashioned airman's goggles, and the other men parted as he approached and informed Byron that there was room on the helicopter for him. Byron looked up at the canyon, trying to imagine flying any aircraft through the equally dangerous air currents, sheer cliffs on either side. Other rescue workers were by the river, talking in low voices, and Byron suddenly realized he was alive. He saw Suzi's young beautiful face and began to laugh. After a moment, he put down the cup of coffee and smiled at Judson who was lighting an inevitable cigarette. The old pilot stood at some distance.

"Where is Martine Coke Brown?" he asked again.

"On the bank," the old pilot said. He walked down to the river. "We'll take the scenic route out." Byron shook his head.

"Can we trust an old bush pilot, Judson?"

"Byron, he's not an old bush pilot for nothing. Trust him."

"I thought you were gone," said Suzi.

Byron stood up. He felt strong but suddenly, Judson was holding him.

"A doctor will have to check you out," he said. "They got you in time, but you suffered some shock."

Byron looked around for the chopper and saw the men carrying a heavy body in a plastic bag. Judson lowered his head and other spectators removed their caps or helmets.

"If the Old Man River wants you, he'll git you," one of the men said. "Other fools get spared."

"Ain't that the truth?" another said. "Martine was one of the best, too. Ole Coke Brown was good, real good—but not at flood stage."

"He got caught underwater against a rock," Judson said.

Byron stared at the curving body bag, remembering Martine's wrinkled face and red hair and blue eyes, the fingers constantly reaching for or lighting a cigarette. Now he was dead, drowned.

Jesus Christ, thought Byron. *Not him.*

"Those worthless clowns without life jackets made it all the way downstream," a third man said. "Imagine!"

Then they were packed into the small helicopter, Martine's body wedged into the back, Byron sitting between Suzi and Judson, the old pilot flying the rescue aircraft up through the dangerous windy currents of the canyon, the cliffs rising on either side. Below was the Salmon River cutting through the canyon where it would flow into the Snake River as it had for centuries past. Byron held Suzi, trying not to think of the dead body. He saw the forested cliffs and etched Indian drawings from another epoch.

Near the end of the summer, they sat in the Ketchum cafe. Looking at Suzi, Byron realized he had not felt this way for anyone, even his ex-wife, since leaving high school. The fact they were fifteen years apart seemed irrelevant, though he couldn't easily imagine the years ahead. Thoughtful, Judson leaned back, watching Byron's angular face, then glanced around the cafe, one of his favorite haunts when he was in Ketchum. The place reflected simple plain taste, with pine-knot walls, wooden tables and concealed speakers playing folk and blue grass music.

"You came close to death," said Judson. "Tell me about it. You see the tunnel? Hear voices? See old relatives?"

"I heard music. It filled my body."

"What kind of music?"

"Country," said Suzi, laughing.

Judson repeated his question.

"I don't know, Judson. You *are* the music while the music lasts," Byron told him, his blue eyes glowing in the light.

"That sounds like T.S. Eliot."

"It is. I can't describe it. I *was* the music."

"Well, then, let's drink to the music and Martine Coke Brown's memory."

Judson took out a flask and spiked his coffee. Suzi drew her lips into a slight pucker and dragged off the cigarette. She stretched, her breasts pushing against a halter top. Byron smiled, thinking of Suzi in bed, then saw the tall, frail young man with purple streaks in his hair walking toward the table. He carried two cameras, one slung over his shoulder.

"Excuse me," he said, looking at Suzi. "My name is Brad. I'm a photographer."

"Obviously," said Suzi, popping her gum.

"I like your face. Do you mind if I shoot some pictures of you? I can shoot your friends, too."

Byron observed Brad's sickly-white face, spoiled by blemishes. The young man smiled, and suddenly blushed.

"No autographs, today," said Suzi, grinning.

She stood up and introduced Byron and Judson, then shook out her luxuriant hair from beneath a bandanna.

"Where does this shooting take place?"

He won't blush again, thought Byron, but Brad did blush as he aimed one of his cameras and clicked one off. "I can shoot here, or outside. Hey, that's nice!"

Byron and Judson enjoyed the show as Suzi made some theatrical poses, Brad firing away with his camera. Then she relaxed, and finally they walked outside where he snapped more, sometimes moving in for a tight shot or a different angle.

"Who is that puke?" asked Judson.

"Just a kid. He's under Suzi's spell."

"So I noticed."

Byron heard a warning in Judson's voice.

"I know Suzi looks great in cut-offs. Be careful, old buddy."

"I will," he said, remembering her sculpted body in a bikini.

"Heck, I'm what ya call a romantic," said Judson. "Get all the loving you want, but don't fall in love, not with something that pretty and *that* young."

Brad came into the cafe and shot a group portrait around the table, then gave Suzi his card and left. Suzi sat down, smiling, watching Judson finish his coffee, then reached across and took Byron's hand, and for a moment, he could see and hear the river, again. It brought back his moment facing the unknown. Suzi leaned her elbows on the table.

"Brad wants to shoot a series."

"I get feeb vibes," said Judson. "But maybe you could use some photos. Do a nude for me."

Judson laughed, and Byron could tell he was getting tipsy. Suzi reached over and playfully slapped Judson on the shoulder. It seemed they would be friends forever. Then they paid the bill and walked outside where they saw Brad driving down the street. Byron embraced Judson, and then shook his hand. It was time to say good-bye.

"I got to get back to Pocatello," he said. "I got school work, and so do you, Byron. Don't be messing around up here too long." Byron felt Suzi's strong hand sliding up his back.

"Don't let that hippy photographer hump your woman."

"I'm not his property," Suzi said. "I take care of myself."

"But can he?" Judson winked at Byron before getting in the car and driving away. When Byron turned, he saw Suzi walking away and thought of Judson's parting words.

Suzi and Byron spent a wonderful month in Ketchum, living in a cabin with an old collage of the Beatles on one wall and Suzi's butterfly collection from all over the world displayed against another; her face and voice filled his days and her body filled his nights, the rapid breathing against his neck, the lovely breasts, the female articulation of thigh and buttock that would stay with him. Byron felt they had little time; with the fall came his return to teaching, and Byron knew it would be hard to leave Ketchum when the leaves were turning. Brad often came by to shoot more pictures. He was a presence, a being who was suddenly and simply there. It was easy for Byron to ignore Brad. Byron had his fishing and afternoons spent by the Hemingway Memorial, gazing at the bust of Papa and listening to the murmur of the small stream running beneath the plaque, or evenings when Suzi would take off her clothes and stand naked by the window and listen to the night sounds, then slip into bed and reach for him. In the morning, they would walk to the same cafe and have breakfast and read the paper. One morning, shortly before he was to leave, he sat and watched Suzi, unusually quiet.

"What's up?"

"Nothing."

"Nothing? Really?"

Suzi smiled and looked away.

"I plan to take a riding lesson, today."

"Good."

Suzi reached over and took his hand.

"Byron? It might be best if I stay here for a while."

Byron was surprised at a sudden surge of panic.

"Oh? Why is that?"

"Mother is freaked out. She thinks I'm being corrupted by an older man. She *is* something of a religious fanatic, you know."

"That never stopped you before."

Suzi shrugged and finished her food, devouring fries and a cheeseburger. Byron read the paper. Then Suzi gestured with a last piece of her burger.

"Byron, it took you awhile to take me seriously. I mean, as a *woman*, not a girl. I was lonely and hung up on you for a long time."

"Okay—let's make up for lost time."

Byron studied her face, trying to read her mind behind the blazing rich green of her eyes, waiting for the words, remembering Judson's warning.

"I think I should camp here for a while, and maybe we should stay apart...maybe a month, you know? I got some thinking to do, Byron. I can join you in October."

Byron nodded and put down the paper.

"That's a good idea," he said.

Suzi reached for a cigarette, knowing smoke bothered him.

"I don't want my mother to get you in trouble with the school. She's a puritanical Christian Scientist. She never quits."

In the cafe, other lovers had breakfast or an early lunch. Suzi dropped a manila envelope on the table and pushed it toward Byron.

"I want you to see some of Brad's photos of me. He thinks I should be a model, you know? Maybe I could work as a model and even support you."

"I can support myself," he told her.

Suzi smoked as Byron took out the photos and examined them, the images clear and provocative. Brad had captured the elusive innocence of Suzi, and her arrogant sexuality, alluring, secret, even as Suzi smiled in the rough outdoor setting, glowing with health and a vulnerable sensuousness. Byron found himself seeing the nudes as though they were pin-ups of another woman, some in profile, her face and breasts highlighted, some with Suzi dramatically confronting the camera with a raw little girl toughness and power, perhaps a sleeve in the corner of her wet mouth with shadowed legs slightly apart. A cafe group portrait captured them in a past moment.

Byron caught Suzi watching his face. She ground out the cigarette.

"Well?"

"Brad is good. I see a lot of you and him in these photos." Byron took a deep breath. A family passed by the window. "I bet he jacked off to these, a few times. I don't blame him."

"Don't be so creepy, Byron."

"It's all right. Brad knows what he's doing."

Byron was amused as Suzi attempted to control her anger.

"We're gonna do a photo session later this afternoon. In fact, I told him to pick me up, here. I hope that's all right."

Byron didn't know he would speak so quickly.

"Move in with me."

"Not right away, Byron. I don't wanna argue this, okay?"

Byron slid the photos toward her. Suzi brushed some hair from her eyes.

"Byron, it's okay."

"I think Brad wants to get into your knickers."

"He's probably a fag."

"With purple hair, that's a possibility," he said.

"Please don't *ever* be jealous," Suzi said. "It's uncool."

Byron saw the anger in her eyes, and glanced down at the paper. The news of the day was fairly boring.

How can I be jealous? he thought to himself. He felt a little sick. They sat for a long time.

"Maybe Brad can make you a star."

"What's wrong with that?"

"Will I see you tonight?"

Suzi blew her nose and laughed.

"Of course. I ain't goin' nowhere."

Looking at the beautiful woman across from him made his silent fear of foolishness and loss more concrete, but Byron finally shrugged, slipping into another reality mode. Why did love only hurt when it was over? Or was it over? If so, he had been given something. It seemed only fair. Byron suddenly felt Suzi holding his face and kissing him. She was wiping away tears, and speaking into his face, trying to smile.

"Byron, I'll see you, tonight! I love you."

Byron gently pushed her away, then they saw Brad nervously standing by the door, afraid to approach the table; Suzi scooped up her envelope of photos and was out the door. Byron sipped another cup of coffee and looked out the window.

That night, they undressed before a mirror and drank champagne, then got into bed and made love, Suzi's face pushed into the pillow. Byron saw his image in the darkened mirror, feeling something wild and savage and even vengeful in his being; later, they were lying side by side, feeling empty.

"Baby, that was fine," she said, echoing a line from a B picture.

"Yeah," he said.

During their lovemaking, he had imagined fantasies from Suzi's photos, conjuring sexual moments that would engulf them. It was an irony that Brad's art would be a sexual aid. Suzi began to cry but wouldn't say why. Byron went to sleep with a ghostly presence between them.

When he drove back to Pocatello to start his next semester of teaching, the leaves were turning; he thought of Hemingway and the trout filled streams, and reading Faulkner in college, then reading Hemingway to balance the Faulkner. There was a song on the car radio. It was "Baby, Please Don't Go."

What difference does it make, he thought to himself. You were given some time, and it was good, and now it is over and something else begins. Just be accepting. Isn't that great advice?

Sure, he thought to himself. But who can take it?

He drove down the narrow highway through Hailey, Idaho. The blues song was still throbbing on the radio, a plaintive bottleneck sound that Byron liked, but this time, it was too harsh. He reached over and turned off the radio. He had forgotten about the river. He had also forgotten his promise to drive back to Pocatello and wait for Suzi to call. Byron drove back to the cabin and found a note and a pencil drawing of a building: "Dear Brad, here is where I'm at. Suzi." Even as he realized how stupid it was, Byron drove to Sun Valley, looking for Brad's car, finding it in front of a weathered building once used for horses.

They were inside. Suzi was posing against a screen, wearing only a filmy gown, the room bright from lights and reflectors, Brad giving directions behind the camera. Suzi saw Byron and cursed; later, he would remember Brad's frightened face.

"Get in the fucking car, now!"

Suzi struck him once in the face. Byron ripped off her gown, tearing it away from her beautiful sudden nakedness, then he hit Brad, pounding the pock-marked face, knocking the now whimpering man to the floor. Byron crashed out, Suzi shrieking invectives.

A month later, Byron still heard Suzi's cries as he visited Judson at a rehab center. Though Suzi didn't speak to him, her mother, a tiny woman in black, had kicked on his door, one night, threatening him with rape and kidnapping. As usual, Judson found all this intriguing. He was baking a pie—sober, now.

"You explained, I trust, that Suzi was off with yet *another* degenerate, one her own age?"

"Yes," Byron told him. "Her mother, Myrtle, is a piece of work."

Judson had lost weight since his arrest for drunk driving, but had more vitality. Byron was covering one of his classes, filled with students who worked so hard to write mediocre papers. Byron found himself in class staring at freshmen girls, thinking of Suzi, feeling the regret.

"You ever sleep with Suzi?"

"No," Judson said.

"Why did I hit Brad? He had nothing to do with it. I was just sick and jealous. He got in the way."

Judson waited to hear more.

"One night, Judson, I got drunk, myself. Listened to an angry Dylan song, then went out looking for a girl or a fight."

Judson studied the mess in the pan.

"And?"

Byron remembered the chubby young woman in the nameless bar telling him that she did not go to motels, certainly not with anyone like him, that she might step over him but never sleep with him. Judson was amused. Byron sat, pressing his hands together.

"Of course, her boyfriend was the captain of the football team.

I escaped without injury."

Judson was silent. He lit a cigarette, and Byron could see the slight tremor in his hands.

"I could use a drink," Judson said. "But you? Lay off the sauce. I'm the drunk!"

Byron stood up.

"I'm checking into a monastery. Or maybe I'll jump back in the Snake River. See you."

They shook hands. Byron left.

His mind seemed more clear as he drove past the bleak countryside. The fall was always beautiful but they had missed Indian Summer. Soon, the rains would set in and the leaves would fall from the trees. The advancing cold would kill everything, and they would wait another month before snow covered the barrenness. With the winter feeling of death and dissolution, Byron felt what he called his "Dostoyevski" mood of guilt. Byron wanted to ask Suzi and even Brad for forgiveness, and was rehearsing a speech with similar sentiments when he saw the police car in front of his house. Byron approached the officer.

"What's the problem, sir?"

"You live here?"

"Yes."

"You had a burglary. We took a Myrtle Johnson into custody. Her daughter identified her. I guess nothing was taken, but you'll have to come down later and make a statement."

"I would like to take out a restraining order on that old woman," said Byron. "She's a witch!"

The officer stared at him.

"You can do that at the station, sir."

As Byron walked up the steps and into the house, he realized that Suzi Johnson was in town, and entering the front room with its familiar paintings and photographs, Judson's clothes and books scattered everywhere, Byron saw Suzi sitting on the sofa. She was well dressed, a tinge of pale gold in her recently cut hair. A pile of shredded photographs lay on the floor, bits and pieces of Suzi's face and body parts on glossy paper, torn up, tossed—scattered at random.

"Hello, Byron," she said.

He examined the photos: a leg here, a breast, there.

"The mad mother strikes again?"

"Yes."

Suzi picked up a mug shot from the floor.

"They may keep her in jail overnight. I hope so."

"You seem more sophisticated and confident."

"Tell that to mom. The cops found her in a dead faint on the floor after she broke in and found some of the photos I sent to you, which you *never* opened. They included two nudes."

"So mom got an eyeful?"

"Byron, the photos were meant to show you how I'd grown." Suzi crossed her legs and took out a cigarette. "I *am* sorry about what happened to us."

"So am I. You better leave."

Suzi stood up. Byron couldn't read her expression.

"I'll go. Meet me at the pizza joint, tonight. I wanna tell you what's up. Brad is a lightweight. You taught me everything, Byron. Believe it or not, I still love you."

"See you tonight."

"I wanna see Judson, too. I am glad he's drying out."

Suzi left. Byron sat on the overstuffed, ragged sofa. Seeing her again brought back the emptiness, then anger and frustration. Of course, Judson had been right from the start. Suzi was fun to sleep with, but serious love was meant to be with a mature woman. They would marry, live in the suburbs, and he would write novels about the human condition after the inevitable divorce.

Byron shook off this thinking and stood on the back porch, staring at the empty back yard.

Later that evening, Byron pushed into Buddy's Pizza; there were the same tables and a long bar, with a television screen showing endless sports or cartoons. Byron was nervous, and felt a shock when he saw Suzi sitting at one of the tables; he saw a frightened young girl hiding behind the green eyes, the skillfully applied makeup, the beautiful dress she could now afford, her breasts full and outlined against the filmy fabric, the hair cut close and stylish. Then Byron remembered the rugged but gorgeous female digging into a wild river, or hoisting a pack and keeping a fire going while trees dissolved into driving rain.

He sat down. Suzi picked at a salad.

"Hello," he said.

"I'm glad you came, Byron. I wanted to see you, again. I'll be doing a show in Salt Lake, and then I'm off to New York with a photographer named Malcolm. Brad's good at shooting human interest shots, but Malcolm can shoot meat on the block."

Byron was silent.

"Byron? You and Judson are the only reality I know."

Byron ordered a soft drink.

"God, I don't know if that's a positive reality. I'm an idiot."

"No you're not."

She reached over and grabbed him.

"Byron?"

"Yes?

"I thought maybe we could drive to Lava Hot Springs, dance, have a few drinks."

"It's a possibility." Byron smiled. "How are you, really?"

"I'm fine. Of course, if I get a pimple anywhere, it's a disaster. Brad is not so happy about Malcolm. He doesn't like Malcolm's leather and jewelry, but that's the business."

"Do you like the business?"

"I tolerate it," said Suzi. "It's a ticket outta here. I learned how to love and how to write from you. Now I am learning how to model clothes. Who knows? Maybe I'll go into acting."

She hesitated before speaking and Byron saw the vulnerable child, again.

"I admit, I can be a flighty bitch, but no matter what happens, you were the first and most important influence in my life. I didn't say the things that you needed to hear. We weren't meant to marry and have children, but I hope something good can happen."

It seemed strange they were having this intimate conversation in Buddy's Pizza.

"Byron, will you *ever* forgive me?"

"Sure. Perhaps we should call it a night."

She didn't answer, but slipped an envelope across the smooth table. Byron was not anxious to open it. He could hear indistinct conversations in the bar, so many talking heads and clinking glasses. Finally, he took out the photo. It was Brad's three shot of them at the table in Ketchum that afternoon after the river trip, and seeing the photo brought back a rush of memories and feelings. He would see the photo in future years, remembering what they had shared and lost.

"It's nice," Byron said. "I'm touched."

His eyes moistened. Suzi eyed him in shock.

"Sorry," he said. "I didn't know that would happen."

"Oh God," she insisted. "It's all *right*."

They drove to the Wagon Wheel Saloon in Lava Hot Springs, a noisy cowboy bar, Byron still drinking soft drinks, and Suzi got tipsy on bourbon and seven-up. A band played country rock. Steam rose from the outdoor public baths.

"I'll be back here for Thanksgiving," said Suzi. "I want you, me and Judson to get together before I'm on the road, okay?"

"Whatever you say, Suzi."

"Let's rent a private hot bath at the old hotel. I don't mind the smell of cats and kitty litter. Do you?"

"Suzi? We can't do this, again."

"For old times. Okay?"

"Sure," he said, knowing the consequences.

Perhaps Suzi realized she was entering a new stretch of river, another stage, and that sex with Byron would be another step toward a final farewell, an escape. They got a bottle and rented a subterranean bath, undressing and walking into the large tubs of hot mineral water, the steam enveloping Suzi's naked body. They drank. Perhaps somewhere was the real Suzi who would always need him whenever the magic faded. For now, they could listen to the heart's whisper, surrender to the body's prurient ache. They half crouched in the hot water and embraced, kissing. Byron felt the sexual escape in her arms and open thighs, rocking in the hot baths.

Waking up in the hotel the next morning, sunlight coming through a crack in the shade, Suzi was gone, the night before only a memory. She had escaped again into whatever broken world she was trying to enter. Hungry cats hunted the faded hallways.

It was a different Suzi they saw at Thanksgiving, sitting at the table with Malcolm in his plunging V-neck and gold chains and leather jacket and pants, staring at Judson and Byron with not so much contempt as detached curiosity. Perhaps Suzi didn't see the arrogantly handsome Malcolm as just another brute in the glittering world of fashion. Byron watched her across the table, remembering the river and Brad's group photo, and Suzi floating open thighed, smooth-bellied in the hotel basement hot baths.

"If I stay sober, I'll get my daughter back," said Judson. "But I find reality very depressing without a drink."

"I drink mineral water," said Malcolm, smiling. "You know, I really like this town. It's kinda quaint. I like simple people. I mean, I deal with so much flash and glitter. Tits and ass. It's really nice to see *real* people. Plain girls, overweight women. People who can change a tire."

"Suzi can change a tire. She's a very talented girl." Byron grinned at Suzi, her eyes on her food. "Suzi jacked up a lot of cars until the world of fashion grabbed her. Knows how to handle tools—isn't that right, Suzi?"

"That's right," said Suzi. "Malcolm, did I tell you that Byron was one of my lovers?"

"I think so."

"Before that, Judson."

"This is excellent turkey," said Judson, quickly.

"We forgot Brad," said Byron. "Where is he?"

"He's shooting a cattle auction, somewhere," said Malcolm, grinning. "Excuse me, I gotta buzz my agent. I'll use my credit card, okay?"

Suzi glared at Byron and Judson. Byron was silent for a long time, then finally spoke in a low voice.

"Would you like another piece of meat, Suzi?"

"No!"

"Byron, let it go," Judson said. "Please."

Hours later, Malcolm was sitting in the rented car outside while Suzi stood at the door, staring at Byron. There was something in her dark eyes that Byron didn't recognize. Was she even thinking of him? Then she blurted out a good-bye and was gone.

"You want to punch me out?" Judson said.

"I'm mature," said Byron.

"I hope so," said Judson, drinking an iced tea. "We need women who are adventurous, but not promiscuous. We want order in a world that is patchwork to begin with."

Byron closed his eyes, remembering Suzi's walk. "I'm going to bed," he said. "And you can stick your platitudes up your ass." He turned and swung at Judson's face. Judson blocked the wild blow. "I could break you in half," he barked. Byron backed away.

On Christmas Day, Byron stood in the outdoor public hot baths of Lava Hot Springs. Judson brought his eight-year-old daughter, Joan; she was a pretty child with clear eyes and a quick, nervous smile, her blonde hair tied in a pony tail. She watched her father when he spoke. Snow fell on the steaming water. Many elderly people and children came to the baths, and Byron thought of the old hotel with its many retired residents and wandering cats belonging to no one..

"I learned a new word," Joan explained. "'Sarcastic.'"

She stood in the hottest pool.

"It's a good word," said Judson. "Excuse me."

He walked toward the dressing room. Joan waded over to Byron.

"Is daddy going for a drink?"

"I think he needs a smoke."

The little girl ignored other children, many of them too young for her.

"It's very pretty when the snow falls on the steaming water," said Byron. "Usually, it's sunny on Christmas."

"Do you have any kids?" Joan asked, moving her hands through the hot mineral water, looking at no one.

"No."

"Why not? You don't like kids?"

"I love children. I just never had any. I bet you'd like someone to play with so you wouldn't be so bored."

He could feel Joan watching him, and later, sitting on the steps, she asked questions.

"My mom back home is very sick. Is your mom sick?"

"No," Byron said. He pointed. "See? Your dad's returning."

Face and shoulders red, Judson McGee was walking back to the hot pools.

"We're going to Disneyland next week," said Joan.

"Just what I need," bellowed Judson. "Mickey Mouse and Southern California."

"I like Minnie Mouse," said Joan.

People drifted through the hot pools in the mist and falling snow. It gave a surreal impression, and Byron thought of Suzi again.

"California surfers give me hives," growled Judson.

He was breathing heavily from exertion.

"Let's go on the river, again."

"Maybe."

After Judson and Joan left, Byron walked to the Wagon Wheel. The band was playing a plaintive country blues that touched Byron, but quickly depressed him so he left.

On New Year's Eve, the call came from Suzi. Brad's group photo hung on the wall. Moments later, Byron bellowed into the receiver at the woman so far away, no more than a disembodied voice.

"Byron, you don't need to send me money, okay? I can take care of it. It might be yours or Malcolm's, I don't know. I always thought I was sterile from Pelvic Inflammatory Disease, but so much for *that* thought. Byron, calm down!"

"Think of what you're doing," Byron said.

He listened to the strong voice hammering back at him over the line.

"I *know* what I'm doing. I can't raise a kid with a career just taking off. Since when are you against abortion?" Suzi's calm voice went on. "The kid may not even be yours."

Outside, it was beginning to snow.

"I'm concerned about weight gain."

Byron reacted with anger. "Weight gain?" He stared at the wall. "We're talking about a child, a new life!"

"Your Catholic upbringing ruined you. Get modern, Byron."

"You may never have another chance at this again."

"Good," said Suzi. "I don't want a kid. I'm getting my tubes tied."

There was a long silence. Byron felt a little sick, remembering his pro choice arguments.

"Byron, I have to run. I'm going to Paris and a baby would cramp my style." Byron held the phone, his breath going shallow. "I still love you."

"I don't care."

"You *should* care!"

"We're through, Suzi."

"What else is new? Byron, please don't let it end this way."

Byron closed his eyes. "How can I *not* be angry?"

"Okay, then *be* angry. I know farmers have saved more lives than beauty queens, but that's what I do for a living. I've made a choice, Byron. I think we...I...am doing the right thing. I can't believe you're so conservative about this—so unforgiving."

Byron held the phone. He felt something pounding in his head and there was a tight feeling like an iron bar across his chest.

"You're right, Suzi. Maybe your dog can get a book deal."

"I don't have a dog. Byron?"

"What?"

"I'm serious. You think I'm an airhead, but I'm a lot smarter than you think. You will *always* be special."

"Wonderful, Suzi," Byron said. "I feel just great to be so fucking special."

"I'm sorry you feel this way. Talk to ya soon," Suzi said. Her voice was choked. He could tell she was about to cry. A new year was only a few minutes away.

"It's all right."

"Are you sure, Byron?"

"I'm sure. Good luck."

"Thanks."

"Good-bye, Suzi."

"Good-bye."

He hung up the phone. Byron sat down on the sofa; he felt as though he were entering a dead sterile time, a harsh savage flow of reality that was like a river, relentless and going nowhere. He looked out the window at the falling snow, floating through the dark sky. It should make everything cleaner. He imagined lovers kissing and celebrating the New Year all over the world while the harsh river of time flowed, strong and brutal.

THE WRECKING CREW

THAT MORNING, BYRON SURPRISED HIMSELF by driving to the Owl. Earlier, he saw Chan walking across the quad, tearing up pieces of paper and littering the dead lawn.

"Chan, what are you doing?"

Chan stopped, his body short and muscular, his mustache black and bristling beneath an aquiline nose. No one knew why he had a Chinese sounding name since Chan was an Arab. He held up another piece of paper, perhaps a letter.

"Rejections," he shouted. "No bananas, today."

Chan turned and continued across the open university space, ripping more rejections.

Byron drove to the Owl Club and the now doomed yellow house on the hill. As he waited for Dale's big dozer to begin demolition, Byron was more surprised to see Shanahan, wearing a heavy jacket, staring with a morbid fascination at the house. Dale talked with a group of men in a circle as Becky and Ted drove up to the Owl. A keg sat on the hard earth, and people drank beer at eight in the morning.

"What are you doing here, Shanahan?"

"I once read some Chaucer out here for the hippies. It was part of a summer solstice." Byron glanced at Ted and Becky who clung to him, shivering, her breath blowing steam in the cold air. One of the men from the night before stared at Ted.

"We got a real live hippy, boys!"

To Byron's shock, the man giggled, a strange demented sound.

Shanahan began drinking beer. A group of people gathered around Ted and watched as a young boy fired the dozer, the engine roaring. A few in the crowd cheered, and Byron noticed two distinct groups among the spectators — the former hippy residents and the local militia cadre. Ted was silent. Dale nodded once to the boy.

"That's Dale's son," said Shanahan. "He has the honors. I hope he survives."

"Survives what?" Byron said.

Sheriff Dale proudly gave an order and the youth, barely sixteen, moved the controls of the bulldozer. The giggling man clapped. Ted took out a sixteen-millimeter camera and began shooting footage of the house's final moments.

"Screw it on!" shouted the giggling man. "Get her done!"

Byron found himself watching, equally caught up in the minor drama.

The young boy, wearing a straw hat and overalls, drove the bulldozer into the old house, tearing through the wood, breaking up the home into sections, rolling over the timbers, so that the dozer looked like a puny but ferocious termite gnawing away at a bigger structure, each bite and grinding motion pushing the house further apart, the heavy metal tread crushing the fractured wood into the muddy earth. The spectators drank beer and cheered. The bulldozer roared and rolled back and forth over the broken timbers while Ted shot his film.

Then they saw the smoke seeping from under the house. Shanahan made a whimpering sound as smoke poured from a shattered basement window, a gust of wind blowing through the broken beams as an explosion of flame engulfed the laboring bulldozer and the boy stood up. Dale cursed. The entire house exploded, as though it had been soaked in gasoline. Converging men suddenly jumped back from the flames burning around the boy who finally jumped, his shirt on fire. Shanahan's lips blew over his beer as he watched, Ted's camera clacking loudly. The dozer disappeared in flame, and clouds of smoke swirled across a single cottonwood tree in the background. Dale's son rolled on the ground, screaming as Byron pushed through the crowd, covering him with his coat. He elevated the boy's feet. The house had become a gutted ruin, and Ted stopped filming.

"That calls for a beer," he said. "Good footage."

A gaunt man with a rifle shouted: "Who started that fire? Who?"

The giggling man, somber now, walked toward Ted while the men flaunting a military toughness observed the fire. They wore steel-toed boots and cut-off sleeves exposing their muscular tattooed arms. Dale called for help on his police radio, but no one saw Maria arrive.

"Gimme that film!" the giggler screamed, suddenly advancing on Ted.

"Take it," said Ted, decking the man with a right hook. He and Becky ran to his car and drove off as the giggler got up, the Meridell Park residents quickly blocking his path. Byron saw their love beads, bell-bottoms and long hair from another era.

"Peace brother," a man with shoulder length blond hair said. He made a V sign. In response, one of the soldiers pulled out an army issue .45.

"Let's settle down," Byron said. Maria tugged at Byron's sleeve even as he backed away from the impending fight. "An ambulance is on the way. Meet me later."

The giggler reached inside his jacket, then stopped as Maria drove past him. For a moment, Byron assumed Maria was afraid of the weapon displayed. Shanahan trembled, watching the smoking house, his lips pursed in a silent whistle. Some tipsy spectators cheered again and the gaunt man cocked his rifle; they grew silent.

"Shanahan, are you all right?"

Shanahan met Byron's eyes. "I'm fine," he said.

They could hear the distant ambulance as the bulldozer burned on the gutted ruins of the house and the self-styled soldiers quietly circled the crowd. The gaunt man fired his rifle in the air, teeth flashing through his beard. "Who started that fucking fire? I'll burn *him.*"

Sheriff Dale knelt by his son as the ambulance turned onto the muddy road. Another keg was rolled out and a few Owl Club patrons gathered around thrusting forward empty cups. The rifleman lowered his weapon. Byron gently touched Shanahan on the shoulder.

"I'll see you at school."

The small band of hippies watched him as he drove down the deeply rutted road. Byron imagined the same people dancing around a May Pole while Shanahan read from Chaucer. He had to admire them. He could visit Nepal or hike in Paraguay and suddenly a bright psychedelically colored van would appear and some latter day hippy would know every lyric of the Grateful Dead. By tomorrow, they'd be driving a caravan of overloaded vans down the road to start another anachronistic commune. He had been there and done that, but Byron Duffy could meditate on sunsets for so long before he wanted action, usually in the form of some dramatic change.

Then he sat in Maria's house, drinking coffee.

"How could Ted just film the whole thing with someone on fire?" Byron said.

"Maybe he's a cinematic cannibal. Maybe he wanted the whole picture, you know, a complete record. Maybe it was arson."

Byron thought about Shanahan and the glow in his eyes that no fire could explain.

"The boy will spend some time in the burn center. I know what happens. It's awful."

Byron was curious about burn centers but asked another question: "What the hell is wrong with Shanahan?"

Maria shrugged. "I don't know."

The small cottage had stuffed animals, many quilts and wall hangings. It had a feel that Byron could only describe as "female, cute," though Maria moved like an athlete. Somehow the cottage didn't fit her. She had changed into jeans and a work shirt, unbuttoned. She didn't wear a bra, her brown hair clean and bright.

"Some students have complained about Shanahan coming drunk to class," Maria said.

"He mentioned something about the boy surviving."

"*Before* the fire?"

"Yes."

Maria was silent. Then she touched his shirt. "You left your coat back there."

"I'm sure Dale will have it at the investigation."

Byron finished the coffee. Maria looked out the window at the clear cold day.

"I feel like a swim at Lava. I hear you went there a lot with your under age girlfriend."

"She wasn't under age and what is this, published information? Why do you care?"

"It's none of my business, Mr. Duffy." She put away the coffee cups and dishes.

"What caused the fire?"

"A spilled can of gasoline, friction, a leak. Who knows?"

They drove to Lava Hot Springs; it was a nice drive down the two-lane blacktop and then a turn through open country and along a stream until they saw the hill with a big L in the top. At the upper end of the small town were the hot pools. Resting in the hot steaming water, he thought of Ted's filming. What did he shoot while secretly roaming the Meridell Park grounds—posse military maneuvers? Perhaps there was a conspiracy after all. Would they be distracted from bigger battles by a local race war? Byron saw some Latino children wading in the pools and he addressed them in Spanish: "*Buenos dias.*" The round brown faces smiled and moved on. The steam from the hot mineral water gave everything the appearance of a surreal Hollywood set. Byron turned and saw Maria watching him.

"I used to work as a substitute teacher in LA. I had a lot of Mexican children. They're lovely kids."

They went to the Wagon Wheel Bar for a drink. Maria studied him as he sat at the bar, listening to the country band. Couples danced on the small dance floor. Then they danced. He liked the feel of Maria's body against him, and remembered how athletic she appeared in a bathing suit, not a bit of fat, her breasts small and firm, her legs smooth but muscled.

"You're in good shape for an English teacher."

"So are you." Maria saw his expression change. "What's wrong?"

Byron looked up at the television screen showing a fashion show. A number of models in heavy make-up and beautiful dresses paraded in front of the camera. One of them, wearing exotic Asian make-up and a tight fitting silk dress, was Suzi. "I guess you can't escape her," said Maria. "And it still hurts."

"I can't escape, but it no longer hurts."

He didn't think it hurt anymore, but he still remembered finding Suzi at her photo session that afternoon with Brad, a young photographer with a bad complexion and purple dyed hair, and how he suddenly ripped off the gown exposing her nakedness and then struck the frightened Brad in the face, and for no reason, really. The session was legitimate. Suzi was working, after all, and Byron had to thank her later for not pressing charges.

49

When they drove to Maria's house, a gentle wind blew outside the cottage; they sat on the sofa and were silent for a long time. Maria poured them some drinks. Then he talked about his affair with the younger woman. It had seemed so right, at first. Maria listened quietly.

"It was not so complex. Boy meets girl, boy loves girl, boy loses girl."

"Always a rival."

"The minute I saw his partially nude photo of Suzi with that coke in her mouth, I knew he had also captured her soul and it was over."

"I see. He captured her soul *and* her body?"

"Another mule kicking in my stall."

"The macho man's nightmare."

"The rest is boring and not pleasant."

"Try me."

He could've talked about the small cabin they shared with a Beatle collage on one wall, shots of George, John, Paul and Ringo forever young out to conquer the world, and Suzi's butterfly collection on another wall, and the way she dropped her clothes and stood to face him, her naked beauty always breath-taking, and then the fierce savage passion of their lovemaking.

But he didn't discuss the sexual details.

"Every moment of life was a gift after I almost drowned on a river trip. Even my morning coffee at the café was a supreme revelation."

"Perhaps that's the main lesson here," Maria said. "Live."

Byron took her wrist and held it, looking into her eyes. "Have you ever been close to death?"

"Yes."

"Tell me about it."

"Maybe later."

He released her hand. "Savor life, yes—but to have and lose a young beautiful woman and know you're entering a new phase of life. Daunting."

"So you suffered an early mid life crisis?" Maria finally asked.

"Maybe."

"Are you the jealous type?"

"Negative," he insisted. "I hate jealousy. In the past, I would've shrugged and walked out the door. One woman leaves, another appears. We spend our entire lives saying 'Good-bye' and what's the problem?"

Maria's eyes seemed haunted in the lamplight. "Good-bye?"

"I think the German poet, Rilke, said it best." Byron recited:

"'Alone he climbs to the mountains of primal pain.
And never once does his step ring from the
soundless destiny.'"

Byron's voice faded to silence.

"That sounds so depressing."

"And very German. We go out with the tide and where we end up is anyone's guess. Things fade. Nothing's permanent...except pain."

"And no mere woman will ever tie you down?"

"That's right, baby," he said with a smile. "Destiny awaits."

"I don't believe you."

"Believe none of us." He finished his drink. "Great art is permanent, but I don't know if I can create that."

Byron liked her handsome features in the soft light. He also realized that he still knew very little about her.

"I hope we don't say 'Good-bye' too soon. Byron?" She leaned forward. "I would like to seduce you," she said. "However, maybe we should wait. I don't know how professional such conduct might be viewed by...by the English Department." She smiled at Byron. "Can you wait, or am I presuming too much?"

"I think you're right," said Byron. "That we should wait, that is."

He kissed her good night. He liked the feel of her lips and the clean smell of her hair.

"I am also curious to hear about what caused the fire," said Maria. "Keep me posted. I'll ask a few discreet questions about Shanahan."

"You know," said Byron, "Ted's conspiracy theory might be accurate."

He left, but didn't drive home. He drove to Shanahan's house, surrounded by cottonwoods, and finding the door unlocked, looked in and called out. The wind moaned outside. The house was dark.

He called Shanahan's name, then heard a match strike behind him, and even as he felt a sickening drop in his stomach, he realized it was all right. Shanahan, lighting a candle, stared at him in the flickering light.

"Mr. Duffy. I was about to go to bed."

"Sorry to disturb you."

"Quite all right."

Byron asked about the fire.

"An accident, I guess."

"You seemed worried about the boy."

"Yes—I hate to see an attractive young man or woman growing up in that foul environment."

"Really? Who is the Wrecking Crew?"

Shanahan smiled in the weak glow of the candle.

"Let me put on a real light."

"That's okay."

Shanahan put the candle on a table next to an open pint of whiskey. He resembled some ghost out of Dickens.

"I think they have a big ball and wreck condemned homes." Shanahan laughed softly. "Would you like a drink?"

"No," said Byron, sensing another presence in the dark room.

"I think *some* wrecking crew is going to destroy the English Department, Mr. Duffy. Regarding the Wrecking Crew, the Posse and the Klan once boasted of some assassins using that name."

The wind rattled the windows.

"Really?" A wooden Indian stood in the corner of the room, watching them in the candlelight. A sad expression came across Shanahan's small face.

"I am ashamed to admit that while growing up in the South, I became too acquainted with the Klan. My father was a member. This is very embarrassing to me."

"I can understand," said Byron. "But surely *you* have no—"

"—ties? No. But the department would be very nervous if they ever suspected I had a father who was a man of the cloth."

"I won't tell, Shanahan. I *am* concerned about that fire, though. How did it start?"

"A spark in an old building." Shanahan gulped his bourbon. "Heat from the dozer. You know, something big *is* going to happen.

Warn Ted Bear to be careful."

"How do you know about him?"

"This is a small town, Mr. Duffy. The sheriff will want to question him. *And* you." Shanahan yawned. "I'm so tired."

"Good night," Byron said. He stopped at the door. "You know, if you ever need to talk to someone.... you see, drinking problems run in my family."

"I don't have a drinking problem," said Shanahan. He snickered. "I can get all I want. Calms me down when I look in the mirror. Good night."

When Byron returned home, he found Judson very drunk, holding his coat. His daughter had left.

"Our fat little sheriff friend was by, and left this. He said thanks, and he's also going to subpoena you and Ted. Thought you should know. Too bad about that old house."

Judson blinked, slurring his speech; Byron was afraid he would suddenly crash into the wall.

"Go to bed," he said.

"Ted called and wants a secret meeting," said Judson. He had a big voice that filled the room. "Secret from whom? He's glad you're on his side. *What* side?"

"You got me. Good night," added Byron.

He went to bed. Judson followed him into the room.

"I'll be sober for class," he said.

"You ought to start a band with Shanahan," said Byron. "Play ukulele or guitar, have Shanahan play the wax comb. Maybe Ted could film it."

"You have to stay drunk to be normal in this town."

Byron felt an anger rising in him; he had drunk heavily in earlier days and grew up with drunks and knew all the excuses. While working on a novel, Byron had shot pool in San Francisco with a celebrated author who also drank late into the night, drinking to the point even the inevitable young girls willing to sleep with the celebrity and his friend no longer seemed as attractive as the endless bottles of whiskey. One day, the celebrated writer, his long but thinning hair and mustache famous from many book covers, found his books not selling while critics insisted he was a simplistic writer from another era and had become passé. He and Byron continued to make the rounds at San Francisco's North Beach, staggering into the famed Beat bar, Vesuvio's, the writer bellowing, "Kerouac has left the building; I'm his replacement," while Byron pretended mock horror. The now fading writer spent time in Montana and drank heavily like Kerouac and then shot himself one afternoon, lying across his desk for a week before anyone noticed he was gone.

"You are my friend and I love you but you drink too much, Judson."

"I have a big thirst."

"Good night."

Judson put on Dylan's "Watch the River Flow" as Byron lay on his bed, remembering Judson on the river, a vibrant, almost elemental figure. If Los Angeles swallowed people like Michael Wells, this small town seemed to diminish individual lives. In the morning, Byron stepped over Judson, passed out on the floor, and walked to school.

LATER THAT WEEK, Byron viewed Ted's footage of Posse military maneuvers, and strange initiation rituals, young boys swearing allegiance, their faces satanic in the torch light. The coarse quality of Ted's old stock and primitive conditions gave his footage a cinema verite look. There was an eerie resemblance to foreign terrorist training films. Then he saw the sentry's corpse, the throat cut, his head leaning at an unnatural angle, the mouth grinning in light from the nearby dump, a dark stain on his chest. The image blurred as the cameraman fled.

"Ick," said Becky, her cigarette smoke drifting across the beam of light.

"I just stumbled upon him, then heard footsteps and ran. Something is going on, out there."

"I would say so," said Byron, "but what?"

"Whoever he was, his death wasn't reported."

"Ted? Did you stage this footage?"

"Hell no. I'm an artist. I don't fake anything."

"That's not an actor in makeup?"

"No."

"Then take this film to the authorities," Byron told him.

"Not yet," Ted replied.

The next morning as they crossed the street, Sheriff Dale picked up Ted for questioning. As they drove Ted away, Byron tried to comfort Becky. Maria stood across the street.

"They only want him for questioning."

"What happens if fat old Dale sees his Posse film?"

Before he could answer, Maria came up to them. "Hello," she said.

Frowning, Becky quickly walked away.

"What's wrong with her?"

"She and Ted think you're a cop."

"Really? I care about students, including Becky. Next time, I'll mind my own business."

"I'm glad you care about students," Byron said.

She regarded him. "You think I'm a cop?"

"Would you tell me if you were?"

"You suggesting I'm a liar?"

"Let's get lunch."

They had lunch at Juck's Bar, a dark establishment with pigeons roosting in the rafters and day-glow rock star images painted on the black walls. Everyone eventually went to Juck's: students, professors like Rex who was a champion chess player and challenged anyone, Indians, rock musicians, drug dealers and disaffected intellectuals.

"Who is Juck?"

"No one," Byron said. "Two people bought it, Chuck and Jock, and they called it Juck's. Jock died of an overdose but Chuck is still around."

Maria watched as a man went from table to table offering drugs for sale.

"That gentleman is named Methedrine Pete," said Byron.

"Why don't the police shut down Juck's?"

"Because they can keep all the misfits in one place."

Judson joined them, sober now, smoking, listening to Chuck Berry music. A few patrons sat at the bar, discussing the weather, boats, dogs and the recent fire.

"It was ruled arson," Maria finally said. "It's in the police news.

The fire chief won't say exactly how it happened, but they'll round up the former residents for questioning. They'll also want to see Ted's film."

"Ted may have hid it away," said Byron, remembering the dead sentry.

"Have you seen the film?"

"Of the fire—no."

"Is there *another* film?'

"No," Byron said, lying. "Why?"

Maria did not comment.

"I have no sympathy for Sheriff Dale or his little army out there," Judson said.

Maria sipped her beer. "Maybe he's afraid someone is gunning for the Posse. That would be an interesting twist."

Byron kept silent. He stared at Maria's shining face and bright hair and listened to her voice, knowing he did not want to believe she was an undercover cop. The drug pusher who carried drugs and drug paraphernalia in his long coat had suddenly left the bar. Judson took out a cigarette and lit it with a graceful motion. After a moment he said, "Maria? Would you like to see a movie, tonight?"

"Sure," she said. "Byron? Maybe you could join us. You like movies?"

"Never interfere with a friend's date," he told them, smiling at Judson who watched him to see if it was all right.

"I didn't know it *was* a date," Maria said. "Byron's friends think I'm a cop. Do you think I'm a cop?"

"No," said Judson. "And if you are, so what?"

Maria met Byron's eyes. "I occasionally watch out for troubled students. I guess I shouldn't give a shit. That way, I won't scare off paranoid men."

"Who isn't paranoid?" commented Judson.

"We hide, they seek," joked Byron.

Maria didn't laugh.

"Shanahan seems to be doing very well, paranoia or not," Maria finally said. "He's even going to AA. That's a step toward sobriety."

"Why—when he could drink, instead?"

"I'll see you, Judson," Byron said, and left the table.

When Byron arrived home, he thought about the dead sentry and wondered if there was a rival assassin out at Meridell Park; if so, who was he and what was his target? It sounded like a film treatment, and Byron imagined himself driving to a Burbank studio to pitch the story. Later that evening as he graded essays, the phone rang. Byron picked up.

"They grilled me and let me go," Ted said, "but they want my Posse film. I'm claiming privilege as a reporter. I don't want them to see it."

"Show them everything. Why not? The police will have to investigate."

"And spoil the fun? We got a big underground about to explode, partner."

"Explain that," Byron asked, but Ted hung up.

Byron considered what Ted suggested. That night, he drove toward Meridell Park, driving past the Owl Club. Many trucks and motorcycles were parked in front of the bar. He knew the location of the dump surrounded with a cyclone fence. Byron had binoculars, but the few lights only revealed mounds of earth in an open devastated area. As he focused the binoculars, he saw a few oddly shaped cisterns, half buried. He drove his car along a road and got out, walking to a hill where he could see a small airport near the barracks. Byron knew from Ted's film that a target range had been set up. Thinking of the corpse gave him a sick feeling, and for a moment, Byron felt someone watched him from the darkness. He listened but heard nothing.

When he returned, three men with rifles stood around his car. Their faces and eyes were hidden in the partial darkness, the scene illuminated by distant lights and the moon. One of the men flashed a light in his face. He had a chipped tooth and darting eyes.

"What the hell do you think yer doing?"

Byron backed away. "I got lost, gents."

"Like hell. You spying, out here?"

Another guard stepped close, putting his rifle under Byron's chin.

"You were at the fire. I remember you."

"I helped save Dale's son. You remember that?"

The second rifleman stared at him. "I remember. Yeah."

There was the sudden staccato of echoing gunshots. The men cursed and ran toward the airstrip. Byron got into his car, the men suddenly scattering. As Byron drove from the area, he saw a guard wearing a gas mask. A bonfire was smoking, and as Byron drove past, the sentry looking like a warrior from a monster movie lifted his rifle; Byron turned onto the highway.

He felt a sudden powerful nausea. Byron was throwing up by the side of the road when Sheriff Dale's police car pulled up, blue lights flashing. The sheriff and his deputy approached Byron.

"Jesus, you drunk?"

"No, just sick."

Sheriff Dale peered at Byron's face.

"Look, I appreciate what you did for my boy. It could've been worse except for you, but I got to know what the hell you were doing out at the landfill. That's where we dump trash. That area's restricted." The sheriff waited as Byron recovered, taking deep breaths. "What were you doing out there?"

"Looking for the Owl Club. Turned too soon, I guess."

The deputy walked to his car to run a check on Byron.

"We gotta question that sum bitch, Ted Bear. He's a crazy sucker! Tried to burn a Mormon Seminary, some years back. You know that?"

"No," said Byron.

"You don't seem drunk so I'll give you a break, okay? But don't go near that dump. Nothing out there but trash, anyway."

"What kind of trash, sheriff? I inhaled some smoke. I think I've been poisoned by chemicals."

"Maybe you had some bad dope."

"I don't do drugs," said Byron.

The deputy came up to the car. "He's clean."

"We got things to do, Mr. Duffy. Don't trespass, no more, all right? It's unhealthy!"

They drove off. Then he saw Maria driving up behind his car. She got out and embraced him. Byron pushed her away and vomited one more time.

"I'm going to the hospital," he said.

——— ———

IN THE MORNING, Maria made Byron some soup. He remembered Maria slipping into bed with him, but he was too weak to make love and woke up with a headache. His stomach had calmed down.

"I'd like to know what unknown chemical was competing with my blood cells," Byron said.

Maria walked around in her robe. She brought the morning paper.

"There was a shooting accident at Meridell Park. One of the Posse boys shot himself, evidently."

"Dead?"

"Yes."

Byron glanced at the headline. He remembered the distant shots from the night before. Maria smiled. "What *were* you doing out there?"

"I was on a drive. Why do you want to know?"

"Sorry—you get nervous when I ask questions." She sat on the bed.

"Why were *you* out there?"

"I like Judson, but I was looking for you. I'm afraid our date didn't go very far."

"How far did you want it to go?"

Maria spoke quietly. "Not as far as he wanted. With Judson, I want to talk, that's all. I love his mind. You better go to school if you feel better."

Byron got out of bed.

"I feel better now," he said. "Thanks for helping me. I was damn sick."

They embraced. Then they kissed. Maria responded with an urgent hunger, and then pushed him away. "You better go," she said. "I've got work to do."

Byron held her and kissed her again, feeling his desire coming back. Maria gently stroked his face. "Please go," she said. "Call me later."

———

THE FIRE DEPARTMENT called in Byron to answer questions; they had used dogs to sniff ignition points at the site. Sheriff Dale stood in the hall as Byron passed.

"Seems like Mr. Bear took off."

"He'll be back," said Byron.

"He was seen sneaking around at my place a number of times," said the sheriff. "Do you know if he was shootin' a film *besides* the fire?" Byron was silent. "I can subpoena evidence, and I can call you in anytime."

"I'm always willing to help, sheriff. I got a few questions myself."

The sheriff watched Byron as he entered the fire chief's office. The chief was a large man named Chuck, his once muscular body now stocky; he had a round pleasant face, warm eyes, the voice level, revealing nothing.

"Mr. Duffy. Have a seat.,"

Chuck looked at some papers as they discussed the weather and the school football team. It was a few minutes before the chief mentioned the fire.

"You know anyone who was out there that day?"

Byron told him.

"Right. Mr. James Shanahan and the student, Ted Bear. You know them well?"

"Not really. Shanahan keeps to himself. Ted is a creative, gifted student. I suspect he wants to be an actor or maybe a filmmaker."

Chuck had a neutral expression. "He shot some grim footage of the fire. We're going over it." The chief settled his bulk in a leather chair and stared out the window. "Sheriff Dale claims Ted was out at his place trespassing."

"Really?"

"Did he talk to you about it?"

"He may have mentioned watching them."

"Them?"

"Those self styled commandos out there."

Chuck smiled. "They are a caution, aren't they?" Suddenly, the chief met his eyes. "Mr. Duffy—do you know anyone who would want to kill the sheriff?"

Byron was surprised. "No. Why would anyone want to do

that?"

"Maybe Ted or one of his fellow residents. John Dale was their landlord. I know Ted has publicly condemned those extremist whack jobs, and I don't blame him. They're bad for the state. Still, as you have probably heard, that fire was deliberate. The heat and friction from the dozer set off some gasoline soaked straw in the basement."

"Why would anyone want to burn down a house that was set for demolition?"

"You tell me."

"Are you saying—?"

"Sheriff Dale was the target. His son happened to be at the controls, that morning. Nice boy. I like him." Byron remained silent. "Maybe your colleague wanted to hurt the sheriff?"

"Shanahan? God no. He's too nervous."

Byron caught himself. Chuck studied him, his gaze steady, his voice still level and warm.

"He *is* a bit nervous, isn't he?" The chief stood up. They shook hands. "We'll call you in if we need you, Mr. Duffy. I thought we were finished with those racist nuts when they left the compound up north, but we don't need a range war, do we?"

"No."

"If you discover any new information, call me."

"I will," Byron said, thinking of the dead sentry.

When Becky heard the details of Byron's interview, she exploded in Byron's small cubicle.

"Fuck him," she shouted, lighting a cigarette. He asked she extinguish it, and after a puff, she did. "They can't push us around. They can't prove Ted is an arsonist!"

Byron leaned back in his chair while Becky raved.

"You know what I think?" Becky's voice had a strain of hysteria in it. "I think Ted should turn *all* his film over to the FBI. *Let* them see the Posse maneuvers. Then let those Posse assholes explain why some guy shot himself to death, accidentally."

"If it was an accident."

After Becky left, Byron corrected a paper titled, "The Right to Bare Arms." He imagined a strip show with pistols. Maria did not come to her office, but later in the afternoon, Shanahan, his eyes lustrous, poked his head into Byron's space. He seemed happy as he sat down.

"I'm sorry you're one of those getting the ax. Maybe I can help. I have some pull with Sterling."

"I'll be all right. Anything else?"

"No," he said. Shanahan smiled. "The Negroes are doing well."

"Did you hear one of the Posse boys at Meridell Park shot himself?"

"Yes. I heard. You believe it?"

"I guess. What *should* I believe?"

"I have an appointment with Chief Chuck."

"Good."

Shanahan glared at him with something of suppressed mirth about his lips and eyes. Then he remained in the hall while Byron waited for the professor to speak; moments later, he was gone. Two hours later as Byron walked across the quad, Sterling motioned him over; they sat in Sterling's Cadillac, looking at the cold driving day. Sterling had lost some of his cheerful manner.

"I really did want to start a great English Department in the wilderness. I mean, Massacre Rocks and the Birds of Prey area are so close. Timber up north. Desert to the west. Plus the Fort Hall Reservation. They suspect Shanahan of arson."

"Really?"

"He was acting strangely when that house went. I'd dance on the ashes, and I don't *care* about those extremists. They seem so petty and passé with the horrific terrorist attacks on New York, but really, it's getting *crazy* around here." He shot Byron a side-glance. "I may have to hire you back. Tell Mr. McGee to slow down. We have little money but enrollment is climbing."

"Of course," Byron agreed. "Californians know we exist."

"You think Shanahan is a threat?"

"No," Byron said. "He's afraid."

Byron walked home. It was quiet in the house until he heard Judson and a woman laughing in his room. Byron did not want to see anyone, so he put on a warmer coat and walked toward the door. The phone rang.

"Tonight is the night," Maria said.

"For what?"

"This I have to explain? After tonight, my friend, the milk train don't stop here no more. *Comprende?*"

He drove along south Main until he came to Johnny Creek Road, then turned up a mountain road, driving with a view of Pocatello. On the radio, Tom Waits sang about "Saturday Night" and its elusive heart. He liked the bluesy sound, and the rough whiskey voice of Waits. Byron could put himself into songs. He had walked Dylan's beach in "Tambourine Man", and even imagined the white Christmas of Bing Crosby, a favorite song of his father's. Sometimes, he saw the large luminous eyes of Shanahan in the windshield, glaring at him. Byron drove to the cottage.

Maria was inside, something dark in her face and eyes. Did she want to be there? Did she not want to be anywhere? Then she unbuttoned her dress, kicking off her shoes. She unhooked her bra, a Star of David hanging between her small firm breasts. She walked toward Byron and began to unbutton his shirt. They kissed, and kneeling, Maria pulled down his pants after taking off his shoes. Food was still on the table.

Wearing underpants, they walked to the bed in another room, and turning to face him, Maria put her arms around his neck, pressing against him, her mouth slightly open, her hips moving. She ripped down his underpants and slipped out of her panties, sitting on the bed, Byron standing, looking down at her upturned face. She held and softly kissed his erection, and then they slipped under the covers to make love quickly, sleeping for a while, then attacking each other with an animal hunger. Byron felt the urgency of the moment, as though it would be their last. Her body was firm but soft, their lovemaking intense; she knew how to revive him, using her hands and mouth. In the morning, Maria smiled, watching his face in the new light. Then her expression was somber, betrayed, as though some code had been broken.

"I was afraid of falling in love," she said, her face passive.

"And?"

The answer never came.

They did not have much time to even enjoy the fresh breakfast she cooked, for already, Shanahan had taken an old World War II Carcano Italian rifle and from atop the Business Administration building, began shooting at students, firing in a random pattern. As

Maria took a call, Byron realized it was something he had suspected but never really believed would happen. A pattern of violence had opened up, like Byron's recent nightmares of Custer's Last Stand, the Indians closing in to slaughter and castrate the invading white troopers while blood darkened the Montana grass.

Maria kissed Byron and said good-bye as he stepped out the door.

"Be careful," she said, a strange resignation in her voice.

"Why? Ted and Shanahan are nuts and we have paranoid racists ready for war. I'm just a boring English teacher."

"This place is nuts and you're *not* boring."

"Who would want to hurt me?"

Without smiling, Maria said, "You'd be surprised. I'll see you."

The sky was overcast, the air a steely gray. Driving past a few homes and cottonwoods, he thought of Ted's cryptic remark about the underground and a possible confrontation with the well-armed white supremacists; would Ted put down his camera and fire rounds instead? Would peace loving "flower children" from a dead era be a match for a trained fanatical militia? Why had Byron kept silent about the dead sentry, and why had no report been made? Byron tried to picture the face of the sentry's killer who possibly cut the guard's throat while he slept only to wake, choking on his own blood. What was he guarding and how would conspiracy minded civilian soldiers react? Something had changed, and not just because of Shanahan's desperate action.

THE SNIPER

THE NEWS MEDIA CONVERGED ON THE SCHOOL, though from the first gunshot until police surrounded the school and set snipers on Red Hill overlooking the campus, Shanahan had hit no one, not even during the early morning rush hour. The students scattered toward trees, buildings, and the cafeteria. When Byron pulled up, he saw flashes of gunfire from the window just below the roof; he ran toward the cafeteria. Classes were canceled for the day and Byron planned to use his house or the library if they convened the next day, assuming Shanahan held out. Becky found Byron drinking coffee. Police sirens screamed in the distance.

"He can't hit shit."

"Maybe he doesn't *want* to hit anyone. Maybe he's making a statement." Byron stirred his coffee. "I hear Ted gave the fire department his footage."

Becky snorted. "He wanted the sheriff to see his kid going up in smoke."

"For God's sake, the boy is innocent."

"But Fat Sheriff Dale isn't."

"Becky? Do you think Ted planned it? The fire, I mean?"

"Hell no!"

"He's not planning to bump the sheriff off?"

"He doesn't need to. Maybe the Posse footage could be used to blackmail those suckers."

"Or have them hunting him down," said Byron. "That dead man was a Posse member."

More shots rang through the campus.

"That poor guy," said Byron.

"Poor guy? He's a symptom of this school's sickness," Becky

said. She reached over and took his hand. "Look, I just hope I can get Ted outta here before a redneck blows his ass away—or he blows some dirtbag to hell."

"That might be a possibility."

Becky got up. "I *can* tell you this. Ted's been staying at a shack on the reservation. He's got his Posse film hidden there." Becky nervously met his eyes; hers were dark and frightened. "You don't really think they'll come looking for him, do you?"

"No," said Byron, lying.

Becky left through the rear exit, even as Sterling ducked into the cafeteria; police shouted at him as a bullet ricocheted off the pavement. He saw Byron and sat down.

"There goes his tenure," said Byron, as a second shot went off.

"Very funny," said Sterling. "This looks *awful*. How could he *do* this to us? We'll make the national news for a scandal. This will *trash* our image."

"What image?"

"I'm serious!"

"So am I."

Sterling regarded him with his petulant stare. "Well, I knew Shanahan had problems, but I had no idea he'd do this."

"It might get worse," said Byron.

Sterling gazed at him with his striking eyes. "Really? It gets *worse*?"

They saw the running police outside, a few hiding in bushes, carrying radios and watching the window where the sniper sat. Byron was about to leave when he saw Maria running across the quad. There was something very different in the way she carried herself, as though she had a private mission. None of the police stopped her. She ran into the nearly empty cafeteria, spotting Byron almost instantly. He did not recognize the expression of anger and urgency in her face as she walked up to his table, and he thought of Becky's warning even as Maria seized his arm with strong tight fingers and lifted him from the chair.

"Byron, we think you can help. Shanahan wants to talk to you."

Byron pulled back.

"He won't cooperate with our negotiator," she continued.

"*Our* negotiator?"

Maria, with a quick snap, flashed her badge. He saw her photo, the hair shorter, and the letters: *FBI.*

"Well, well. Hello, Agent Goldstein." He tuned and faced at the department chairman. "Did you know she was FBI?"

"Yes," Sterling said. "If you can help, get that man down from there."

Byron nodded. "Let's go."

They approached the building, the rifle silent. Then he stood in an elevator, riding up to the sniper's floor, looking at Maria's face; she had assumed an official self that had no connection with the night before. They were both on a mission to stop a demented sniper. Agents were at either end of the corridor, and many uniformed police. Maria pointed to the door leading to the room where Shanahan had chosen to make his last stand.

"Listen up. He's probably low on ammo. He's got a bolt-action rifle, which is a clumsy gun. I think he's too chicken shit to come out shooting. If he doesn't remember me, he does remember you."

"Maybe he thinks you're a traitor."

Maria glanced at him, dropping her professional mask for a microsecond.

"Maybe," she said. "Rap on the door and find out what he wants. We have to keep him immobilized. Distract him—we can do the rest."

"Sure," said Byron. "No problem."

"Talk him out in the hall."

"So you can shoot him? I don't want him to die."

"I don't want him to die, either. Rap three times." He walked toward the door. Maria stopped him. "Talk to him, but don't go inside." He walked on. "Byron?" He turned again, seeing the semi-automatic pistol in her hand. "Be careful."

Byron walked toward the door. Another shot came from inside, then he heard the bolt action driving home another shell. Byron stood outside, hesitated, then gently rapped three times. He could hear the man inside listening, and imagined Shanahan's terrified face, the small hands gripping the rifle. Byron glanced down the corridor, seeing Maria in a crouching position, her gun out. Byron rapped again.

"Who is it?"

The voice was high pitched and quavering.

"It's me, Byron Duffy."

"Liar!"

A bullet ripped through the door. The agents and police, including Maria, fell to the floor, guns pointed. Byron could hear another round being fed into the chamber.

"Shanahan, what the hell are you doing? You *asked* to see me."

"Go away!"

"I'm coming in."

Maria got up, waving to Byron to stop, but he suddenly kicked open the door and walked in. Shanahan held the rifle, standing by the window.

"Oh, it's only you," he said.

Shanahan's face was pale, with heavy dark bags under his red eyes, the shaking hands holding an old World War II rifle.

"Of course, it's me. You *asked* for me. What are you doing?"

"Close the door."

Byron closed the door, hearing a scurrying in the hall. Then he saw a photographer suspended from a rope, swing past the window. Shanahan turned and pointed the gun, and the man with the camera vanished. He turned again, grinning, holding up the weapon. He had not slammed the bolt home on his next bullet.

"This is an old Italian war rifle," he said, proudly. "It's the gun that got Jack Kennedy. Some of the boys prefer newer guns, but I grew fond of this one." He slid home the bolt. "It will do fine, though it has crooked sights." He nodded at Byron and stepped away from the window. "I thought it was time the world realized we existed."

He glared at Byron with a strange triumph.

"Who existed?"

"The Wrecking Crew. Only this time, we're turncoats. We're going to bring them down!"

"And who is 'Them'?"

A cameraman appeared outside the window again, shooting video. He was suspended beneath a flexible rope, like a bungee jumper. Shanahan turned and fired a round through the window, even as the cameraman bounded away. Byron had seen the face, and the same wispy hair. It was Ted Bear, shooting more of his cinema verite, two hundred feet up.

"I bet that was a Republican," said Shanahan. "You want to know who the enemy is? The Posse, the K.K.K., the Aryan Nation. We've declared war on their obscenities."

"We?"

"All my life I felt guilt for what my father did. Well, it's payback time! All their worst nightmares are coming true, even to nigger police on campus." Shanahan glared at him in the poor light. "I got help, too. Lots of it. Even International help!"

Byron slid down the wall and sat, watching the sniper.

"They are out there, Shanahan. Police. If you don't give up, they'll kill you. Give me the gun."

Looking at the weapon, Byron could not imagine him hitting anything, unless by accident.

"I *won't* give up! It is time to stop all of it! It's the end of the line, brother. I am God, and I have decided."

Shanahan began shrieking with laughter, and Byron felt a cold sick fear. He had never heard a voice capable of these kinds of maniacal sounds, not even in horror movies. Finally, Byron spoke: "Shanahan, you asked to see me. What do you want?" He could feel movement in the hall beyond the door. "*Talk* to me, Shanahan."

Shanahan's face was working in the light of a dying afternoon, his expression like that of an injured or frustrated child, the grimace of sorrow and frustration tightening the facial muscles. He began to weep, his narrow shoulders shaking.

The cameraman appeared, shot some footage, bounded away. Byron took a step.

"Stay there," he shouted in a shrill voice.

"Did you plan that fire?"

"I didn't need to."

"What do you mean?"

Shanahan held up a fresh round. "I've got the ultimate dum dum bullet. I shove this baby home, pull the trigger, the whole university and the fucking world goes, KERBLAM! Understand? It will go in a big bang. Won't Sterling be surprised?"

Byron took another step. "Shanahan? They'll gun you down!"

"Who? The police? The Posse, whom I betrayed? The Israelis? They've become Nazis, themselves, but for this operation, they're on *our* side."

"Give me the rifle—now!"

"I'm not alone. I got snipers out there who *really* know how to shoot—including warriors of the Indian Nation. Byron—you got to carry on."

"Carry on what?"

"The liberal revolution you assholes started in the sixties." Shanahan grinned at him with something sick in his face, his eyes going suddenly white in his skull. He slipped the bullet into the chamber. "The US military can take out those Islamic extremists, and we'll exterminate the local paranoids. Stand back and watch some true style," he said, slamming home his marked 'dum dum' bullet. "Kiss your ass goodbye. It's time to end the *shit*!"

Shanahan's face had the exaggeration of a cartoon. Then he closed his eyes, as though frozen in a grim meditation, and Byron dove at him. Shanahan screamed as they rolled on the floor, struggling, Byron grabbing the rifle, firing into the ceiling even as police charged into the room. Shanahan moaned in despair and disappointment as the police handcuffed him, shoving his face into the floor. They dragged him screaming from the room, pushing Byron against the wall.

"It's supposed to blow up the world," he shrieked. "Now!"

Byron saw Maria, heavily sweating. She glared at Shanahan being carried off, and then turned to face Byron. For a moment, there was a glimmer of communication.

"The rifle?"

"What?"

"Hand me the weapon."

"Yes. Here."

He gave her the old rifle. Then Byron forced his way out, passing Sterling holding out a manicured hand. Shanahan's desperate cries echoed down the corridor. While a TV anchor interviewed Ted Bear, Byron quickly rushed toward his car to avoid the media, but they saw him.

"There he is. Professor Duffy, we have some questions! Sir!"

He said nothing.

Driving away, he could still see Shanahan's pale gleaming face in the light reflected from the window. Judson McGee waited at home. His new woman was a short stocky graduate student named Darlene. She had short blond hair and a sharp focus in her eyes as they shook hands. They watched Shanahan on the news, his gun and face seen through the window, then the police dragging him in cuffs from the building. The clips were followed by Ted's account of his dangerous taping. Byron wondered if he was acting.

"Perhaps there's a conspiracy here," announced Ted from the screen.

"Oswald *did* use an old Italian war rifle," said Judson.

"It's a bad rifle. If Shanahan was serious, why would he use *that* antiquated weapon?"

"Why did Oswald?" Judson asked.

Byron found himself watching the local coverage after Judson and Darlene had gone to bed. He called Michael Wells long distance but there was no answer. Byron did not want to remember Shanahan's mad face the next day when they questioned him, and he didn't make eye contact with Maria who sat with a beefy agent from the Bureau. Chief Chuck sat, quietly observing him. Then they asked the same questions in a different way: "We are concerned Shanahan was part of some conspiracy, not just another schizoid."

"He ran with The Wrecking Crew."

They studied him, expressionless. He could feel Sheriff Dale's eyes going to his face, then meeting his eyes. "Come again?"

"He mentioned some former Posse assassins called The Wrecking Crew. He said he had become a counter assassin, out to destroy the Posse and other extremist groups like them."

Maria and the agent leaned forward. "What you're saying is significant."

Sheriff Dale interrupted.

"Wait a minute. Hold your horses. Are you telling me there's a secret underground out there taking pot shots at some good old boys who get a little riled now and then? I never heard of no Wrecking Crew, before."

Byron felt like an actor delivering an important line.

"He said there were others—and that it would not stop." Dale continued to stare and Byron could see his mind working, the jaws stopping, the breath suddenly quiet. "There's more. He said there were Indian snipers."

Dale exploded. "Warhoops? He's nuts! We got Sitting Bull about a hundred years ago."

"How many have you lost in your little army, sheriff—two?"

"There ain't no army." He paused. "One. An accident. Why?"

"Just asking. I'd like to go." When Byron stood up, the fire chief held up his hand.

"Is there anything *else* we should know?"

"You better talk now," the sheriff warned.

Byron made eye contact with Maria. "All I can say is that Shanahan is a frightened man. I have never been favorably disposed toward the FBI. I don't like them."

"Why not?" another agent asked. "We like you."

Maria was more blunt: "You're out of fashion, Byron. Who broke the Civil Rights case in Mississippi? *We* did."

"Who will stop the next major attack? We will," the other agent said.

Chuck reached over with his card. "Call me."

Byron left the office. Ted waited outside.

"How's the television business, Ted? Are you a star, yet?"

"Come on, Byron. It's just karma. Shanahan was a warrior. I caught his greatest moment."

"They may be coming for you next," said Byron. He walked down the corridor. Ted watched him leave, then entered the small office. Byron saw Becky outside but brushed past her.

"Byron, wait a minute."

"I'm not good company." He walked on.

Byron found Judson and Darlene at Buddy's. He hoped he would not see Shanahan's face in his dreams, the desperate man cowering in a darkened room with police closing in.

"Maria was right," said Byron. "I guess the milk train don't stop here no more."

"What's that?"

"It's gone—smokin' down the track."

"What are you talking about?" said Judson.

Byron didn't answer. He saw Soumya sitting with students at another table. She smiled and waved at him, then they whispered among themselves in the language of India. Byron heard Duncan bellow his name and took a phone call. It was Maria. "We have to talk," she said.

"I got nothing to say," said Byron.

"I may have information you could use."

"Don't tell me you'd rat on the FBI, too. Don't you have some code of silence?"

"I'm sorry you feel that way, Byron. A job is a job. I teach and I work for the Bureau. We protect lives."

"Whose lives?" said Byron. "It's over."

"*This* is not over. They know about Ted's Posse film. Shanahan may have been into a bigger scope than we thought."

"So? I'm out of it."

"No you're not," she said, but Byron hung up.

From across the table, Darlene studied him with bright, penetrating eyes. Suddenly, she laughed loudly, grinning at Byron with a joyous arrogance. She poked Judson.

"Where did you find this clown?"

"I don't know. Where did *you* find him?"

Darlene laughed again as a few people turned to look.

"Actually, I found her," Judson said. "At a poetry reading."

"You're a poet?"

Darlene leaned on the table, her round face close to his.

"That's right...but not some chicken-shit liberal poet. I think Ronald Reagan was a great man and a great President except he wasn't conservative enough. I hate these left wing, pot smoking, faggot poets who write limp verses about how fucked up they are and the country is while they're collecting welfare. Please—*don't* mistake me for those punks."

"I won't," Byron said.

"Ironically, most poets *are* chicken-shit liberals," Judson boomed, his resonant voice breaking over them. "Your hobby has you with some strange company."

"It's *not* a hobby and I think the image of the liberal 'sensitive' poet is a cliché."

Darlene knew she always disturbed listeners at poetry readings; recently she followed a woman reciting poems about the human condition, delivering lyrics with closed eyes and a quavering voice, only to have Darlene launch her short poems about God, country and the annihilation of the left wing. On a good night, patrons hissed.

"Look," Judson said, "Regarding Shanahan, someone should kill a few *more* of those supremacist pricks."

"Racists go too far," Darlene offered. "But if they bump off a few Democrats—good."

Darlene and Judson drank while Byron listened to some blues on the jukebox. Judson lifted the pitcher and poured a beer for Byron.

"It took courage, what you did. I feel bad for Shanahan, but he could've shot you."

Looking around the bar, Byron grew a little anxious.

"What do you think of Ayn Rand?" Darlene asked with an edge in her voice. "Isn't she wonderful?"

"I'll tell you later. Right now, I'm going for a drive."

At the door, Byron glanced at Soumya's table. "Who won the Cricket game?"

"The Pakis," Soumya said.

Byron drove to Scout Mountain along some railroad tracks, listening to the wind and the heater hum, enjoying the solitude. Then he played a cassette. John Lee Hooker was singing a Robert Johnson song called "Terraplane Blues." He made a big circle and came back, driving past the Owl Club. A truck full of men followed and pulled close behind him. Byron turned off onto the main highway heading toward Pocatello Creek Road and numerous restaurants. It was here that the pickup turned toward town. Perhaps the men inside did not recognize his car. Perhaps they were not ready to strike, yet. He had talked Shanahan alive into the hands of the police, but if Shanahan were telling the truth, and not merely having a manic episode, the Posse might want him dead.

Byron stopped at the Sandpiper for a drink. The restaurant, like Buddy's, had a certain predictable sameness that tonight he found comforting. A well-known guitarist was singing love songs, and the people at tables drank and talked loudly over the acoustic music.

"Talk to me, man." The voice was Ted's. Behind him stood Becky, her thick frizzy blonde hair combed out. Ted shuffled his light sinewy body on one foot. "The media asked me to get some footage, and I did. Wait until the FBI gets a gander at the sick little Posse maneuvers I filmed. Byron, we got a *case* against those racist mothers."

"What case?"

"I identified with Shanahan," Ted continued. "A warrior against the world. I'm a warrior, myself. I *like* confrontation!"

"Since when do you exploit a man's tragedy?"

"I'm an artist. That's my job. I think I made it hot for the Posse."

"They got weapons," Byron said. "Do your drama on the stage."

"I'm like the mad Artaud. My *life* is theatre."

"Let's do it someplace else," Becky said. "LA. New York."

The guitarist took a break, and Becky moved close to Byron, holding his eyes.

"I got you into this, Byron," she drawled. "Sorry."

"Forget it," Byron said. "For God's sake, be careful."

When he arrived home, Judson and Darlene were in Judson's room, drinking and laughing. Byron went to his room. They were quiet for a while, and he managed to sleep, waking at some point to their loud lovemaking in the night. He also heard another sound, and recognized it, the slapping of a hand against bare flesh before Darlene came, her vocal carrying beyond the wall.

———————

DAVID STERLING held his meeting in an empty classroom. Judson had forgotten to comb his hair and he looked hung over. Shanahan's tragic incident had left an opening, and one MA would be retained. Then Sterling regarded Maria, who stood opposite Byron in a circle.

"We may be losing Maria since her FBI cover is blown. She's the spy who came in from the cold. That means, I may be able to keep *two* of the MA candidates."

"Lies," barked Chan. "We're all being sold down the river."

"That's not correct. I know it's *awful* that we play with lives and careers, here, but *that's* education." He smiled. "That's all. Don't forget the Hemingway seminar, this summer. We get to pick over Papa's literary bones."

Rex took out a cigarillo. "White writers are retrograde," he said. "Anyone for a game of chess at Juck's?"

"Playing with you isn't playing," Byron told him.

The gathering broke up. Maria wore a man's suit to the meeting. Outside, he watched her walk to her car, stopping for a moment to talk with a graduate student. Then she turned to face him.

"Byron, why don't you grow up?"

"Why don't you?"

"You will need my help," she said.

"I have to visit a sick friend."

Byron walked past her and drove to the new courthouse that also housed the jail. He walked through the metal detector and met with Shanahan, dressed in an orange jump suit; he seemed stable and clear in his thoughts and smiled at Byron, no hysteria in his voice.

"I *am* sorry about what happened. They plan to come for me at noon. They'll move me to Blackfoot South—the hospital." He smiled again. "Are you all right?"

"Yes."

Shanahan leaned against the glass, speaking into the phone.

"They're listening in on our conversation. That's all right. When the cops dig up the body, maybe you better lay low for now."

"What body?"

He pressed his hands against the glass. "Listen. I have a pair of shoes I want you to keep for me until I get out."

"Talk to me about the body. I saw Ted's—"

"I *am* sorry for bringing you into this. When I don't take the lithium, I literally go crazy. Of course, I know a lot of things. When I get out, we can get the band back on the road."

"What band?"

Byron could see another image sliding up into Shanahan's face, the eyes suddenly gleaming with an inner light. "What band? Why, Neil Young and Crazy Horse, of course."

"Shanahan, I am *not* Neil Young."

"You're not?"

He saw tears spilling from the man's eyes; as Shanahan wept, Byron felt he was staring into a face of all the world's pain and despair. Shanahan took off his worn shoes, but he could not pass them through the glass. A guard came over as Shanahan whispered into the phone.

"I got guards outside my cell. They want to kill me. When they take me to Blackfoot, you got to stop the truck and save me, Byron. Then we'll liberate Ireland."

"Okay. But first, take your medication. I'll talk to your lawyer."

"He's a Zionist," screamed Shanahan. "A charlatan!"

"Keep your voice down."

"I will." The guard touched him on the shoulder. Shanahan reacted: "Why don't you fuck off?"

"This visit is over," the guard said.

Shanahan lowered his head. "I'm sorry. I think they gave me the wrong medication, this morning. Sometimes, I don't know what I'm saying."

The guard motioned. Shanahan held the phone, trembling on the other side of the glass. "They *will* kill me."

"They?"

"Time's up," said the guard.

"Shanahan. Is there another avenging hitman out there?"

Suddenly in control, Shanahan smiled at Byron.

"Of course. That could scare the hate groups, make them dangerous for a while." After a pause, he said, "Don't worry. This hitman will protect you."

"What hitman?"

"Never again." He waved goodbye. "Never again."

"I'll pick up your shoes next time," Byron said.

Then Shanahan was gone. Byron could hear other prisoners and family members talking loudly in the small room, separated by a glass partition. He walked outside into the too bright street. Sheriff Dale drove by. The flow of traffic seemed normal with people entering or leaving the state building. Byron didn't want to admit that he had to talk to Agent Maria Jones, AKA Goldstein, but he called her from Buddy's Pizza.

They met at the Fort Hall Reservation. It was a cold clear day, and from the entrance to the river bottoms, he could see a distant herd of buffalo grazing. He liked to watch them, thinking of what America had been, indulging in a romantic fantasy of Lewis and Clark's America. Byron drove down Sheepskin Road beyond an orange sign warning against illegal hunting, fishing and trespassing, driving out into open prairie. Wild horses ran in herds, driven by a stallion. Beyond the open country were the Snake River and the plaque marking the original Fort Hall of 1834, a meeting place for Jim Bridger and Kit Carson. Byron had come out with Ted once to watch some Bannock Shoshone Indians driving buffalo into a vast, penned area. The Indians used pick up trucks to herd the bulky, ill tempered, shaggy animals, the bulls occasionally turning and charging the bouncing trucks. Byron saw Maria pulling up and parking; she walked across crunching gravel toward him, smiling as though they were two lovers with no cares.

"Hello" she said.

"Hello."

"You packing your gun?"

"Of course, Byron. And I guess you'll never forgive me for having a job with the Bureau."

They sat on a hill, overlooking the prairie.

"Maybe you're right. Times have changed. Shall we skip all formalities and cut to the chase?"

"Sure," Maria said.

Byron related his conversation with Shanahan. He told her about the footage of the dead man. Sometimes, he felt like a traitor, but he wanted Maria's story. Her eyes studied his face. When he finished, he waited patiently.

"Talk," he said.

"Some of what I know is classified," she told him.

"So you lied to me? You said you had information."

"I do. Listen to what I *can* give you. Shanahan's father *was* a member of the Klan. The Wrecking Crew *did* exist, and claimed hits from King to even foreign leaders. Some hits were untrue, of course. Some weren't."

Maria spoke in the clipped speech of a dossier, and as Byron listened, he saw Hollywood producers already planning a movie of the week.

"We have an informant *with* the Posse who says they think Shanahan's a Jewish infiltrator, and that the Wrecking Crew is some hit squad from Israel. They could make a hit on Ted and steal his film of their maneuvers before we take possession of it. Remember, running paramilitary maneuvers is not a crime. If we have Ted's film as evidence of a murder, we have an excuse to investigate further. The dump could be tied to a mob operation."

"Mob?"

"What's left of organized crime has been reduced to the toxic dump business, now. We've picked up a minor Jersey mobster in the area."

It was growing warmer. Byron stared out over the beautiful country, not yet green.

"What about an Indian hitman?"

"Not on our radar, but the Posse doesn't take the tribe seriously."

"One more question. Remind me. What does 'Never again' refer to?"

Maria reacted to the phrase. "Why?"

"Shanahan said it before they took him away. He said, 'Never again'."

"It's a reference to the holocaust and the six million Jews who died."

"Of course."

"He said that, meaning revenge?"

"I don't know. Shanahan is Irish. He isn't a Jew," Byron said.

"But I am." Maria nodded, suddenly amused. "My real name is Mary Goldstein. My mother was Catholic, father Jewish. I'm half Jewish and half Christmas."

Nearby, cliff swallows were flying in and out of caves in the hill. She gently rubbed her hand on his shoulder and along his thigh. Once again, he was struck by the beauty of her eyes, the intense warm gaze that could turn suddenly bright like a jewel in dark earth.

"I was afraid of getting involved again, but I did."

"Are you involved with someone else?"

Maria didn't answer at first.

"I was close to an agent named Dalton. Hell, we're *still* close. There's also a possibility I made some enemies along the way."

"Someone put a hit on you?"

Maria shrugged. Viewing the open country, they might have been waiting to lay out a picnic. "It's always a possibility."

"Can you tell me about it?"

"I had my Tarot cards read. There's a dark intruder in my

future."

"You're joking, right?"

"No. Listen, Byron, let's work together. I need to get Ted's film before they come for it. These Posse people are threatened, which makes them more dangerous."

"Shanahan said that."

"Everything that has happened is proof to them that Jews *are* taking over the country, not to mention blacks and black police." Byron recognized a catch in her voice. "I am their worst nightmare, a Jewish agent of the FBI."

"Why did you become a fed?"

"My father was a cop in Detroit. I wanted to be like him. I was always in competition with four brothers, all older, but they didn't go on the force, I did. I wanted to serve. I wanted to help people."

"Through a spy organization?"

"We gather intelligence, and you better hope we're successful."

Byron observed as the herd of buffalo came closer, remembering a conversation he had with his ex wife on a beach in San Francisco, the waves breaking on the sand; the winter air was biting as she told him she was leaving. Then she began crying. He had stared into a future that seemed empty, without meaning, like the distant ships at sea. Sea gulls watched them. He now studied Maria, feeling vulnerable, seeing not the armed agent but another fragile human being. She spoke first.

"I missed you, Byron."

"I missed you, too." He took her hand. "So now what?"

"I have a job to finish."

"Then you leave?"

"The Bureau could ship me to another location tomorrow." She kissed his cheek. "I don't want to lose you." They embraced.

"I guess if I can't find you, you'll be able to track me down. You have my dossier."

"True."

"*Would* you track me down?"

"I'd always want to know where you were."

"I've seen some other sides of your face."

"You don't want to know everything." A distant jeep drove down a side road. "Byron? We *have* to get Ted's film and *you* need

80

a guard."

"I can take care of myself," said Byron.

"We are dealing with fanatics," said Maria. "Let's walk."

They walked down the gravel road to the Fort Hall monument and stared at the plaque commemorating the original fort from an earlier century. She took his hand.

"Byron?"

He glanced down at her face and nodded. They found a lovely meadow and lay down near the river. Maria leaned over and kissed him, undoing his shirt button, and then they quickly undressed and made love to the songs of wild birds. Her head and shoulders were pressed against the wild flowers as he thrust inside, kissing the curve of her throat, her head flung back, her breasts open to his lips, her eyes closed, hearing her rapid breathing, smelling the earth and trees and young honeysuckle. They came together. After a while, Maria and Byron sat up and dressed. The Snake River flowed quietly, and wind blew in the trees overhead.

"Unprofessional conduct, but I needed that."

"So did I. Did the earth move?"

She laughed. "Yes, it did."

Maria looked toward the road where they had parked and Byron suddenly felt a chill; the birds stopped singing and an unnatural hush fell over the meadow. He stared toward the river and saw a man watching them. Standing in high grass, he was short and heavy-set, wearing a blue Union Army jacket and a black hat with a broad brim that kept his Indian face half in shadow. A white feather glowed in the sunlight. The single dark eye was fixed on him.

"My God. Maria?"

"What?"

"We got company."

"Where?"

But as Maria turned and they faced the river, the apparition had disappeared.

"I saw an Indian man watching us," he said, "wearing a Civil War jacket."

"I hope he got an eyeful," said Maria. "Let's go."

They drove across country that would soon turn green, crossing a bridge over a narrow stream, passing some abandoned corrals. No

Indians fished. Maria turned onto a gravel road.

THE night before, three armed white men had driven to the remote cabin of the Eagle Man on the reservation. His weathered shack sat along a stretch where the asphalt road turned to gravel, and distant potato fields lay beyond the cabin. Beyond that was the shot-up sign warning unauthorized people to proceed no further down the gravel road that ran through meadows and curved near the Snake River and open fields where buffalo and wild horses still grazed. It was dark on the prairie and the air was lit with occasional flashes of sheet lightning in the night sky.

The three white men in the pickup truck felt uneasy driving toward the river bottoms knowing the Indian Police might stop them, though they could argue they were lost. One of the men was John Dixon, thin and in his mid-forties. He had a weathered face and a broken front tooth; his young companion, Brandon, was compactly built with nervous eyes now watching the light playing over the gravel road. Both men wore jeans, Levi jackets and Stetsons, but the driver was different. Wearing leather pants, Rusty was a big man with thick blond hair in a ponytail and a wide mouth; a silver stud flashed in his tongue whenever he laughed. Earlier in the day, he had swallowed the last of his beer and placed a lead weight on a chain and swung it from a hook slipped through the hole in his tongue. It was an impressive display.

"You get more girls with this here stud in your tongue, boys. This tongue of mine drives 'em wild if you know what I mean."

"I'm a man, Rusty," Brandon said.

"What's that supposed to mean?" Rusty said. "You think eating pussy is unmanly?"

John Dixon said nothing, staring ahead at the deeply rutted road illuminated by the truck lights. A light wind blew through the highly flammable cheat grass. All three men were armed, and a shotgun lay in a rack behind the driver. Rusty took out a bottle of Jack Daniels and the two men drank and continued to argue the merits of tongue studs.

"I seen girls with 'em," Brandon said. "Made me sick. They look like Dykes."

"What does that tell you?" Rusty asked.

"I've been down this road before," Dixon finally said. "I don't like it. Why do we care about this squirrely hippy with a camera? I heard that crazy Injun moved down by the river."

"We don't care about him," Brandon said. "And that squirrely hippy has a film we need."

"We lost buddies," Rusty said. "One thing the military taught me, you take care of and avenge your own. Now if it's real good money, I'll even work for niggers."

In the cab of the truck, all three men sat in the darkness, bouncing with the ruts in the road.

"You don't think he suspects something?"

"He's probably stoned."

"And there's three of us," Rusty said.

"His girlfriend is sure pretty," Brandon said.

"I'd do her," Rusty agreed.

"This could be a trap," Dixon warned. "I heard this psycho fruit packs a gun."

"We're at war," Rusty told him. "Shit, you lost a relative out at the compound."

"My brother was an idiot," Dixon insisted. "Talked to himself. Heard voices."

"Idiots got a right to live," Brandon argued. "Somebody cut his throat."

"He coulda fallen on his own knife, knowing him."

They followed the gravel road in the dry darkness, once seeing a deer in the headlights. Brandon wanted to shoot but they couldn't risk alerting the Fort Hall Police. A single vehicle driving across the restricted area might draw enough attention. Rusty suddenly told a joke.

"You know what's significant about buffalo?"

"No," Brandon said, taking a drink. "What?"

"It's proof Indians fucked niggers."

They laughed except for John Dixon who stared out at the black prairie. They passed an abandoned gas station. Then Rusty took the truck off the road, killed the lights and coasted down a path toward a small cabin. A kerosene lamp glowed inside the crudely built shack and they saw wavering shadows through the window. Rusty pulled on the brake.

"Showtime," he said.

Carrying pistols, the three men exited the truck quietly, Rusty bringing along the shotgun. He had black leather metal-studded bands around his thick wrists. They spread out and advanced on the cabin. The night air was still. Rusty moved like a military commando on the lonely shack, the lamp glowing weakly inside. Dixon held back but Brandon waved him on with a head toss. They heard the occasional sound of roosting birds and other sounds they couldn't identify. Dixon sensed another presence in the darkness as they advanced.

——— ——

MARIA DROVE along an open field, the tires throwing up gravel from the road.

"The tribe has a lot of stories about avenging spirits on the reservation."

"So I heard. Ted's hiding out here, somewhere," Byron said.

"The game warden mentioned a shack owned by The Eagle Man. He's a slightly regarded old guy who cares for sick birds."

Maria's scanner was tuned to tribal police frequency, and they heard voices:

"Shot up the Towersap place..."

"...Edmo Road. Need a backup..."

"...dead birds..."

Placing a flashing blue police light on the car, Maria pressed the accelerator, driving over ruts in the gravel road. As they came over the ridge, Byron felt nauseated.

"If anything happens to Ted—"

"Quiet. I'm listening."

It was hard to clearly understand the Indian voices coming over the police radio.

Then they stepped out of the car, walking toward the Indian police vehicles and the group of cops who stared at the many dead birds. Billy Towersap, the Eagle man, his bony frame racked by sobs, howled—the mouth an open circle of black teeth. Someone had riddled the shack with gunfire. Ted's desk lay open on the ground, split with an ax. Maria touched a dead bird and shook her head. "Well," she said.

Teton, a huge burly game warden, approached her. As they spoke, Byron realized that many people knew Maria as a federal agent.

"One truck full of armed men," said Teton. "Shot the place to shit, then ran inside looking for something. I don't know why they killed the birds. Who do you think would do this? Were they gunning for that crazy white boy?"

"The Posse—and yes, they were. Where is he?"

"Who knows?"

Still howling, Billy ran toward the river like an emaciated spirit; they knew he couldn't tell them. Byron examined the feathered carnage, including one bald eagle. It was a grotesque still life of dead birds blown off their perches. Maria talked over her car radio. Teton approached, his huge brown face and brawny shoulders hovering over him.

"This is just no good. The Eagle Man is an innocent." Teton turned away from the crime scene. "Billy's touched by God, you know? Birds were his only life. This will destroy him."

With Ted gone, Byron ran the grim possibilities through his mind, including kidnapping, torture, or murder. Maria signed off her police radio and walked toward him.

"Let them come out here again," an Indian officer said. "We'll blow their white asses away."

Maria gently took Byron's arm. "Let's go. I'm afraid we both wasted a lot of time, today. It was fun but..."

"What's up?"

"I'll drive you to your car," Maria said, eyes averted. "I want you to stay out of this. Let me handle it, okay?"

Once again, the agent was replacing the Maria he took naked in the meadow by the Snake River.

"Handle what?

They drove on through the beautiful country.

"Byron, when they finally shoot me down, or blow me up, scatter my ashes out here, all right? On the reservation where we made love. Do that for me."

"Maria, what *else* is going on?"

"This country is so pretty, but the people are so violent.

Tomorrow, we'll be digging for a body at Meridell Park." Maria finally looked over at him. "They broke into Becky's place, ransacked it, beat her up. She's in the hospital. No sign of Ted or the film."

Byron clenched his fist.

"Byron, I want you to go home and stay there. We'll send a police guard." She touched him. "And listen. There's something else—"

Byron got out and walked quickly to his car. "I don't need a guard," he shouted over his shoulder. He drove toward the hospital. On the radio, the announcer was suddenly talking about a former English instructor who had hanged himself in his cell after holding the school at bay with an old war rifle. Byron drove, feeling something foul and helpless rushing through him, remembering Shanahan's old shoes.

Oh the bastards, he thought. *Oh Jesus Christ.*

Byron drove past Becky's house. Police were there, taking notes, gathering evidence, shooting photos. He continued on to the hospital.

After confronting a nurse, he found her room. Becky had been struck in the face; she had blackened eyes, some chipped teeth, and a dislocated jaw. Seeing her battered face on the white pillow, speech difficult with the wired jaw, Byron could only recall Ted's face and remember the gun Becky had mentioned. He talked to her, holding her hand.

"Look, I'll find Ted, and I'll stop him, okay? These animals won't get away with this."

Becky stared at him, unable to talk, gripping his hand. He gently touched her forehead. Outside in the corridor, no police stood guard. Byron watched her puffy, swollen face, recalling her urgent tone that day she told him about Ted's strange nocturnal wanderings and obsession with the Posse. Becky began to cry, and Byron called out for a nurse; the nurse informed him that Becky was all right.

"All right? Have you ever been beaten up? Give her some pain killers."

"The doctor has to prescribe them," the nurse said, leaving.

Byron gently wiped Becky's bruised lips, kissing her on the forehead. When he left the hospital, he could see storm clouds coming in over the mountains. As he drove, he saw more images: the shrieking Eagle Man, the dead birds, the battered face of Becky. At home, Judson waited for him. He was unusually subdued.

"What's up?"

"You got a call from a female agent in London."

"Ashley Roland."

"She sounded very nice. Wants one of your short stories to adapt for the BBC."

Really?"

"That's the good news. Ted called from Salt Lake. He took his film to be transferred to video."

"And that's the bad news?"

"He's coming here to shoot the sheriff," he said bluntly.

Byron sat down and closed his eyes. "We can't allow that."

"We can't stop him, either." Judson snapped open his lighter and lit a cigarette. "There's also a memorial for Shanahan being planned."

Byron got up and walked toward his bed, feeling weak and confused; he collapsed.

Outside town at the police firing range, agents Dalton and Goldstein fired pistols at targets. He had a .45, she a 9mm. Then they took turns with a .22 semiautomatic AR. It had little recoil and a scope. Later at lunch, Agent Dalton, a ruggedly built man with a square face and sapphire-colored eyes, regarded the unusually silent Agent Goldstein.

"We got a problem. Our snitch was shot and dumped in the reservoir. Those survivalist nut jobs know we're watching them. Your little fruit friend in the English Department could be a target."

Agent Goldstein smiled over her coffee. "He isn't a fruit," she said, knowing it would irk Dalton. "But you're right—we better move and soon."

"Not without solid evidence. The snitch was a drug dealer. Anybody couldda whacked him. They could be watching you," Dalton added.

Maria, AKA Mary Goldstein, looked out the window at the passing traffic. It had been a good day of shooting.

GHOST WARRIOR

THE DEPARTMENT CHAIRMAN WAS BLUNT: "Take some time off, Mr. Duffy."

"I'll be all right. I can finish the semester."

"We have had enough operatic drama to last a season," Sterling said.

In class, Byron did feel burn-out. He found himself repeating sentences, and at one point, could not spell a simple word on the board.

"Start on *Gatsby* for tomorrow," he said.

In the hall, Soumya faced him, holding her books, her dark eyes penetrating, her smile warm and still seductive. Students milled around them.

"You are a brave man," she said.

"Not really. Dr. Shanahan is dead."

"I had him for a teacher. I didn't like him but I'm sorry he died."

"How did you do in his class?"

"He gave me my only C." Her expression changed. "These people—the white supremacists?"

"Yes?"

"They hate all people of color?"

"I suspect they do. Maybe even Pakis."

Soumya smiled, her cheeks close to a blush. He noticed she wasn't wearing a bra. "You embarrass me. You must teach me," she added.

"I hope I *am* teaching you."

"About life," she said. She gave him a card. "Call me."

He watched her walk away.

88

That afternoon, Byron sat in the empty school theatre that would soon be destroyed for a new theatre-concert hall complex. He had done a summer series in this small black box, but now only one row of seats remained, and the stage was littered with broken lumber, a single out of tune piano pushed against a far wall. Byron sipped from a half pint of Bourbon. He liked the feeling of doing something dangerous and inappropriate, getting drunk in the afternoon. Now he needed Judson or even the sardonic Michael Wells to drink with and remember a summer of comedies and brief romances. For a moment, he imagined calling Soumya and taking her in the back of the theatre, the girl from India straddling his thighs in a seat marked for the dump.

Judson said nothing when Byron went home, drunk enough to sleep past sundown. It was dark when—exhausted—Byron pushed back from a meal of Kentucky Fried Chicken and answered the door. Three missionaries stood on the porch wearing cheap dark suits that made them resemble waiters or undertakers. Two were blond; they carried a Book of Mormon and wore placards with their names. The third missionary was an Indian.

"Hello," the first missionary said.

"There's no God here," Byron said. "Sorry."

"All the more reason to let us in," the second missionary said.

"Not today, gentlemen."

"Wait—what religion are you?" the first missionary demanded.

"None of your business."

"Just let us talk for a minute," the second missionary said.

"I'm a neo pagan, lapsed Catholic, Existentialist with strong beliefs in the Albagensinist heresy," replied Byron. "Now if you'll excuse us—"

"I heard the word 'Catholic'," the Indian said. "That is a venerable old trusted religion. What we represent is a new religion—a fresh new vision of Christianity, if you will."

Byron examined the handsome brown face. He knew it was fruitless to argue but he felt anger pushing him into a confrontation. "Are you a Bannock Shoshone?"

"Yes."

"You believe you're descended from the lost tribe who didn't except Christ when he preached in America after that crucifixion incident—correct?"

"Well, that sounds funny out of context but—"

"—and your people were punished by being turned into Indians...the Lamanites, I believe? Does that make you a traitor to your Indian brothers and sisters? An Uncle Tomahawk?"

The Indian smiled. "No. I am just spreading good news."

"But I *am* glad black skin is no longer the mark of Cain."

Byron could see suppressed anger in the dark penetrating eyes.

"Nor has it mattered for a long time."

"Our church has changed," the first missionary insisted. "The president had a revelation."

Judson suddenly appeared in the doorway. He was smoking and had a beer in his hand.

"We're going to a Catholic wake," he barked. "If you'll excuse us."

"Just give us a moment of your time," the Indian said.

"Due respect," Byron argued, "but my religion is the theatre. In the name of the Beckett, the Brecht, and the Chekhov."

Judson pulled Byron back into the room. "Gentlemen, we don't have time to argue the merits of religion with you."

The three missionaries had not moved when they saw Darlene who had stepped from the shower. She opened her robe and they glimpsed her stocky but voluptuous body and the large firm breasts. She smiled and spoke in her theatrical May West voice: "You've come to the right place, gentlemen. I may be pure as the driven snow but I drift. Step inside and let's party!"

The three missionaries retreated.

An hour later, Byron, Judson and Darlene sat in a Catholic Church. A priest gave the rosary, and David Sterling delivered a flamboyant eulogy to a sparse audience before the altar. Sterling spoke like an egotistical actor having a showy moment on stage.

"Now I wish to read a poem that Professor Shanahan adored. It starts with a conjunction, but *despite* that flaw, it is a fine piece of work. It is the poem of Dylan Thomas called, "And Death Shall Have No Dominion." As Sterling read in a sonorous voice, Byron stood in the back of the church, thinking about the paranoid man holding the police at bay, and also thinking about the brief flash of Darlene's body. He knew he was also meant to see her nakedness.

Byron didn't feel competent to speak extemporaneously at the wake, so he remained seated when the priest encouraged audience members to say a few words. No one else spoke in remembrance of Shanahan, either. No students attended. There would be no funeral. Maria was not at the service, possibly because she was Jewish. Outside the church, Sheriff Dale approached Byron like a cliché movie sheriff, holding out his fat hand.

"You got a lot of gall coming here, sheriff."

Dale dropped his hand. "Mr. Duffy, I ain't the enemy! I wanna prosecute these bastards myself. I have nothin' to do with them Posse lunatics."

"As long as they pay the rent? Tell that to Ted Bear."

The sheriff stuck his thick finger into Byron's chest.

"As a mater of fact, I *do* rent the place. Ted bear is a nutcase. Listen here, I had to watch as they scraped the dead skin from my boy. You don't think I got nothing at stake?"

"How's the dump?"

"We got feds snooping around private property. I tell you, no citizen has got rights anymore. Condolences on your loss."

The sheriff tipped his hat and left. Another police car was parked outside the church. It had started to rain; lightning broke in the sky, followed by claps of thunder. Judson came up to him, dressed in a suit; he opened an umbrella.

"Byron, if I die before you, don't let Prince Sterling deliver my eulogy, okay? Please."

Moments later, Sterling approached them. "I think it went well," he said. "A good show. Maybe the department *will* recover from all this dreadful publicity."

Sterling gave a little wave and walked away, the rain falling heavily on the parked cars and moving umbrellas.

"I got a bad feeling," said Judson.

"Why wasn't Shanahan on a suicide watch?"

"I don't know. Let's go home."

"I'll go home later."

"Don't drink anymore."

"I won't. See you later."

Byron did not go home. He went back inside the church and sat for a moment, looking at the glow of soft lights in the stained glass windows and at the statues and altar, enjoying the quiet of the near empty church. He needed to think. So much had happened. So much of it seemed unreal, like a bad movie of the week.

Organized religion had lost its meaning for him, but he liked the drama of the Catholic Mass and remembered his days as an altar boy and the priest donning the vestments, the surplice, the Alb, the robes of office, and lifting the chalice before the congregation, a chalice they believed held the body and blood of Christ. It was shortly after the Church had discontinued Masses in Latin, and Byron found himself debating if dumping the Latin was a mistake. Why not hear the ritual in a language one didn't understand? It added to the mystery and power. Byron felt the same sense of awe and worship staring at the swirling colors of Van Gogh. Years before, Byron attended Sunday Mass with his father, something they shared. He and his ex-wife had once gone to a Christmas Mass, but she sat, bored with the service, expecting a rock band and believers holding their hands to the vaulted ceiling.

An elderly woman sat near the front of the church, quietly praying as the rosary beads moved through her stiff fingers. As Byron sat quietly, he noticed another man dressed as a farm worker enter the church. He wore a cap and sat across from Byron, occasionally glancing his way. Byron saw a brief malevolence in the eyes. Another man in jeans, boots, and a heavy jacket, also entered and walked down the aisle, stopping at a pillar to Byron's right. Byron noticed the second worshipper didn't dip his fingers in the holy water and cross himself. He now sat between two strangers, either of whom could be armed. He remembered Maria's words about Posse members growing paranoid.

Byron got up and walked down the aisle toward the altar. He turned quickly and exited out a side door, passing a rack of burning candles and a statue of the Virgin Mary. Glancing over his shoulder, the two men had met in the aisle and were walking toward him. Outside, he ran to his car and drove in the heavy rain and hail to Maria's house, but she was not there, so he drove along the tracks, knowing he would have to make a U turn and come back on the other side, passing the Owl Club. Would it be open? Would the Posse be making plans for the next strike? Would citizens start shooting back, or was it all some underground Pynchonian conspiracy? He passed a faded billboard promoting a politician long dead.

As he drove across the tracks in the darkness, he saw the white van coming up behind him, filled with men, the van moving fast in the heavy downpour. Byron gunned his engine, but it was an old car, a Chevy six in need of a tune-up. Then he saw the flashing red light atop the white van, and Byron pressed the accelerator. He drove down Frontage Road, the van closing on him, its red light flashing but with no siren, the white van moving like a ghostly presence in the rain.

Sure, he thought. *The last thing you want to do is put on a siren.*

The van rammed him; he heard shots being fired into the air. Byron kept driving, not slowing down, the van pulling alongside. He saw a bearded face in the window, screaming at him.

"Pull over. Police!"

Byron sideswiped them and kept driving, the heavier vehicle almost going off the road, then closing on him, again. The rain was heavy on the empty narrow highway. They were coming up fast on the Owl Club. Looking into his rearview mirror, lightening flashed and Byron saw the driver and two other men pulling on woolen cap masks. Ahead lay Meridell Park, and the old cottonwoods looked shadowy and blurred in the rain. For an absurd moment, Byron imagined ramming into the crowded bar. It was important he drive into town and well-lighted streets. He did not want to be stopped on a dark road.

One of the men in the pursuing van shot out a rear tire. Byron felt the car swerving, then lurching from side to side in a rut along side the road; a small twisted tree was coming up fast, and Byron couldn't stop, the car hitting the tree as though it would run up the bark, the vehicle bouncing back, then slamming into the tree and partially turning over. He slid out of the tilted car, one wheel still turning, even as the van stopped and the bright spotlight came on him. He heard three rifles being cocked, but he could see nothing except outlines of the men in the sudden light. He shielded his eyes, and one of the men struck his arm down. Byron was pressed against the tilted car. A gun was shoved against his ribs.

"What's going on?"

"You shut up!"

"Where's your friend? Where's that Goddamn spy?" another voice asked.

"Who the hell are you?" Byron said.

"The police, asshole"

"They have blue lights." The men, wearing wool masks, pushed him back against the car.

"We're the real po-lice! Where's the punk with the camera?"

The curtain of rain gleamed in the flashing lights, water blowing over them.

"Ask the Wrecking Crew."

One of the men slugged him. "What? What did you say, you little bastard?"

Byron blinked in the glare, suddenly more angry than afraid.

"Let's take him for a ride. Get in the car, now!"

Byron lashed out, kicking one of the men who groaned and fell to the wet pavement. Another was upon him, trying to drag him into the van, the red light still turning. Byron felt the third man jab him in the ribs with his rifle.

"You're comin' with us, Jew boy! Get in the van!"

"I'm Irish, you stupid cracker," Byron said, struggling.

He and one of the men went down, then a sudden burst of light came across the dark night sky. Byron felt the wet pavement beneath him. They tossed him into the van and another man tied his hands. Byron started to complain when a rifle butt came across his head.

When he woke up, someone had ripped open the van door and pushed Byron outside. He saw a small fire and three men standing on the bank in a light rain. Beyond, the prairie was in darkness. The men looked sinister in the firelight, rifles cradled in their arms. A tall gaunt man stood like an old fashioned western preacher, wearing a wide brimmed black hat, his teeth white in a thick beard. Byron was shoved to the ground before the fire.

"You better tell us where that shithead is, and what happened to his film," the bearded gaunt man said. "Where is it?"

"I don't know."

"You better remember real *quick*."

Another man shoved a pump gun into his ribs. Byron stared at the legs and boots gathered around him. Their voices were muffled, and for the first time he heard the distant whisper of the river.

"What the hell is this, a fuckin' field trip?" a different male voice said. He had a eastern accent and was wearing a suit. "What are we doin' out here?"

"You should see the land."

"I seen it. We got a deal."

"We got us a problem," the bearded gaunt man said. "Someone took out one of our boys. Done cut his throat."

"So he got whacked. We whack people all the time."

"They done shot another. Then we caught a druggie spy. We don't want no feds snoopin' around. Buck's underwater, but if that film gets in the wrong hands—"

"Look, I'm goin' back to New Jersey. We got an agreement, and we got the connections. *You* deal with the feds." The overdressed man, his new shoes covered with mud, stared at Byron. "What's a smart guy like you doin' out here with these crazy throwbacks?"

Byron didn't answer. For a moment, the Jersey man seemed almost sympathetic.

"In fact, what am *I* doin' out here?" He turned and addressed the gaunt man. "You got a problem with evidence. Stuff him in a barrel with cement and dump him in the river. They'll never find him."

"We gots to kill 'im?"

"You kidnapped him. *You* brought him here. This ain't exactly a legal operation, you know. Think—he's a fuckin' witness."

The tall man stared into Byron's upturned face. Byron watched his red lips move in the firelight. "You know where that film is?"

"No."

"You *better* know."

"Fuck you."

The man pulled back. He laughed.

"Our boy's got some balls. Guess he don't know nothin'."

"Won't this fire tip off the Indian police?"

"We can take care of them," another man said. "Injuns is afraid of the dark."

The gaunt man reached down and took Byron by the collar. "I

guess you're goin' for a swim. Dixon? Brandon?" Two men appeared. "Tie his feet and weigh him down. Let the Snake do the rest."

"There's some quicksand nearby," said Brandon.

"Even better. Hope you're all right with the Lord," the leader said, a forced concern in his voice. "They call me Reverend Parrot, and I got a brutish army gonna do you harm. Too bad. I *like* English teachers. Where would I be without no English teachers?"

The others laughed. The man in the suit walked carefully toward his rented car, outlined against the black night. He saw the sheriff pulling up. "I ruined my Florsheims. How can you people *live* in this shit?"

"We live here because this is *our* land. You gonna help us kill feds, nigger police and Zionist Jews?"

Backing away, the Jersey man shook his head. "Hey, I'm just here to promote business. Now—how do I get the hell outta here?"

"The road eventually turns back to the highway. You just git on it, Tony. If the Injun police stop ya, tell 'em you was going to Blackfoot and got lost."

"You can't get away with this," Byron said.

"Sure we can. Maybe you jest got drunk or lost and done got careless. We'll figure out a story about your car." Reverend Parrot pushed his hat back from the lean bearded face. "We're at war. Dump 'im, boys."

But for the bruises on his cheeks, Byron would have felt as though he were in a nightmare. He had brief thoughts of Maria, 10mm blazing, coming to his rescue. She would eject an empty clip and shove another home before blasting the bad guys. He was still thinking this and feeling dead inside when Dixon and Brandon escorted him toward the river. It was dark beyond the fire and they turned before reaching the river, following the beam of a flashlight toward a wide gray bog. It was barely discernible in the partial darkness, but had a viscous look different from the surrounding ground. The older man knelt before him and took out a short rope.

"Hurry up," Brandon said.

"I don't know if this is a good idea," Dixon said. "Killing unarmed people?"

"Tie his legs and stop whining," Brandon said.

96

"This place is spooky. I always feel like I'm being watched."

"Then let's do it and get outta here."

He placed a flashlight on a rock. They couldn't hear the men around the distant fire, though Byron remembered clapping his hands, once, the sound ricocheting down along the river. As Dixon bent to tie his legs, Byron struggled, feeling Brandon's hands under his armpits tightening, and then there was a quiet *thuck* sound and Brandon let go. Byron kicked and Dixon stepped back, his feet sinking with a sucking sound. "Goddamn," he said, trying to lift his boots.

Byron rolled away and looking up, his arms still pinned behind him, saw Brandon standing before the bog in the focused light, staring now at an arrowhead protruding from his sternum. "Shit," he said. Brandon tried to pull the arrow out and then staggered into Dixon struggling to escape the quicksand. With a gurgled cry, Dixon caught Brandon's body and both of them slipped into the gray bog. Dixon screamed but his words were swallowed in the night air. Wet gray sand crept up his legs.

Byron struggled to stand when he felt someone behind him; he turned. An Indian warrior from another time stood in the weak beam of the flashlight, dressed in an old cavalry jacket, chevrons on his sleeve, wearing a black hat with a white feather, buckskin pants, holding a bow in his hands, a quiver of arrows over one shoulder. The Indian's face was marked with red and white paint, and Byron saw the huge pistol in his belt. He gently pushed Byron to one side and turned toward the distant low fire.

"Help me," the struggling man said, throwing off Brandon's body. Dixon was up to his waist in quicksand. "Please!" He reached out to the Indian warrior who put his big hand in Dixon's face and shoved him further into the bog.

The others talked around the fire but their voices seemed to die on the night air. They were concerned that Rusty was missing since gambling at the Indian casino. Of course, with a hired gun like Rusty, anything was possible. The sheriff, wearing overalls, talked about moving to Sandpoint, a haven for retired police. He was discussing a new life after his son left the burn center when something came whizzing out of the darkness; Sheriff Dale stared at the arrow imbedded in the thick log he was about to drop on the fire. The general discussion continued.

"I bet Rusty got drunk and got himself some Injun tail." The tall reverend produced a cell phone. He was dialing a number when the Indian apparition appeared in the firelight. "What the hell?"

Another arrow came out of the night. The sheriff stared with some surprise at the feathered shaft going into his stomach. He fell heavily. Dropping the cell phone, Reverend Parrot cranked his rifle as another arrow struck and a second man screamed, clutching his leg. Parrot fired a round at the ancient warrior, resembling some atavistic demon from hell. It was very much like a western film, the Posse members seeing the Indian in a cavalry jacket advancing upon them; they fired and he staggered once, dropping the bow and whipping out a huge pistol. They saw the long barrel rising in the flickering light.

Tony stood by the car. "What the fuck?"

He pulled out a .45. There was a loud roar as the Indian's pistol flamed and Reverend Parrot seemed to break in two, his body hurling back into the fire. He rolled clear soundlessly. The Indian calmly began shooting rounds at the other men. Using both hands, Tony fired, the pistol kicking back against his palm, but the savage in his mismatched cavalry and Indian clothing didn't fall. Brass casings lay around Tony's feet.

Byron watched from the edge of the fire as two remaining Posse gunmen backed toward the van, one shooting a deer rifle, the second, limping with an arrow in his thigh, blasting with an AK 47. He suddenly danced a bizarre pattern, tiny explosions of blood appearing along his chest as he dropped the automatic weapon. The other rifleman tossed the 30.06 and opened the van door. The huge pistol roared and the car horn sounded like some avenging ghost. Byron saw the warrior then turn toward Tony who emptied his clip into the Indian's body. The huge pistol slipped from the Indian's hand but he kept walking, his face like a painted devil in the firelight. Blood leaked through holes in his chest and stomach, wrapped in cloth. The avenging warrior, his left arm partially gone, took a few steps and collapsed on the grass. Byron saw the flash of a bowie knife, and even as Tony opened his car door, the blade sailed through the air and buried itself in his back. He slid down the car with a grunt. The noise of the guns had now faded into a rushing silence.

The Eagle Man walked into the clearing. Five men lay dead, one slumped over a steering wheel, his head blown apart. He walked over to the dead gangster known as Tony and pulled out the bloody knife. He lifted his head and howled once, and then approached Byron. The wild Indian in soiled animal skins and eagle feathers, gibbering and shaking his head, reached out the blade and cut the ropes holding Byron. He made a few more crying, inarticulate sounds. Byron heard the cars and the primal spirit, wraith-like, vanished. Maria ran to Byron, gun drawn, observing the carnage. Teton turned over the Indian's body.

"It's Hernandez," an officer named Hayball said. "I thought he drowned."

"Byron—my God, what happened here?" Byron saw Maria's pretty face and tried to speak; he touched his bloody head and felt dizzy. "We found a severed head in the dumpster behind the casino. Then we got an anonymous tip," Maria said.

"Jesus," Teton said. "Look at that pistol. It's a Raging Bull. Shit, you could take down an elephant. Where did Hernandez *get* that sucker?"

Teton touched the old army cavalry jacket, riddled with bloody holes.

"There's more," Byron said, trying to point toward the quicksand. Then he fainted.

There was more. Teton suddenly jumped back from the Indian's body. In the last bit of firelight, they saw the body falling in upon itself, the face collapsing, turning into an ancient shriveled mummy as they stared in shock.

———————

A MONTH LATER, Becky came into Byron's office. Her jaw was healing, the teeth now capped. Byron's headaches had gone. They embraced.

"Ted's Posse footage was a big hit at the American Film Institute. Got him in as a student, anyway. He's adding some voice over."

"And you're moving to LA?"

"Yes," said Becky, her lips tight. "I never thought I would move there. I hate the place, Nothing but earthquakes, ego maniacs and nuts."

"But you're *going* with a nut! Of course, who'll know the difference?"

Becky didn't laugh.

"At least we're going somewhere *else*," she said. "I'm thinking of being a movie and theatre critic. Hey, did they ever explain that Indian dude?"

"Fingerprints proved it was a guy named Hernandez whom they presumed drowned. Why his body mummified is still a mystery. He saved my life. One of the dead men was a New Jersey gangster. Another was a local hitman named Rusty."

"They guy who lost his head?"

"Yes. I guess the Posse had an illegal toxic waste business going with organized crime. The Eagle man disappeared but I really don't think the Fort Hall Police want to catch him. A few tribal members say they hear him howling at night."

Becky shuddered. Maria was not in the adjoining office.

"And the standoff continues."

"Right," Byron said.

Since the shoot-out, feds and the Posse were locked in a confrontation with neither side budging. The agents had decided not to rush the compound but to starve out the remaining Posse members.

Becky reached out her hand and then kissed him. "Thanks, she said. "Come to our party. Bring your cop girlfriend."

Byron attended the farewell party for Ted and Becky but without Maria. He did not consider her leaving Idaho. She had finished her class load for the spring and Sterling had offered her a summer class. They still met and made love from time to time; there was no reason for her to leave. Judson and Darlene came to the party but they were fighting. Perhaps Judson's left wing politics had finally pushed her too far. Ted greeted guests, his hair cut short, wearing a stylish sport jacket and slacks, shirt, vest and without the familiar broad-brimmed hat; he shook hands, happy to be leaving. For the moment, Ted's voices were quiet.

"Tybo, you're real pretty," Edmo said. "I like pretty white

boys. Artistic, too."

Ted smiled, somewhat embarrassed. "Artistic and I hope commercial," Ted said.

Teton walked among the guests, tall and massive. At one point, he took Byron to one side.

"They're doing tests on the body of Hernandez," he said. "DNA tests. How could a modern man die and turn into an ancient mummy?"

"Do you know why?"

"Maybe the old legends are true," Teton said. "The Indian babies left out to die who become Water Babies are like vampires...maybe if you kill the host before the sprit escapes to the water or another host, they leave withered mummies. Some things are beyond our philosophy, right?"

"Are you saying I was saved by a ghost?"

The huge game warden shrugged his broad shoulders. "An *old* ghost who took over Hernandez when he fell in the Snake. We still haven't found the Eagle Man. People hear him if they're brave enough to visit the river bottoms at night." Teton held his eyes for a long time. "Byron, where's Agent Goldstein?"

"She's with the agents surrounding Meridell Park. I guess the standoff is still happening."

"They have a new agent who's good."

"Who's that?"

"Agent Dalton."

"Did you say Dalton?"

"Yeah. He and Maria worked together before."

Byron felt a sharp pain of jealousy run through him. He had heard that name; Maria and Dalton had been lovers. Now he was here, on the battle lines, two Federal agents fighting for truth, justice and the American way.

"Something wrong?"

"Dalton and Maria used to be close."

"They still are," Teton said. "I thought you knew he was here."

"I didn't know."

At some point, Byron found himself sitting next to Rex, his round pleasant face smiling, the hair red and trimmed. Rex smoked his cigarillos and held forth.

"People tell you to live a healthy life style. Samuel Johnson smoked and drank all his life and lived to be an old man." He slapped Byron's thigh. "Cheer up. Romantic love is a crock."

"Who said it wasn't?"

"You look upset."

"I'm fine."

"I fell in love and got married. Big mistake. And now I have twins...young boys always crying for bread."

"Rex, children get hungry. They're *supposed* to cry for food."

"They should learn to fast...even at three." Rex puffed on the thin cigarillo. "An era has ended," he said.

The night before, they played chess at Juck's, sitting beneath a replica of a Michelangelo painting which Rex felt "assaulted his sensibilities." Usually, Byron surrendered after a few moves. While they played and a rock band blasted away, Methedrine Pete entered the dark bar with a gun and fired through the bathroom door at a customer behind on his drug payments. The customer was leaning over the toilet and Pete's bullets whizzed by under his arm. Perhaps it was the reverberations of the gunshots, but the attic suddenly caved in under a ton of pigeon shit, the white foul-smelling mass showering the bar and scattering patrons. A demolition crew did the rest. Now, even as they spoke, Juck's lay in rubble, one black wall left standing with painted day-glo rock stars to greet the cruel daylight.

"Juck's is gone," said Rex. "That is the *true* tragedy. Not terrorism. Not war. But the passing of a surreal bar in a small railroad town."

"I'm going for a walk."

Byron left the party and walked along the road in the moonlight. He knew he had to confront Maria, and knew it would go badly. She hadn't mentioned Dalton and why not? When he returned to the large cabin where the party continued, music and voices heard through the widow, he saw Darlene sitting on the front steps, crying.

"I can't change him," she said.

"Why bother?" He sat down next to her. "Darlene, why aren't you at some young Republican's fund raiser or something?"

Her face was tear-streaked, the eyes swollen.

"Because I *hate* those conservative assholes. I'm drawn to liberals, anarchists, drunks, even though my father died a drunk. I don't get it, either. I don't think I even *like* poetry, let alone poets."

Byron nodded to himself. It was time to drive to the police line.

"I like you, Byron," Darlene said slipping her arm into his. He could hear Judson's loud laugh inside. Byron said goodbye and left for Meridell Park. It was a short drive and agents and police stopped him. Flickering police lights bathed the scene. As he walked back to his car, he heard Maria's voice.

"Byron, what are you doing here?"

"Why do you think? You need back-up?"

"What?"

He confronted her. "Teton tells me Agent Dalton is in town."

Maria stepped back. "He's on this assignment, yes."

"Why didn't you tell me?"

"Why should I? He works for the Bureau. He's an expert negotiator." Maria gabbed him by the arm, suddenly angry. "Byron, for God's sake, Dalton and I are not an item. And I don't like jealous men. It's a turn off. Now go to my place and I'll see you there when we're finished here. I have work to do!"

Byron backed down. "Okay."

"Dalton is a good agent. We have to contain a dangerous situation, here. He also offers protection. Word on the street is that Tony's Mafia boys want revenge."

"I can protect you, Maria."

For a moment, she watched his face. "Call me Mary, Okay?" A siren blasted and she pushed him. "Shit! We got a poison gas warning. Back off! Leave—now!!"

Maria pulled on a gas mask and other officers did the same, running toward the front of the perimeter. Another officer pushed Byron back, directing him to leave. Moments later, Byron could hear loud noises blasted at the compound as he drove past a line of police and federal vehicles. This standoff was costing a lot of money, but Byron suddenly imagined the horror of poison gas clouds drifting toward a school.

Maria came home late that night and slipped into bed.

"Did they have poison gas?"

"It was a false reading."

She turned to him and they made love and in the morning, lying in bed, talked about spending a summer together in Ketchum, perhaps in the same rented place where he had lived with Suzi. He enjoyed the soft resonance of her voice.

"Byron, I'm thinking of quitting the Bureau and maybe getting an advanced degree in English so I can teach here."

"Really? You won't miss the FBI?"

"No."

"You won't leave town?"

"Leave?" Reaching down, she stroked his thigh and circled his aroused cock. With her other hand, she pushed back a lock of hair. Running her tongue over her upper lip, she said, "Baby, I'm not going anywhere."

As her love engulfed him, Byron could not imagine Maria ever leaving, but one day, she did leave. The exit strategy had been set from the beginning without any explanation. They had enjoyed a short affair, making love in a field full of wildflowers. Then Byron heard the news: the stand-off at the compound had ended. The Posse finally surrendered without a shot fired; containers of Anthrax and Mustard Gas were found and destroyed. Maria was now free. One afternoon strolling through the shopping mall, Byron saw Soumya with Richard, an exchange student from Africa. He was handsome with thick sensuous lips, dark skin and thick curly hair; Byron could see they were in love with their secret smiles and constant touching. Soumya saw him and smiled, waving. Maria lowered her eyes.

Byron and Maria left for Montana to spend a last weekend in Absarokee. The town was small and intimate with two bars, one restaurant, one café, and a nearby stream for trout fishing. They drove to the Custer battlefield and walked along the windy ridge where Custer's men had dropped from lathered horses until the few remaining soldiers reached the small hill where Sioux and Cheyenne warriors handed them their scalps and testicles. A stone monument rose over the bodies. Though a marker showed where the boy general died, his body was buried elsewhere. Looking at the grass-grown desolate field and the river below, Byron and Maria could see the battle, imagine smoke and the raining arrows, the terrified troops shooting themselves before the Cheyenne and Sioux reached them. In the museum, Byron examined Custer's white leather shirt and realized how small the man who wore it.

"He picked a good place to die."

It was only in the small motel room with a bed on wooden logs that he saw something elusive and sad in Maria's eyes. She began to weep softly.

"What's wrong?"

"Nothing," she said. "I'm tired. I always feel deflated when the job's over. We have time, now."

"What happened to James Bond?"

"Who?"

"Agent Dalton."

Her face was passive.

"He got reassigned, I guess."

They drove back to Pocatello in silence.

Byron drove to her cottage one afternoon when she failed to make a lunch date. Roses were starting to bloom in the front yard. Her car was gone. He walked to the door, knocked once, and then walked in. The house was empty, stripped of all furniture, his footsteps echoing as he walked through the cottage. He called out: "Maria? Maria!" As panic rose inside, he heard a noise. A well-built handsome man in a black suit appeared at the back door. If they had been in Los Angeles, Byron would have assumed the man was an actor.

"Mr. Duffy?"

"Who the hell are you?"

But Byron knew before the intruder flashed his FBI badge.

"My name is Dalton, Tom Dalton. Mary was called away on another assignment."

The agent spoke in a cold, level voice.

"So you are the famous Agent Dalton?"

"Yes I am. Pleased to meet you at last."

They did not shake hands,

"Where is her assignment?"

"That's classified. Agent Goldstein instructed me to give you this."

Byron took the note but didn't read it.

"Why did they send you?"

"You got me, partner. I only follow orders."

The agent turned to leave.

"Wait. We talked this morning. How could she be suddenly gone, just like that, without even telling me?"

"She told you nothing?"

"No." Byron suddenly imagined the movers filling a truck with her stuff even as she talked to him on the phone, planning to meet for lunch.

"How could she just—leave without a word?"

"I wouldn't know, sir."

"Will I see her again?"

"She may be in touch. Maybe not," he added.

"So you people simply move in and do your job, and then exit? Is that it?"

"We are given assignments. We do them, we leave," he said, pausing for a moment. "Do you want us to be *always* around?"

"We had an affair," Byron said. "She's very talented, don't you agree?"

Byron expected a reaction but the handsome agent regarded him, his eyes revealing nothing. "Mary is a professional."

"Where the hell is she?"

Byron could see a sudden hard glint in Agent Dalton's eyes. He spoke with careful measured enunciation. "I can't give out that information. I was instructed to inform you she had been transferred and hand you her personal note. Those duties executed, I have to go."

Agent Dalton left, closing the door behind him.

Byron stood alone in the empty cottage. He finally read the note:

Dear Byron. I've been given another assignment. I'll never forget you and will always love you. Maybe that German poet was right, we are always saying good-bye. I will miss you. Take care of yourself, Byron. No one else will. Good-bye and good luck. Mary.

Byron read the note a second time, noticing "Mary's" beautiful handwriting. He carefully folded the note, and then walked to his car.

BOOK TWO

THE SEMINAR

STERLING THREW A FAREWELL PARTY for the fired instructors.

A few arrived early, drinking heavily, waiting for a chance, or possibly the nerve, to confront Sterling over his decision to retain only Byron and Judson. Byron sat in a corner, brooding over a beer. He stared at the huge clock dominating the large room, filled with antique and ornate furniture. It was an old clock, and Byron imagined the tension in the hidden springs like the tension gripping the party, itself. Byron had tried to get information on Maria from Sterling, but Sterling claimed ignorance, and the Federal Bureau of Investigation wasn't talking. He had studied the FBI web page for general information.

Byron walked out into Sterling's impressive rose garden, thinking of Maria.

It was never until death do us part, thought Byron. It was only meant to last for a few days, or even a few months. It was not meant to last a lifetime. That kind of relationship is out of the question. Sure, that's something *other* people do.

Holding a drink, Judson joined him in the garden. They heard angry voices of departing teachers; waves of Beethoven piano music crashed over them from the spacious front room as Chan played with a maniacal fury. Someone broke a glass.

One afternoon, he watched the main desk as the secretary went to lunch, and searching through files in one of the cabinets, found Maria's. She was under Maria Jones, but her maiden name was Mary Goldstein from Detroit, and Byron would have to accept 'Mary.' He found no mention of the FBI, only that she had a separate "dossier." He examined an early photo of her from her graduate school days; he studied her college transcript. Byron wondered about the separate dossier. Shanahan's file was not included in the cabinet, as though he had never existed.

Byron planned to call Mary's parents in Detroit. He could disguise himself as an old friend, tracking Mary down. Just what was old Mary up to, these days, and why did a nice Jewish girl bolt, like that, without a face to face good-bye? He was worth that.

Who are you, Mary Goldstein? he thought.

Once again, he remembered that expression in her face as her official self took over and the woman retreated into a silence. It would happen in an instant, the familiar lover disappearing, as though they never had met.

"I'd be afraid to see what they got on me," Judson later said.

The real files were not on the Internet but in the basement of the FBI office, where Mary's history was documented in binary codes, every move recorded in file and dossier after file and dossier: copious documents, folders, photos, typed reports, audio tapes, computer chips, print-out sheets. Byron was part of her file; they had everything, from the face off with Shanahan to their brief romance, though no photos.

Byron thought of Mary as he left with Judson for a Hemingway seminar in Sun Valley. He tried to imagine what assignment she was on, what strange underground she was infiltrating, or if she had enrolled in a graduate program while investigating another drug culture. Her investigation of the Posse had resulted in the death of a Mafia boss, Tony Galindo. The strange story of the avenging Indian gunman was still studied and disputed.

In a Sun Valley Lodge room, Byron lay on the bed; down the hall was the parlor suite where Hemingway had written *For Whom the Bell Tolls*. One of his last letters, written shortly before his suicide, hung on the wall downstairs. Byron tried to imagine those last moments, Hemingway's hands on the gun, the twin barrels pressed to his forehead. Was there a final question before the blast that ended everything? From Hemingway, Byron thought of Mary. He still had fantasies of coming upon Mary in the middle of a major sting, the drug thugs drawing their weapons, Byron driving up in a jeep, both of them shooting their way out, pistols blazing.

This is ridiculous, thought Byron. *The hell with her.*

He read, and then went to sleep. It was late when Judson came to the room. Byron could tell he was drunk from the way he fumbled with his keys.

He will need a shot of whiskey to get him going in the morning, thought Byron.

In the morning, Byron had an early breakfast in a western styled cafe while Judson prepared his lecture to professors, critics, other instructors. Byron visited the Hemingway memorial in Sun Valley and meditated on the bust in profile gazing across the river to distant hills. A narrow brook ran under the plaque and bust. Bald Mountain was now brown and barren of snow, where thousands of skiers would be soaring down the slopes in the winter.

Sterling had scheduled an afternoon brunch for all the instructors, and Byron sat across from Judson who helped himself to the champagne. A few celebrated guests were curious about a local poet who had just found a major publisher and would read a select few poems.

"After Hemingway," Sterling said, "we need, a seminar on Faulkner—in Mississippi."

"Faulkner was a dirt farmer," said Judson. "Had a thing for corn cobs."

Sterling rolled his eyes. "That is true in a sense, but we are here to honor Papa."

The critics and instructors began arguing the merits of Hemingway and Faulkner; Faulkner was doing well but Hemingway was taking a beating.

"Think of it," a critic argued. "I'll give you Faulkner's southern gothic, but Hemingway was something of an exotic adventure writer compared to Thomas Mann and Tolstoy. Like Conrad, he's a bit masturbatory, wouldn't you say?"

Byron gazed at the critic. "Oh really? And how about your last book, *Grooving The Symbol*? Isn't that a kind of fantasy hand-job?"

The critic, bald and bearded, glared over his drink.

"Fantasy hand-job?"

"For my money, Mickey Spillaine and James Cain have them all beat," Byron insisted.

"*Please*," said Sterling. "They are *bad* writers!"

Judson laughed, his shrill, high-pitched guffaw so different from the deep voice; the others stared at him. Then he took a drink of coffee. Only Byron knew what else was in the coffee.

"No one can easily touch Conrad *or* Hemingway," said Byron. "Not even critics with no originality."

"I'm a critic," admitted a heavy set, pleasant looking man, addressing Byron. He had made a fortune editing Hemingway's letters. "And I'd be curious to hear what you think of the so called lesser novels of Hemingway."

"I leave that to Judson McGee," said Byron, "but I love all of them. I even love the worst, *Across the River and Into the Trees.* It breaks my heart."

"*Across the River* is awful," insisted Sterling. "Dreadful!"

Later that afternoon, Byron talked to a famous actor and watched the swans on the pond while Judson sat on the lawn, drinking a beer. The presentation had gone badly.

It was after the critics and instructors left the brunch that Judson consumed more drinks; he held his glass carefully, waiting for refills of Vodka and 7-Up, lifting them and draining them in one fluid motion, setting them down. He would recall images of that afternoon in bits and patches, a handsome poet in a tweed jacket reading poems about finding God on the river and in the forest and on the mountain ridges and even in the eye-pecking savagery of hawks devouring their prey, the poet's hair bright and shiny in the spotlight with just a slight breeze lifting his locks, the poet's voice, so rich and sweet sounding, and then Judson was aware of the full auditorium, blobby faces watching him as his voice bellowed into the microphone, his notes and cards suddenly scattered on the floor. He wanted to tell them about the lesser novels of Hemingway. He was still trying to tell them when he left the stage to vomit into a toilet. He was even telling them when Byron and another man helped Judson outside.

Judson sat up, vaguely remembering certain details. He got a cigarette, but his hands shook, and he had trouble getting the cigarette to his mouth. Then Byron was striking the match and Judson inhaled the smoke. Judson examined the cigarette, then took another sip of beer and felt better. "Jesus Christ, what the hell happened?"

Byron looked at him somewhat sadly and shrugged. "You tell me."

"Did I get through the lecture?"

"You started out okay. Then you belched into the microphone and what followed...."

Byron quickly described what happened.

"I have to admit, you destroyed the effect of the pretentious poet who preceded you. I did like your rendition of the Presley song, 'Are You Lonesome Tonight'?"

"I sang a song?"

"Yep."

"I made a fool of myself?"

"You said it, not me."

"I passed out?"

"I'd say blacked out. You passed out on the lawn."

"I guess I'm out of a job."

"Ask Sterling." Byron gazed at the swans and ducks floating through the glare on the small pond. "Maybe you should go back to the lodge and sack out."

"I am. I am taking one beer with me, and then I'm going to sleep. Tomorrow, it's a hike up to Twin Lakes for about a week. I'll dry out in the woods."

"That's quite a hike," said Byron.

"Maybe you could join me."

Byron considered it. "Not this time."

"I wanted to prove something to those stuffy critics." Judson finished the beer. "I forgot to tell you. Mary called."

Despite the shock, Byron hid his feelings and said nothing as Judson related the sparse details. Later, as Judson slept, Byron tried to reconstruct Mary's brief call to Judson from a Montana pay phone. Restless, he went to the Sun Valley Inn bar and saw a number of the critics still drinking and discussing literature. The heavy-set critic sat down next to him, while a celebrated movie director played the piano, banging out show tunes.

"I think your friend had a lot to say. Too bad he was so drunk. He possessed a certain spark."

"Yes, it *is* too bad. I don't want to talk about it."

"Hemingway was a drunk, but he didn't like rummies."

Byron listened to the romantic piano music, thinking of Mary, wishing he had taken the call, not trusting Judson's memory of the late night conversation. In another dimension, he was beginning to feel her spirit. He could see her in some small room, somewhere, shadows on the wall like in film noir pictures as she waited for an assignment. They were out there, waiting to nab her.

"Virginia Woolf didn't like ole' Ernie too much—nor he her."

"Really? Well, I better be going," Byron told him.

"I prefer Tennessee Williams to Ernest Hemingway, but I agree with you about *Across the River*," the critic said. "It has less technique but *so* much feeling." He touched Byron's thigh. "The old man's doomed love for the young girl is heartbreaking. Love is love however it's described. We could discuss this further over a few drinks."

"No thanks," said Byron.

He felt the hand withdraw and left the critic sitting alone. Judson was asleep, and Byron paced the room. Just before sleep, he thought about a Dylan song celebrating a lover being back in a familiar bed, once again.

The next morning, Judson and Byron had breakfast in Ketchum. Judson had bought a backpack and some supplies, including a knife, fishing line, and a sleeping bag. He drank coffee with the breakfast.

"I'd go with you, but I've been having nightmares, lately."

"The woods can absorb any nightmare."

"No, that's not it. I know Mary's in trouble. I can see her getting attacked in some furnished room. Damn, I wish she had called me."

"I don't think she needs you to defend her."

Byron agreed. They finished the breakfast. Judson was trembling and nervous, but they walked to his car. Byron agreed to follow him to the edge of the forest, where Judson would take a narrow path into the dappled, soaring gloom of the woods, walking up rocky ground to where the trees thinned out and Twin Lakes sat beneath some mountains, looking like two lungs in the earth. The lakes were filled with small trout, starved from overpopulation. They parked the two cars and shook hands.

"When you come out, your car will be here."

"Take care, Byron. Tell Sterling I'm sorry and I'll be in touch."

"I will, Judson. I wish I was going."

"I wish I had a drink!"

Judson hiked into the forest after signing a sheet informing the rangers of his trip; they could search if he failed to return. Byron wanted to hike into the Sawtooth Range, away from even small Idaho towns. He wanted the silence of the woods, and the wildlife; walking in the primitive area, he came closest to some concept of a superior unknown, a cosmic force.

When Judson's big form disappeared up the dappled path into the woods, Byron drove back to Sun Valley. He found Sterling sitting in the coffee shop of the Inn. Sterling was entertaining some critics and writers, and seemed animated and happy. When he saw Byron, he frowned and motioned him to a corner. Byron knew something had happened as he walked over.

"Sorry about Judson."

"I'll work it out with him later. Byron, sit down."

"What's up?"

"I got a call from the department chairman of English at Montana State University."

"Something happened to Mary?"

Sterling looked surprised. "How did you know?"

"I did a little detective work."

Sterling glanced nervously at other hotel guests.

"I have some shocking news."

"Sterling, what the hell happened?"

"Mary was shot."

THE AGENT

LIKE A PROFESSIONAL ACTRESS, Mary had changed in appearance, infiltrating a major drug cartel in this small Montana college town set against the backdrop of mountains. They were a black posse from Jamaica, backed by mob money from the east coast. Mary had a good cover as a teacher with a house set up in her name, phony debts, and even a faked rap sheet. She became an eccentric white chick getting drugs to sell and consume.

One of her contacts was a former agent from England named Neal who had come to Utah, then Montana to join an anti-government, Christian-based cult. The FBI had washed him out after they discovered cocaine addiction. Mary made a coke buy and suddenly, Neal was there. He was a young man with thick black hair, a pitted face, his nose always red and running, a slight blue tinge to his skin. She met her connection for lunch.

"Look, I still believe in God, but I got into this drug thing. Why are you, such a bright young woman, messing with drugs? You'll have to mess with the Man."

"What man?"

"*The* Man. He's connected. He knows everything. A Fed narc was snuffed last month. The Man found out and did torture on his ass. Most awkward. Don't get me wrong, I respect narcs. They are just doing a job, you know?"

Sure, Mary thought. *Like you, asshole, before you cracked.*

Neal's eyeballs gleamed a dull yellow. "Let's have dinner, tonight."

"Later, Neal. You're right about cocaine."

"I can't believe *you'd* do it. You're special."

"Yeah—but I don't see anything wrong with turning a profit, do

115

you?"

The ruined nose flashed at her.

"I *do* see something wrong. You can buy but you can't sell the stuff here. Mary, if you cross the Man, his boys will ice you."

Neal's words trailed off, as though he had lost and now searched for a point.   She wanted to say that she needed *a* man, as well, since Byron was in Ketchum. Lately, Mary often fantasized about Byron at night, lying prone on the bed, her hands between her legs, the belt unbuckled—masturbating to their better moments.

"Neal, selling it *is* dangerous." He seemed relieved. "But I would like to meet this 'Man' you talk about. Maybe we can work together. I hear it's a Jamaican connection."

Neal bellowed: "Right! And why shouldn't blacks make a profit off this racist country?"

Agent Ramon had slipped into the cafe, drinking a beer and watching a folk singer on the stage. Neal spotted him. "Watch out. That guy's no Basque sheepherder."

Mary pretended some surprise. "Really? Seems cool to me."

"I know what I know," Neal insisted, his young face looking bloodless and moist in the light from the bar. Mary made eye contact with Ramon who winked back, giving her a theatrical finger point. Eyes closed, Neal held his palms out as though he were stopping a car.

"That guy is bad news," he said.

"Sorry to disappoint you, Neal, but I have to talk to him."

Neal stared as Mary sat on a red stool next to Ramon. He was a small sinewy man, with a handsome face, dark Mexican eyes and black Indian hair. Mary had seen his skill with a knife and gun, and like so many ethnic agents, he was anxious to prove himself. She could see the other bar patrons reflected in the mirror behind the bottles. Annoyed, Neal got up and walked out.

"What's shakin', Ramon?"

"Everything's fine, but we have to connect with the local police. They could pull a surprise raid and blow our cover." Ramon drank his beer. "How's druggie Neal?"

"Sad. But I think he'll lead me to Carl."

"We got a big one coming down, I can feel it. *Ese.* This is big."

"Bigger than the usual small town drug bust?"

"I think so."

"So does Neal. Carl sounds dangerous."

They sat at the bar, drinking beer. A few students recognized Mary and waved. The recent murder of the federal agent had made everyone in the town aware of the Bureau, and stories of the Jamaicans were taking on mythical proportions.

"Well, *amiga*. Later."

Ramon left. Mary sipped her beer and saw in the mirror police pulling up, throwing Ramon up against the wall. She walked quickly outside. The police were searching Ramon's pockets.

"Where's your ID, greaseball?"

"No habla ingles, Señor."

"What's the problem, officer?" Mary said. "Why are you arresting that man?"

Perhaps it was just what they needed, a public bust before students and citizens. An unmarked car pulled up and more officers converged on them in the parking lot. Mary pushed a detective and then Mary saw the drawn guns and heard her rights being given, even as they found Ramon's berretta.

At the station, she saw Tom Dalton talking to the local police chief.

"Release me," Mary said. "It's perfect. Let me go and they'll contact me."

Dalton shook his head. "Something's wrong."

She sat across from Ramon who glared at Dalton. "Something is wrong. Why didn't you tell the police about us, *cabron*?"

"What did you call me?"

"Nothing. We've been made, that's all."

"Deal with it." Dalton lit a cigarette and sat on a bench. "Boy, these Jamaican mothers will have a laugh about this…they're a major threat in London."

A detective handed Mary her gun. "Sorry, Agent Goldstein. We'll stay out of your way."

Dalton pulled her to one side. "Okay, stay with it but we'll put a watch on you."

She left the station, walking past handcuffed prisoners. That night, Mary sat writing one of her many letters to Byron that she never planned to mail when Neal called.

"Word's out you got arrested. Those feds and the local police are quite stupid, really, but I feel bad about guys getting hurt, you know? Listen, I think the Man is ready to see you, but you might reconsider."

"Why?"

She waited for Neal to respond. She could hear his breathing on the other end of the line.

"Neal? You still there?"

"Yes. I say, these people are dangerous. I got to pay for my habit, you understand? But you're clean."

"I'm not so clean."

"Leave town."

"Neal, I like it here." Neal was silent for a long time. Then she heard him sobbing on the other end. "Neal, are you okay?"

The agents in the van across the street listened to the phone conversation, tapes rolling. Neal's voice had a pathetic sound of whining despair.

"I'm just a bad boy," he said. "I know Carl's boys sell to kids, and I still hump for them. I'm just scum, Mary."

"Maybe you should check into a clinic."

"I don't know if I can do it," said Neal. "I know what that drug money is funding, too."

"And what's that?"

"I talked too much. I better hang up."

Mary sat at her desk. They could wire her, and give her a bullet-proof vest, but the danger was always there. Mary glanced at her hard face in the mirror, at the dyed hair, garish make-up and different cast to her eyes and face. She tried to let innocent Detroit Mary's face show through the lines of the undercover image, like a palimpsest. In the morning, she would wear another mask for the English Department. The lines were getting blurred.

Mary walked to a pay phone where she called the English Department in Pocatello. The street was empty. She got Sterling's information number with a recorded message where they could be reached in Sun Valley. Then she called a popular bar in Ketchum, and asked for Judson McGee. She could hear loud country music in the background. To her shock, Judson came on the line.

"Hello?"

"Hello, Judson. It's Mary, once known as Maria Jones."

"Well I'll be God damned. Where are you?"

"I can't tell you, exactly. Somewhere in Montana. When this is all over, we'll go on a picnic and have fun, and live happily ever after."

"You on an assignment, protecting truth, justice and the American way?"

"Of course. Judson—are you drunk?"

"Yeah, but no matter. Tomorrow, I got to perform. They kept me and Byron on. What a joke on them."

Mary looked down the dark street. "I miss you guys. Say hello to Byron."

"Can we help?"

"No, Judson. You can't. Sober up for tomorrow. Good-bye."

"Take care of yourself, Mary."

She felt tears stinging her eyes and didn't see or hear the van.

"I will, Judson. Love you both."

Jesus, she thought to herself. *I'm breaking every rule of undercover.*

Mary hung up the phone and sensing danger, reached for her gun, even as the van crashed into the booth, knocking Mary out to the pavement. She felt strong hands hurling her struggling body into the van that drove off, leaving a double trail of smoking rubber on the Montana street. A cloth was pressed to her face and she lost consciousness. It had all happened in a few seconds. They had taken her in public without a shot fired.

When Mary recovered, she saw two men and the distant lights of Bozeman. They had stopped at a remote spot and Mary wondered if back-up had seen her abduction; then she saw Neal, and moments later, a tall handsome black man with dread locks got out of a Lincoln town car and came toward her. Mary was handcuffed. Carl spoke in a soft, accented voice, explaining how Mary had simply traded with the wrong people, and now she could work for them, and they would even give her a free cocaine-heroin speedball. It was a jarring kind of high.

Carl held up her gun. "Why you got this?"

"For protection."

"You'll get that from me."

One of the men laughed and Neal looked away. Carl held a small white ball.

"You have no right to do this," Mary said, as they ripped down her pants and she felt the strong probing fingers spreading apart the cheeks of her ass and inserting the suppository. The drugs hit her with a mad rush. Once again, her consciousness began to spin and Mary giggled.

When Mary opened her eyes, she saw Neal sitting on her bed, shaking his head like a mumbling street person. Mary could still see the handsome black face of Carl: Carl's dark eyes, Carl's beautiful dread locks, Carl's flashy car. Neal kept talking. "I told you to stay away from the Man," he said. "I know how tough the Man can be. Once you become Carl's man, you are Carl's slave, period. He calls the shots, Mary." Mary tried to sit up. She was beginning to sweat. "He gets all of his people addicted," said Neal. "Whatever he wants, you do it for your drugs. It's sad."

"Get out," Mary said.

"I got some stuff for you to snort. Then Carl will let you know what's needed."

Mary felt her bones beginning to ache. It was like a touch of flu coming on. Neal began to search the small apartment.

"I've never been here, before. Mind if I look around?"

"Go home, Neal."

"You'll be getting sick from withdrawal so I'll take care of you. That's my job."

Mary rocked back and forth, hands tucked under armpits. "Your job? You get me as payment?"

"Now, Mary, we are in this together. You'll be rich, don't forget that."

Neal walked over the closet. Mary felt the thick sweat on her face. She wanted another hit of cocaine. The rush was short but glorious, and all the pain stopped.

"Stay out of my closet."

"It's standard procedure, Mary. I have to check the place for weapons. You had that nice 10mm. Cops like those guns."

Mary thought about the bullet-proof vest hanging in the closet along with her spare gun in a holster, a small .38 pistol. Neal touched the closet door.

"I need some coke," shouted Mary.

Neal stared at her shining face, and then smiled, almost shyly. "I got some."

Mary nodded, and lay back on the bed, spreading her legs.

"I guess you got an eyeful of my ass, Neal."

"I tried to look away, Mary."

"That's right, you're a man of God." Mary motioned to him. "Hey, I'm getting sick. Why don't you call the corner grocer, for me, and order us some bourbon? I'll buy if you fly."

"We're taken care of." Neal took out a bag of cocaine. "Snort some of this. Relax. For a while, they thought you were a Fed agent, but I never believed it. I *know* undercover cops. I was one. I got nothing against them but they are *worse* scum."

Mary got up and stumbled to her phone.

"Not now, Mary. This first night, we need to keep you under wraps." He grinned. "Once you've had a few more tokes, you can use the phone any time you want, since you'll be calling us."

Mary spoke over Neal's giggling: "I don't want to call anybody important, Neal. But you know, someone might want to call me. I *do* have business calls to make now and then."

"Not this late. Mary, have a snort of coke." He came over and spread out two lines of the white powder. "I must admit, you're taking it very well. Most of them cry and complain, then they get high and end up fucking and sucking the whole gang."

Neal sucked up the two lines in a sudden mad snort. "Sorry. I'll lay out some more. Might as well enjoy your habit."

Mary stared at the beautiful white powder that Neal spread and diced with a razor into three symmetrical lines. She wanted the bone aching, gut sickness to stop.

"Any guards outside, Neal?"

"There might be."

"Who killed the federal agent, Neal?"

Neal confronted her, his eyes and nose gleaming.

"Carl did it personally." Neal managed a weak smile. "Carl kills narcs, Mary. On the spot! He's a soldier in a war." He motioned toward the lines. "Snort this and you'll feel much better. I'll feel better about you."

"What war?"

For a moment, Mary saw a darker turn in Neal's eyes.

"Carl isn't the general. He's a captain, working for an even bigger army. Armageddon, honey. Carl knows people who make him look like a delivery boy…a clerk."

"What are you talking about?"

"One day, all this shit will be destroyed!" The phone rang. Neal dropped the razor, startled. "Who the hell is calling this late?"

"It might be Ramon," said Mary.

Neal's eyes were full of a daring, reckless light.

"Give me that phone! You're protected by the Man. You're now one of us."

Mary knew she might crack and cooperate with Neal and the Jamaican gang, lying to the Bureau, but Neal picked up the phone and the agents outside heard his whining nasal voice telling Ramon before he even identified himself that he was nothing but a low rent Spic and that a new gang had moved into town.

"*Que*? What are you saying, *Señor*?"

"I'm saying your woman is now ours, and you punks are through. *Bugger off.*"

In the van, Ramon listened to the sudden dial tone. He glared at the other agents. They had seen Mary stagger when Neal brought her home. "Let's move."

As they rushed the house, guns drawn, they saw another man running up the stairs. Inside the house, Mary was unzipping Neal's fly as he held the phone, eyes closed, murmuring, "Yes, Mary, yes," even as she brought her knee up and connected. Neal screamed. Mary judo chopped him across the throat, dropping his heavy body. Then she knocked over the table with the cocaine and stumbled to the closet, reaching for her vest and the pistol; she was still holding the gun and vest when Mary saw the tall, thin black man standing in the doorway. Carl wore a full-length black leather coat and wool cap. For a moment, he could've been a black hip-hop gangster from an old-fashioned thriller film.

"What's going on?" Carl said, looking at the fallen Neal. Then he saw Mary fumbling with the vest. "We know who you are, Zionist bitch!"

Mary saw the .32 pointed at her, handle facing the floor; she tried to slip on the vest while raising her revolver. There was a deadly hatred in Carl's eyes that seemed to fill the room, engulfing her. He screamed something in a language she didn't know. For a moment, she imagined a Nazi soldier appearing out of the mist, screaming in harsh German while leveling his weapon

The two guns fired simultaneously.

The door splintered as agents crashed into the apartment. Carl's body hurled backwards, his gun firing a second time with a reflexive action. Mary started to fall, feeling a slamming burning in her guts; she saw the brown anxious face of Ramon and Dalton's frightened eyes, his gun drawn, and then Carl's body sliding down the wall, leaving a red smear.

THE TEMPEST

THE OLD MAN WORE A BLACK SUIT, his eyes hard beneath the crew cut.

"What the hell are you doing?"

Byron stood outside the hospital room. "I came to see Mary Goldstein."

"And who the hell are you?"

Byron told him. Out in the hall, doctors and nurses walked. Visitors searched for patients' rooms. A black officer guarded the door.

"Haven't you Idaho people done enough damage? Her cover was blown. If you found her, so could others. I said this would happen with women in the field." The small wizened man, short but wiry, held an Idaho newspaper. On the cover was a photo of Mary, and a headline: 'The Narc Who Came in from the Cold.' He stepped aside. "Go in. Talk all you want—she can't talk back."

Mary lay on the bed, her eyes closed, her hair dyed a reddish gold, the face pale, tubes going in and out of her body. Byron thought of two lovers in a field in Idaho, and stared at the mask over her face. Mary suddenly opened her eyes. She gave a little wave, and made a sign with her fingers.

"I'll come back," Byron said.

Mary smiled with her eyes and nodded. Then Agent Dalton and a Latino man entered the room, guns on hip, emanating a masculine police authority.

"You better leave," Dalton said.

Byron touched Mary's hand and saw anger and sadness in her glittering eyes that would haunt him on the road back to Idaho. It was the look of grief that sees into the future. Mary closed her eyes. Byron turned to leave. "I'll find you again," he said.

In the hall, Agent Dalton backed Byron against the wall.

"The bullet went under her vest, damaged her spleen. She's lucky her liver wasn't hit. You tell that Idaho reporter I'll make his life miserable. Now look"—and Dalton put his big hands on Byron's collar—"Mary's life is still in danger. She took down some big wise guys, understand? You best scram and leave her alone!"

"I won't go far," Byron said.

Dalton's face drained of color. "You wanna deal with us?"

"Wait." The Latino man, also wearing a black suit, took Byron's arm. "I'm Ramon. I worked with Mary. Come with me—I got something to show you." They walked out of the hospital and Ramon guided Byron to his car. "I have some of Mary's letters she meant to send you. Before surgery, she told me you should have them. Take the letters and take off. Dalton's got a point."

They went to Mary's apartment and Byron examined the sparse furnishings, trying to imagine Mary's other life here. The bed was unmade. He found a batch of unmailed letters addressed to him; Ramon suddenly gripped him by the shoulder.

"Tell her to take a desk job. You reach a point when you just can't do it no more. These letters prove she's getting careless, no offense. Be careful, because if they come after her and we ain't around, they'll blow *both* your asses away. We think this Jamaican Posse group is not just mob connected, but funding terrorist training camps in places like Montana and Idaho."

Byron was impressed. "Domestic terrorists?"

"No, the bigtime folks…fundamentalists who want to destroy everything American…and they use our freedoms to do it. Anyone can buy weapons and train, here. We traced Carl's drug money and some of it is going overseas to suspect accounts."

"Why are you telling me this?"

"It will be in the news, anyway." Ramon turned to go. He stopped and confronted Byron. "I believe in freedom of the press, but if you find this reporter, Ragsdale, shoot the fucker for me."

"I will."

Byron collected the letters. Then he was on the road, rock and roll blasting from the ancient tape deck and watching the Montana vista of mountains and cobalt blue sky. He still had the memory of Mary's pale cheeks and reddish gold hair against the pillow, and a

Mexican agent named Ramon, standing in the furnished room, a gun resting on his hip. That night, a heavy rain on the roof, he read the letters, all of them romantic fragments. Then he slept and dreamed of Mary in the hospital, her face growing larger and blending into something else, a flat broad face with high cheekbones and slit eyes suddenly turning to mummified flesh. Byron woke up frightened, but he heard no gunfire, only the night wind. The rain had stopped and he slept again.

A MONTH LATER, Byron met Darlene at Buddy's.

"What is *wrong* with you people?"

Byron sipped his coffee: "What people?"

"My God, Judson is in the woods living with some hippy commune! I mean, I'm glad Smoky passed her witch's test, but really, Byron. What about sexually transmitted diseases?"

He saw Darlene struggling to restrain her anger. "Why don't you hike into the woods and talk to Judson yourself, Darlene?"

"I can't hike. The woods make me nervous."

Byron felt the words coming out, cold and hard. "Judson is trying to salvage something from the wreckage. I don't care if he paints himself blue and dances around sacrificial fires under a full moon."

"And what's with all this stuff about Goldstein? It sounds like a bad spy novel."

"Life imitating bad art. And instead of criticizing others, why don't you work on yourself?"

Darlene's small eyes peered at him. "Why don't you just go to hell?"

Darlene lifted herself up out of the chair and left. Byron finished his coffee and walked to the university. He had some basic preparation for classes that would start in the fall. He sat in the small office, knowing that Shanahan and Mary were gone, and for a moment, he even missed the crazy rhythms of Ted Bear. Sterling poked his head into the office. "How's our little Robinson Crusoe doing?"

"Judson is just fine, I hear," said Byron. "Any word from

Mary?"

"No. They've got tight security around her. Well, ta, ta."

Sterling's handsome face disappeared. Byron couldn't work so he drove home. The light on his answering machine was blinking; he ran the message, and heard Mary's contralto voice, weak but clear: "Hello, Byron. Meet me at the Utah Shakespeare festival on July sixteenth. Tickets will be under your name. I believe *The Tempest* is playing. This will be our only chance to talk." There was a pause. "If you don't make it, I understand."

He ran the message again, listening to her rich voice.

On the date of performance, Byron drove to Cedar City, Utah. The town had a replica of the Globe Theatre, with semi professional and professional actors brought in for a summer of the Bard. Byron was not expecting an accomplished production. The town was tidy looking with tourist shops, LDS churches and the university with its billiard table lawn and theatre complex.

Byron walked around the campus, but didn't see Mary. Byron waited for Agent Dalton to appear in the shadows, gun under his coat. He went to a cafe and had lunch, then walked back to the theatre, remembering one season of summer stock he had spent as a fledgling actor. He loved the poetry of Shakespeare's plays: the richness, the music, the grandeur, and the large characters.

That night, he found two tickets at the box office under his name. He was seated and waited for the last great play of Shakespeare to begin, a sound of crickets filling the open-air theatre.

A ship appeared on stage. Even as the huge ship split open, spilling out actors over the sound of a theatrical storm, a woman sat next to him, touching his knees, motioning him to be quiet. It was Mary. Byron saw another man standing in the back of the theatre, wearing dark glasses and a suit. Feeling a rush of excitement, they watched the play unfold, and Byron was impressed with the production. At intermission, they finally spoke.

"I can't talk too much, Byron. I am camping out tomorrow, then I may be going to cop school." She gazed at him: "You look good, Byron."

"Mary?"

"My ribs are still taped. I don't know if I can even make love."

"Where are you staying, tonight?"

"I can't tell you yet. I am still under guard. You like the production? Good, isn't it? It's my favorite play. All is forgiven in the end."

They returned for the rest of the play, and Byron found himself caught up the language and pageantry, moved at the final speech of Prospero who decides to drown his book at last. Mary sat next to him, and he knew that all was not over, if forgiven. Once, he touched her and she cried out in pain. The bullet had left its presence. Outside, as the audience was leaving, Byron stared at the now empty stage still feeling the play's spiritual resonance.

"'We are such stuff as dreams are made on, and our little life is rounded with a sleep.'"

"Nice, Byron. You might've been an actor, yourself."

"I was." He touched her cheek. "Now what?"

Mary wore a conservative dress, and the night brought a chill.

"They could trace me through you. If we hook up again, it will be through secret channels."

"What secret channels?"

"You'll find out."

They saw a parked car as they left the theatre and crossed the lawn; two men in suits sat inside. They walked on and stopped under a grove of trees.

"Maybe I can send you an occasional letter."

"Like the last one saying good-bye?"

Mary turned away. Then he realized she was crying.

"I'm sorry. I thought I was stronger." Her eyes were shadowed in the streetlight. "Look, I was born to be a cop or an agent of some kind. I *chose* a life of danger. I *thrive* on it. Thanks to the enemy, I'm a junkie for life."

"I'll help you stay clean."

"Don't count on it."

They could feel the cold of the Utah summer night. The campus was now deserted and still except for crickets.

"Let's get a motel. Your gorillas could guard the door while we quietly hump inside."

"I can't hump. My body hurts even if I tie my shoes."

"We can improvise," said Byron. "Think of the danger."

He liked the rich spontaneous sound of her laugh.

"You always made me laugh, Byron. Except even *that* hurts."

Byron gently stroked her face and hair. "I was so afraid when I heard you'd been shot."

"Thanks for coming to the hospital. I didn't deserve it after leaving you the way I did."

"Let's go for a drive," he said.

"They'll tail us."

"Tell them we both need a drink. There's only one bar open."

They kissed again. He slipped his hands under her jacket but she pulled away.

"Don't squeeze me," she said, gasping. "Let me ask the gorillas."

Byron got into his car and Mary disappeared; moments later, she leaned in the window. "They said okay, but I can't stay long."

She got in. Byron laid a strip of rubber and drove to a tavern on the edge of town. A car followed them. Byron drove through a light as it changed, forcing the other car to stop. He turned a corner and headed toward another part of town, hunting for a dark vacant lot. He drove fast and Mary glanced at him. "What the hell are you doing?"

"Finding a dark place to ravish you," he said.

"Really?" She looked out the window. "My boys are gonna be mucho angry when they catch us."

Byron screeched around corners, driving through the small town that had many reckless teenaged drivers on the road.

""Byron—drive me to the fucking bar."

"We're taking the long route."

They found a road leading to a campsite, and Byron pulled over under some trees. There was a single park light, and when he kissed her, she pushed against him.

"Be careful. Even breathing hurts."

She kissed him as he ran his hand up her thigh, feeling her panties. Mary moaned into his ear, then opened the door.

"Get in the back," she said, slipping down her panties. Her jacket lay on the front seat, and it was cold in the car. They sat in the back and kissed again, Byron struggling with his pants. Mary slid them half-way down and then held to the front seat and settled on him; he felt a rush of desire coursing through him, but even as he began to move, Mary cried out in pain. Her mouth opened with eyes closed, the color draining from her face in the low light. Her voice came in hoarse rapid whispers.

"Oh Byron, please, my ribs are killing me. Don't stop. Wait! Okay. Hurry! Jesus Christ, I love it, but it hurts too much. Stop! Don't fucking *move*."

Byron tried not to move, but it was impossible. Mary slid off and sat next to him, running her hand up between her thighs until she stopped, her fingers now moving in a circle.

"Give me a taste."

Carefully, Mary bent her face down and Byron felt her lips again. He touched the top of her rising and falling head, feeling her lips and free fingers, then a shuddering wave of sudden release; she swallowed, murmuring approval.

They were dressed when the police car appeared moments later, the lights full on Byron's car. A young policeman with short blond hair approached with a flashlight.

"It is illegal to park here," he said. "I need to see a driver's license."

"Certainly, officer," said Byron, blinking in the flood of light. "My friend and I were just discussing your excellent Shakespeare festival. She's off duty, tonight."

Another policeman checked the car on the computer. Byron grinned at the uniformed officers as they stared at Mary.

"Off duty?"

Mary smiled, touching up her lipstick in the mirror. "Yes. I'm on vacation."

"May we see some identification?"

"Sure," Mary said, taking shallow breaths with the pain. It was the moment she always relished, reaching into her purse, finding the badge next to her panties. She flashed her FBI shield.

As the cops stood there, another car pulled up and agents rushed Byron's vehicle.

"We have her in protective custody," shouted Agent Dalton. He glared at Mary, a tremor running through his voice. "Agent Goldstein, will you get in the car, please?"

"We got lost," said Mary. "Byron doesn't know Cedar City."

"I thought there was a bar here," said Byron.

"On the edge of town, Mr. Duffy," the young cop said.

"I admire Utah police," said Dalton. "You're a clean cut, decent bunch. True Americans. Not many of us left."

Mary walked up to Byron and kissed him. "It was nice seeing you, again. I'll be in touch."

Byron watched as they drove off.

"Why is the FBI here?" the first policeman asked.

"That agent just cracked a big case involving a drug cartel invading a small town…very much like your town."

Byron could almost hear the police officers sucking in a collective breath.

"A drug cartel? Here?"

"Not yet. Where's that bar, again?"

"Just keep heading west outside of town if that's your thing," the second policeman said.

Byron drove through the dark night to the half empty bar on the edge of town, and as he drank the weak beer, he still tasted Mary's lips and saw her face. Agent Dalton entered the bar and sat at the table, staring at him, his thick arms lying heavily on the table. A biker shot pool while an attractive waitress in Levi cut-offs served the few patrons.

"Look," Dalton said, pointing, "we blew the case bad in Bozeman, but Mary was able to take out Mr. Big and foul up a cocaine operation. The Jamaican gang and the Mafia have long memories. Normally, I don't have to tell you shit, but I know she cares."

"I care. I could marry her."

Dalton stared at him with disgust, and then motioned to the waitress. She came over and he ordered a beer.

"That means you'd be on the witness protection program, and it would cost the tax payers big money. Listen, Duffy, these guys could show up and stick your head in a bath full of acid while shoving big members up your ass. You wanna be buggered by some big black buck?"

"As opposed to a big white buck?"

Dalton picked up his beer when it arrived and sucked it up; he made a face. "What weak shit." He pushed the glass away. "A lot of drug money funds terrorist organizations," he finally said. "We could have another attack on America." There was a catch in Dalton's voice. "It could even be a nuclear attack. Do I *have* your attention, now?"

"You have."

"We don't need *anybody* interfering with our operations, and that includes Agent Goldstein, understand? She'll go to school under another name and get protection from *us*."

"Why would a low rent drug dealer become a terrorist?"

"Carl, AKA, Lemar Jones, converted to Islam and decided America hated Muslims, so he declared war on the U.S. Instead of being a drug dealer, now he was a soldier of God, funding Al Quaeda. The fact a Jewish woman bumped him off will disturb his fanatical friends."

"The Koran doesn't condone terrorism *or* the taking of innocent life."

"Really? Tell that to those rag headed assholes."

Tom Dalton stood up. Byron could see the bulge of his gun. Dalton glanced at the pool table and jars of beef jerky and hard boiled eggs on the bar and the mirror reflecting patrons in the dim light. He spoke without making eye contact.

"Agent Goldstein was one of the best. We *both* want to take care of her—right, Mr. Duffy?"

Suddenly, Byron understood. He called out: "Are you in love with her?"

Dalton walked to the door, stopped, turned. "Yes," he said, before pushing out the door. Byron sat alone, hearing a country song over the unseen sound system.

THE MEETING

ONE AFTERNOON ON THE FORT HALL RESERVATION, Byron watched a herd of buffalo. He remembered making love to Mary by the Snake River that lovely day. Did spirits live in the water? Byron had grown up with contempt for undercover cops and suddenly found himself drawn to one. Mary was a warrior against strong enemies. Perhaps it was it just her head flung back in the flowers on a sunny day, and the rhythm of their lovemaking. Their magical moment was gone, vanished into thin air, leaving not a trace behind.

One of the shaggy bulls walked up to the fence and stared at Byron, something dull and wicked in the small eyes. Tempted, Byron wanted to climb the fence and touch the animal. The bull finally snorted once and walked back to the herd. Then he saw the two heavy-set Indians walking toward him. They dressed alike in jeans, heavy shirts and worn leather boots.

"Hey," one demanded. "What are you doin' out here?"

"You got to have a permit or a guide to be out here," the other Indian said.

"Yeah, a permit or a guide."

"Is that right?"

The larger Indian peered into his face. "I'll be your guide. Pay up."

"Hey," the second man said. "This was the same Tybo when old Hernandez came back. Just no good."

"Hernandez?"

"Turned mummy," the smaller man said. "Water Baby ate him."

"I don't think so, Hayball."

The other man continued to argue. "You seen it, Edmo. Even this white boy seen it. Old spirit takes your body, and when it

133

leaves, you be *real* old."

"Those Tybos had guns," Edmo said. He pointed at Byron. "You need a guide."

"I better be going," Byron told them. "You know, maybe there's an explanation. I mean, the way the body—"

"Ain't no explanations out here," Hayball said, "everything is mystical. We are Injuns. We got magic powers. Don't you watch television?"

"Yes." Byron backed away, still talking. "Don't forget, those Posse assholes tried to kill me. Your friend saved my life."

"With that big honky gun," Edmo agreed. "The Raging Bull is a pistol for crazy people." He reached out a big hand and grabbed Byron's shirt. "Enough talk. You took my land. Pay me, you white piece of shit."

As the two men closed in on him, they heard Teton's jeep. Hayball seized Byron's hand and studied it as though he were a fortune teller. "They be comin' for you, Tybo. Agents of the Great White Father."

"Kiss your ass good-bye," Edmo said.

"Don't be showing no disrespect," Hayball said.

Teton's massive form sat behind the wheel. He motioned Byron over.

"I know, I need a permit," Byron said.

"Your boys want you. Tell them this is Indian land—Federal Government or no Federal Government. I don't want them out here."

"Boys? What boys?"

Teton drove Byron to the road and then a clearing where a helicopter landed. Three men in FBI jackets got out and walked toward them. One of the men met Byron's eyes.

"Agent Goldstein wants to see you."

"Where is she?"

"You'll find out."

"Is this a secret channel?"

"A what?"

"Nothing. Is she okay?"

"Yes."

"Where are they training her?"

"That's classified. Get in."

He obeyed their commands and boarded the helicopter; they floated over Pocatello and flew toward Nevada, the pilot silent, another agent watching the desert. Byron decided to remain silent. They crossed the border and landed near a rest stop in the desert. The closest town was Jackpot, Nevada.

"Walk to the rest area, Mr. Duffy. We'll be right here."

"This ain't an ambush, is it, boys?"

The pilot and agents looked at one another.

"Take a walk," an agent said, holding an assault rifle.

Byron walked in the heat to the deserted rest stop. A sign warned away motorists, citing closed for repairs. Byron sat at one of the tables and noticed the thin trees set against the expanse of Nevada desert. The bathrooms were locked. Then a black car pulled up near the entrance to the closed rest stop. Two men were inside; a woman got out and walked toward the rest area.

Dust devils swirled before his eyes and then he saw Mary; she wore a nice suit and cap with dark glasses and walked with a graceful, athletic stride. He could tell from a distance that she had recovered from the bullet wound. She came out of the desert and smiled. Byron felt something turn inside; he got up they embraced. Mary pulled away, holding his hands.

"Just like in the movies, Byron."

"How are you?"

"Recovered. In drug counseling and new training."

"For what? Making bombs? Swat Team? Demolition?"

Mary laughed. "No shop talk. I want to hear about *you* and Judson."

Byron spoke, catching up with all he had to tell her, and she was happy, watching him. Her hair was still short but the color had grown out. The suit accented the wonderful declivity of her thighs, snug in the pants. Byron suddenly reached out and touched her face.

"My God," she said. "I can't believe we're here, and that I'm talking to you."

"I'm here. Let me kiss you."

She kissed him and pulled back, happy but blushing.

"What's wrong?"

"They've got binoculars on us."

"Don't those spies ever rest?"

"Byron, relax."

"Okay. What training?"

"For a swat team to stop terrorists."

"Where?"

"I can't tell you, yet."

"Mary, I want to live with you."

He could see her slipping into another one of her official masks, staring back at him, enigmatic, mysterious. Byron shrugged. "Okay, I'll play." The car with men inside still sat on the desert road. "How is Bad Ass Dalton?"

Her expression changed. "Jealous."

"Jealous? Of me?"

"Yes. He wants to be my protector, as well. I guess I've got two knights in shining armor." Mary reached over and touched him. "I told him I love you."

"Then what's the problem? Come with me. I got a helicopter."

"I can't."

"Then I'll come with you. We can hitch a ride to Jackpot, stay overnight, gamble, eat, make love." He wanted to say, "Get married," but didn't.

"Byron, I am still Bureau Property. I am not free, like you. When I sign up for the special training, it will be with a police force. I will no longer be an FBI agent. Then, old friend, we can be together if you still want me. Who knows? A lot has happened, Byron. Love wears out, especially long distance love."

"Exactly," Byron said. "Let's do it, now."

"I need Dalton's...Tom's permission."

"Fuck him."

Mary lifted her glasses, a slight defiance in her eyes. "Maybe I have."

Byron felt a rush of sickness in his stomach.

"I'm sorry," she said. "I didn't mean to say that."

"If you have, I don't want to know," Byron told her.

A wind blew dust across the rest area.

"What about you? No freshmen girls like the last one?"

"No. No one. *Nada*."

They sat like statues at the worn faded table, dust blowing up in little dry circles. Mary stroked his blowing hair. "No one like Suzi, eh? Why not?"

"That died long ago."

"I see. I demanded this talk with you because it's not fair to keep you hanging, like this. The Bureau wanted me to say goodbye, and probably is still banking on it. I know Tom is. That helicopter is costing the taxpayers money, you know."

He closed his eyes against the dust. "So? I *am* a taxpayer.

Mary seized his hands across the table. "Byron, this is more complex than you realize."

"Because of danger?"

After a moment, Mary stood up. "Watch."

Mary took out a 9mm berretta, pulling back and releasing the slide to chamber a round, and then commenced firing rapidly at distant bottles on a ridge. The pistol jogged against her palm. Byron covered his ears as the shots echoed and bottles shattered. Small puffs of sand exploded into the warm air. Mary emptied the clip, the slide snapped back.

"I like this lighter gun." She put up more bottles, shoved home another clip and chambered the first round. "Here, try it."

"Okay."

Byron took the gun and aiming, squeezed the trigger. Nothing happened.

"It's got a squeeze cock."

"I bet your pardon?"

"Squeeze the front of the handle. Then fire."

Byron squeezed the handle, and then began shooting; no bottles shattered.

"You're flinching and shooting high. It takes practice, but you might consider getting a handgun."

Dalton and a second man had jumped out of the black car. Mary waved to them and quickly put away the gun. The helicopter sat in the desert.

"There *is* something sexual about this gun business," Byron said. "I mean shoving in the clip, pulling back the slide. I like that squeeze cock."

Mary grinned.

"Your first gun lesson. They'll fly you back. The next time we

137

meet, I'm on my own. Maybe we can make a life."

"A life? Where's the training?"

Mary studied his face, and suddenly slammed the table with both palms. "I'm not supposed to tell you, understand?"

Byron seized her shoulders. "What swat team?"

"The one in Pocatello—four lousy months from now."

"You'll be *there*? Where I teach?"

Mary smiled, then bit her lip. She slipped into his arms. They rocked back and forth, and it was good to hold her.

"It happens to be a good training program. After, we can go anywhere, provided you can find something to do. Provided the Jamaican connection and Tony's hoods don't track us."

Byron gently touched her on the chin. "It's odd the Bureau put you so close to me. It's almost cruel."

"The FBI has an office in Pocatello."

He slid his hands up her back, feeling the shoulder holster.

"Let's knock off a quick piece in the toilet."

"It's locked."

"Blow out the door."

"Byron, I *have* to go."

"Can't we spend *one* night, together? Come on, even Dalton will understand. Why not?"

"Walk toward the chopper, okay? Say hello to Judson. Believe me, I'm holding on because of you, Byron."

He suddenly kissed her. Then Mary met his eyes for a long time, the dust settling with the dying winds, her expression a mask. Something dark and lost shadowed her eyes as she glanced at the helicopter and waiting car. She turned to face him.

"Kiss me, again."

He kissed her. She pulled away and Mary turned and walked toward the car. Dalton leaned against the door, waiting. Byron trudged over the sand toward the helicopter, the chopper looking like a large ugly insect in the desert. The black car headed toward the small border town of Jackpot. The agents were silent as Byron swung himself up and settled in; then they lifted and turned, flying toward one of the casino hotels in Jackpot—Cactus Pete's. A few pink clouds drifted across the blue sky and a tall agent regarded Byron with obvious contempt.

138

"We're just old friends," Byron insisted. "We go way back."

"We usually don't operate as transportation for whores."

Byron faced the agent. "I won't allow anyone to put down my woman, understand?"

The agent's eyes narrowed, small and fierce. "I was talking about *you*, asshole. When we land, get out. You can take a bus home."

"What?"

They landed on the roof of Cactus Pete's Casino and Byron stepped off after a push, the wind from the blades blowing over him as he ran, stooped, toward one of the doors. Then he turned and watched the chopper lift off and turn west, disappearing into the desert autumn sun. From the roof, he saw the small town of Jackpot, with another casino across the street, some trailers and bars, and a place called Krazy Kates glittering in the distance. A few hundred yards down the street lay the desert and a highway leading to the Idaho border, just a few miles away.

Byron walked into the hotel and took stairs to the casino; he did not like the harsh light and noise of gambling, the pale, unhealthy faces and monotonous voices of the croupiers. Then he met the bulky Agent Dalton on the stairs, blocking his path, pulling him to one side, his face full of outrage. He raised a finger.

"Duffy, if anything happens to her."

"What are you doing here, Dalton? You gonna see I get on the bus?"

"I warn you, Duffy, you're more dangerous than the Mafia. Now walk to the crap table."

Byron could see desperation in Dalton's carved clean-shaven face, thinking, *he loves her. He really loves her.*

"I hate dice," he said. Byron's voice stopped. He suddenly understood the anger of the agents on board the chopper. "My God."

"Scram," Dalton told him.

Byron turned and continued down the stairs and across a thick red carpet past tourists and career gamblers to the crap table where Mary was on a roll. People stood around while a cocktail waitress served free drinks to the players. Mary vigorously shook her hands after the sudden click and scutter of tumbling dice, smiling at him, a sudden hard boldness in her eyes, thin lines of moisture on her upper lip. Then she sipped a drink and retrieved the dice for another roll. She held the cup and saluted Byron as he approached, and then rolled the dice.

"Seven, a winner," the dealer said, catching the flung dice with his curved stick and returning them to Mary. "Comin' out."

"Let it ride," Mary said, picking up and rattling the dice in the cup. "Let 'em fall. This one's the big roll, sweet daddy. Seven come eleven, you son-of-a-bitch!"

Mary tossed the dice across the marked green table.

"Boxcars," said the dealer. "You're out."

A FUNERAL

JUDSON WAS CALLED AWAY TO HIS EX-WIFE'S BEDSIDE knowing he might return to Idaho with his daughter, Joan. Judson and Byron said goodbye at the Salt Lake City airport as Judson stared at the plane taxing on the runway.

"I'm sorry about all this."

"I've been expecting it," said Judson.

"Are you strong enough?"

"If by that, you mean, can I get through it sober, yes," said Judson. "Tell Darlene I escaped to the Amazon." He put out a cigarette. "Any word from our elusive FBI agent?"

"No."

They embraced, and Judson walked toward the gate. When the plane took off, Byron drove back to Pocatello, remembering a trip he had taken with Judson and his wife, Judy, driving in the early morning cold and darkness to the same fogged in airport, singing theme songs from old fifty's TV westerns, Judson bringing out a six pack of beer. Byron did much thinking as he drove to the empty house and sat in the partial darkness, waiting for a call from the elusive woman who dominated his life. The house was deathly quiet. Outside, the full colors of Autumn would soon cover the hills with patches of color, and the streets with red and gold leaves. He knew there had to be a point of separation so that he might live his life, but he was distracted by an impossible love.

Distracted from distraction by distraction, he thought, quoting that wordsmith, T.S. Eliot.

At school, Byron was disturbed by the general sameness of classes. There were so few driven to learn to read and write their own language well. Few students had passion for the works of great literature. Hunting season was beginning, and Sterling wanted to take a few teachers out on a bear hunt, since he was teaching a class on Faulkner's *The Bear*.

"Good idea," said Byron. "Maybe we ought to teach hunting. Who reads literature anymore?"

Sterling gave him his usual reproachful smile. "Why not teach *both*, literature *and* the great outdoors?"

The department chairman walked away.

That night, he found Darlene at Buddy's drinking a diet coke; her dark eyes seemed not to see him. "I feel awful," she finally said.

"Are we missing Judson?"

"Yes. And I have no right to." Darlene examined her salad. "I'm on a diet. I hate to give up beer, but that's part of it. I mean, where I come from, beer is not considered alcohol."

Byron didn't comment.

"What's his ex wife like?"

"Very dramatic. She has a beautiful voice, and worked in radio. Did a very colorful weather program. I guess the weather in Oklahoma can be dramatic."

Darlene sipped her coke. "I see. And I bet she's tiny. Thin. Wispy. Has long flowing hair to match her great voice. If she dies, it will be worse. I can't compete with a ghost." Darlene picked at the salad. "I shaved my legs, this morning. If I have to have fat legs, I'll at least have smooth flab."

"You're not fat. There isn't an ounce of fat on you."

"But I'm stocky. I don't have the traditional female hourglass shape."

"Judson isn't exactly a movie star, you know."

"Right." Darlene managed to laugh, her body shaking. "Why do I find such an unromantic romantic attractive? I'm confused. I don't even like men as a species."

Byron glanced at students sitting, eating, talking, watching the inevitable sports events on television.

"That man *has* got a mind," Darlene continued. "And I *do* love him."

She began to cry. The waitress saw her crying and turned away.

"It will all work out and we'll live by the seashore," Byron said, taking her hand. She met his eyes. "It has to get better,

Darlene."

"You're a good man, Byron. I'm sorry I've been such a confrontational bitch. I've often wondered what would have happened if we hooked up."

"I'm an environmentalist," he reminded her.

"Bad for business," she warned.

"I'm a left wing Democrat," Byron said.

Darlene gagged.

"I want to ship all Republicans to concentration camps," he continued.

Darlene pretended to throw up.

"Not to mention automatic welfare for all liberal artists."

"Stop," said Darlene. "You're *killing* me."

"I was also a drunk. Probably still am."

He could see Darlene turning pale. It was no longer funny.

"I know, I'm sick. I love all the things I hate," she admitted.

"I have to go. I have a 'Save the Whales' meeting, tonight."

That evening, Byron found a message on his answering machine. It was frustrating to hear Mary's voice again, direct, icy, informing him that possibly they might get together around Thanksgiving, and that there was a new complication with "Tom." The message abruptly ended. It would be a similar pattern in her two brief letters, neither with a return address: small talk ending with a sentence that had Byron turning the page, looking for more vital information. Was she really feeling *suicidal*? *Why* was Dalton panicking? She had succumbed to *what*—cocaine? These questions were left unanswered, and Byron lay on his bed, thinking about the Thanksgiving holiday and the bleak feast he had shared with Suzi and Malcolm.

Byron thought of Judson. He might be dealing with relatives he hadn't seen in years, or talking with a child he barely knew, now a year older. Was Judy on her deathbed? Had she already died? Was Judson at a wake, hearing a rosary, Judy being Catholic, the mourners kneeling while Judson either sat in defiance, or knelt out of a new found respect for religion? Byron saw a flow of images. He had written many stories and fragments in his imagination, often featuring coincidental though unseen incidents in the lives of friends. Occasionally, he described details that became true, an eerie element that made Byron briefly stop writing fiction.

At the airport Judson had met Aunt Milly, a small spidery woman in her eighties wearing an old coat and heavy pearls, and Joan—a little taller, now—staring at Judson, trying to smile. She looked as though she didn't want to be present. There had been a tornado warning, and Judson had watched the incoming storm on the airport television, the black funnel cloud with a thin wavering black thread searching the ground. They drove to Stillwater, Oklahoma, the tornado turning away from the airport and destroying another town.

All the time, Judson wanted to talk with his daughter, to catch up and say the things he hadn't said. She sat beside him, her hands in her lap, knowing, perhaps, that her mother was leaving her in a world that seemed unfair with a father she hardly knew. Perhaps she discovered him when Judy Judson lay on the hospital bed, wasted by the disease that had caused her body to fall in upon itself, as though her tiny frame had shrunk to even this smaller measure, and now someone had wrapped the still breathing remains in a bed sheet. Judson did talk to her before the end, and what they said he never revealed. Father and daughter were there when the newswoman known as Judy Judson passed into another dimension, and the nurse gently asked Judson to take his child outside. The little girl left, but Judson refused to go, throwing the nurse out, remaining a moment alone in the dimly lit hospital room. He sat by the corpse, but there was nothing left to say.

There would be time for the funeral Mass and the dinner and the many relatives pressing forward to touch Judson out of consolation. He finally sat in a garden, the still air hot and dry from a fierce late September heat wave, sitting next to Joan, staring at the sparse trees. Joan began to cry; Judson held his daughter, offering comfort, feeling the sudden hot release of tears himself. They sat in the garden, with Aunt Milly and others inside the house talking and eating the post funeral meal.

In Pocatello, Byron imagined the whole scene in his mind: Judson in a black suit, the girl in a blue dress and black shoes, a blue band over her thick, blonde hair. Byron knew he would glean their conversations in bits and pieces, filing it all for some future novel, some outflow of words to capture a moment and turn it into an elusive truth.

He met Judson at the airport. Judson was silent on the way home. David Sterling still wanted to take the remaining English instructors on a bear hunt.

"A maverick bear has been running loose," Byron continued. "Killing cattle, sheep, and he evidently got two hikers, including a woman and an environmentalist photographer."

"Send Sterling. He can handle it," said Judson.

Byron drove on. "Are you all right?"

"I think so. It was good to be back, touch base, however sad the occasion. It was nice to see Joan, again." Judson stared ahead, smoking. "You don't know what it's like to have a child, do you?"

"No."

"It can change everything. It's difficult to describe."

They rode in silence through the fall colors.

"My daughter is proof that I had a serious relationship with a woman, and against odds, we brought another life into the world."

Before Byron could make a comment, Judson had another statement.

"There was love, not just screwing."

"I understand, Judson."

Byron tried to imagine Mary carrying his child; he tried to visualize the spirit of the child Suzi aborted, but it was too difficult. Then they were sitting in the house, drinking soft drinks and iced tea or coffee after the soft drinks, the conversation taking a philosophical turn.

"I think maybe the Catholics are right," said Judson. "They are the first Christian religion. I like that rebirth image. Look at all our classical literature." Byron held his cup, uncertain how to respond. "I know Judy got some comfort at the end. It makes sense, and I need some *order* in my life. Byron, I've been messing around for a long time, you know?"

"But Catholicism?"

"You were mentally buggered by the Jesuits," said Judson, pointing a thick-knuckled finger at him. "I can't cling to art, the bottle will destroy me, and I have no woman in my life. I *do* have a child, and I need to know there *is* something out there in the darkness when I feel naked and afraid." Judson coughed once, then laughed. "I guess that sounds like second rate Sunday school talk."

"It *is* dark, out there. We need love."

"Of what?"

"The universe."

"Jesus Christ," said Judson. "What second rate Buddhism is that? You'll be worshipping sacred cows, next."

"I think Hindus worship cows."

"I need something, Byron. When I sat in that garden, holding my little girl's hand..."

"What was she wearing? A blue dress?"

"Always the writer. I think it was a dark gray dress. I don't notice such things. I just could hear the funeral party in the house, and she was crying and shivering and I was holding her, and then I started to cry. Hey, Judy and I fought to the bitter end, and I didn't even know I was going to cry. When I did, it was hard to stop. Joan held me, and we felt a bond that maybe helped us jump the gap of all those years."

Judson stopped. He took a drink of iced tea, rattling the ice in the glass. Then he lit one of his inevitable cigarettes and began the subsequent nervous pacing. Byron sat at the table with a cup of coffee.

"No Woman? What about Darlene?"

"What about her? I like her. I don't love her."

Judson glanced down at the newspaper photo of an old brown bear reaching out one hooked paw close to the camera and out of focus.

"Boy, the photographer *did* get close."

"His last shot. The bear pulled him off a flatbed truck and ate his face and intestines. A week ago, when he snagged a woman hiker, all they found were her feet."

Judson held his eyes. "You think death is the end, don't you?"

"Yes. Just because the followers of Jesus found an empty tomb doesn't mean his resurrected corpse was walking around. Maybe they felt guilt for abandoning him to the Romans so they resurrected his memory and started a church. Jesus Christ was a rebellious Jew, not a Christian. He was talking about another kingdom."

"What kingdom was that?"

"The one inside." It was quiet outside except for a single car.

"Judson, surely you don't believe that Jesus worked miracles and came back from the dead."

"I do."

"And you'll have eternal life playing a harp among the clouds?"

"I'm not sure about the harp."

"We have to separate the Gospel's history from the Christian myth."

"Maybe *you* have to make a separation. That's what faith is all about." Judson dragged on his cigarette, the end suddenly glowing. "Byron? Joan is my only priority. When she's older, maybe we can be existential philosophers."

"What's wrong with that? Can't we face death without clinging to some deity? Can't we have brotherhood in an absurd world *without* organized superstition?" Before Judson could answer, Byron quoted Beckett: "'They give birth astride a grave, the light gleams an instant, then it's night once more.'"

"I prefer T.S. Eliot: 'In my end is my beginning.'"

Byron shook his head. "In my beginning is my end." After a silence, Byron said: "I'm going for a walk."

"Maybe you should forget Mary."

"Teach me how. She might be in danger."

"And you'll save her? One of the most dangerous things in the world is to put either a tool or a weapon in your hands. You'd probably shoot yourself. Goodnight."

Judson went to bed. The smoke from his cigarettes hung in the air. Byron inhaled the ambience of the masculine apartment; a mounted deer head watched him through dead glassy eyes. A single rug covered the hardwood floor with wall hangings, an Indian painting, and a rifle in a gun rack. No feminine trace remained from the days of Suzi, her pin-ups missing from the kitchen, perfume bottles gone from the bathroom, panties no longer on the bedpost. Regarding Judson's last remark, Byron had bought a gun, a Walther PPK since it was the only famous brand he knew; he liked taking the compact semi auto to the firing range to shoot rounds at paper targets and feel the recoil against his palm. With a steady hand, his pattern of hits improved. Byron found he enjoyed the gun culture, and holding the pistol, wondered if he would ever use it in self defense.

Outside their apartment, it was a lovely night. He could still hear Judson's rumbling voice, see the clear eyes and the slight stubble on his round cheeks, the brown hair longer, now. His lumbering walk demonstrated a cartoon-ish determination. Byron heard the distant trains hooking up, slamming into each other, and the screech of air brakes. He liked the bite of autumn air. For a moment, Byron wanted to call Suzi, hear her voice, even ask advice, knowing his desperate passion for her was replaced by something nostalgic and genuinely warm. Perhaps Suzi might be a good friend after all. They had been good if short-lived lovers; the ending was painful, inevitable, but he had accepted it.

Mary was a different story.

Love affairs could be so intense, shutting the lovers out against the rest of the world, but it was all an illusion, and even the strongest sexual passion faded, killing the magic. It was like walking past an old abandoned movie set where spectacular scenes and vistas had been filmed, but now the crew was gone, no trace left of the film's false world except on celluloid buried somewhere in a vault. The film would celebrate something past, gone, dead.

But what a rush, Byron thought.

He walked through the blaze of autumn color, the perfect setting for his drifting mental images, like ghosts crowding his consciousness.

Judson had discovered his child and found religious meaning at his ex wife's funeral.

Good, Byron thought. *And I'll stand in front of the church giving out tickets to the theatre where the great human dramas are staged.*

Perhaps he'd find his meaning in that.

THE BEAR HUNT

THEY LEFT FOR THE CARIBOU FOREST one clear morning.

It seemed all of Idaho's hunters had converged on the area to hunt a transplanted Yellowstone bear that had gained mythical recognition. Men who had only the day before worked as clerks and mechanics now had new hunting clothes and guns, ready to tramp though the woods for a bear that had killed two people. The Caribou woods were lovely and not as threatening or dense as the primitive area.

They sat in the country tavern, Dr. Sterling drinking while another instructor, Leo, bellowed in high German at the collected hunters and sheepmen in the tavern. They seemed to appreciate Goethe's *Faust*. The bartender was a woman named Maureen, married to Gus, a sheepherder going bankrupt. She was a tall woman with long blonde hair, blue eyes and a quick laugh that the men found appealing. She served the drinks quickly, and drew each customer out, skillfully listening.

"I don't mind the environmentalists," she said. "Too bad that bear ate one, but they kept us from killing coyotes. Now wolves and that bear can run loose and finish off the sheep industry."

"Ain't that the truth?" a herder said.

Sterling drank his beer. He was excited and a slight stubble gave him a more masculine look.

"You ain't a farmer," Maureen observed.

"Education," declared Sterling. "With three of my staff."

He introduced Judson, Leo and Byron. Leo proudly displayed his deer rifle and long barreled pistol used for boar. Maureen examined Sterling's new 30.06-caliber rifle.

"You better be a good shot with that. When that bear starts to move, nothing will stop him but a shot to the shoulder and head, and even then, he can run over you with his heart shot to pieces."

"It's a new gun," said Sterling.

"I *know* it's a new gun. *Too* new. You fire that thing a lot?"

"Sure," Leo bellowed. "We are hunters first, teachers second."

Maureen poured more drinks, and stopped at Judson and Byron who were drinking sodas.

"You could be a farmer and you"—looking at Byron—"you, I suspect, are a poet of some kind."

"God no," protested Byron, "I play in a jug band."

Byron felt Maureen's eyes lingering on him for a moment. Then she moved down the bar.

"It sure was nice of the forest service in Yellowstone to drop that sucker in Caribou," she said. "Now we got to deal with him."

The small tavern was built with logs. A jukebox played country music. During an interval, an old man coaxed his dog onto the piano bench to bang its paws on the keys. A few drunks cheered. Judson glanced nervously at the bottles of whiskey behind the bar, and then he smiled at Byron, who winked, once. Maureen leaned across the bar.

"You don't have to drink whiskey to be macho hunters, boys. Soft drinks are just fine."

"I know," said Judson.

"I'd rather shoot some film in the woods," Byron said.

Maureen lit a cigarette; they heard Leo shooting his boar gun outside.

"I hope your friend can shoot as well as he barks that German, stuff."

"He knows his guns," Judson agreed. "Byron, on the other hand, would be better off taking a novel to read, or maybe a drop line for minnows."

Maureen inched closer to them.

"Fishing's dropped off. Fewer fish, fewer licenses sold. I think the dams have finished the job of any past over fishing. In ten years, there won't be any wild trout. The wild salmon are disappearing."

"There goes my outdoors," said Byron.

He stopped. Darlene had entered the bar. Sterling was holding forth with another teacher and some local farmers. Judson saw Darlene in the bar mirror.

"Don't mind me," said Darlene.

"I won't," said Judson.

"I just came for all the excitement," said Darlene, sitting heavily down on a barstool. Maureen waited for her request, a light beer. "I like hunting, myself."

"I think we got too many hunters," Maureen warned. "They'll probably shoot each other."

Judson said nothing. Darlene was wearing tight jeans that made her look heavier, and Byron tried to make conversation. Outside, they heard Leo shrieking in mock Hitlerian German as he blasted another target with his Buntline Special boar gun. Getting drunk, Sterling blinked at Byron and Judson.

"What the hell is Leo *doing* out there?"

A country song came on the jukebox.

"Dance with me, Judson."

"Later, Darlene."

"Sterling, how about a quick dance?"

"I'm not very good—but sure."

He danced with Darlene. The ballad was about a sad love affair. Leo came back into the bar, followed by some young, impressed hunters. Judson stared ahead.

"I'm sure you'll find time to get away," Maureen said.

"I hope so," said Judson.

Maureen refilled Byron's soft drink.

"I had a boyfriend kinda like you about two years ago when my husband was tom catting around, but he wanted to do his art stuff in LA, and I'd rather die than live in Los Angeles. He finally took off, and me and my fireplug of a husband seem to be getting along, so I guess my old boyfriend can stay in Southern California. I did miss him for a while. I think someone new is always exciting...but I guess I'm pretty square stock when you come right down to it."

Byron liked Maureen's pleasant face. Leo was showing his gun to other hunters. Darlene rocked heavily back and forth clutching the slightly built Sterling.

"Why are you telling me this?"

"I don't know, Byron," said Maureen. "Idaho doesn't have *much* culture, but it does have some fine people. Even English professors who think they can hunt because they have new guns and new clothes to hunt in."

"I can hunt," insisted Judson. "But I prefer not to."

He spoke about missing his daughter living in another state, Maureen listening in between trips up and down the bar. Darlene tugged at Leo's arm, and they finally danced while Darlene switched to whiskey with her beer, tipping it up, singing along with the music.

"I can feel for you, Judson," said Maureen. "I got three kids. One is away at college, and it's lonely without her. Of course, I want her to get educated."

Sterling stood at the bar, beaming. "This is *divine*," he intoned. "A taste of rough reality. After this—fishing. We will drop dry flies to rising rainbows."

Byron found himself growing bored with the smoky bar. Judson drank from a huge glass of ginger ale and when Darlene yanked his sleeve, he took her outside where they shouted at one another. Sterling lifted his eyes to the ceiling. "Lover's quarrel," Byron explained.

Then it was midnight. Judson had disappeared, and Darlene was leading a train around the tavern; she crunched ice between her teeth, lifting her nose and upper lip, snorting like a pig as the drunken shouting patrons hooked up and followed her train in a broken circle.

Gus, a short squat man with thick glasses and bald head, took over for Maureen behind the bar. He decided to join the hunt, though he knew the bear dogs might scatter any sheep left in the area. Byron sat near Sterling who had passed out, his head on the bar. Leo hopped and rocked behind Darlene, singing Wagnerian lines as they chugged around the bar. Byron imagined the morning hunt when he saw Maureen.

"I'm worried that we'll have chaos, tomorrow, what with bear dogs and skittish horses. Why don't we look for your friend at the other bar? We got a sheep camp you can stay in, tonight. It looks like a covered wagon. Might save you some money."

Gus toasted the hunters with a drink as Maureen shouted over the noise: "Gus, I don't want anyone riding my horse."

"*Your* horse? That animal belongs to the ranch," Gus argued.

"But no one else can handle Buckskin. You *know* that."

After they left, Maureen listed her grievances against certain hunters.

"It's just macho chest beating. They get drunk and run wild over the land. They can ruin good horses, scatter livestock, shoot each other."

Byron nodded in agreement, though he had never been on a bear hunt. They found Judson drinking a coke in a quiet bar down the street.

"Of all the gin joints in the world, she has to walk into yours," he said, grinning at Maureen.

"She's now pulling a choo-choo train," Byron said.

"Which will be a real train by tonight," observed Judson.

Maureen lit another cigarette.

"Well, a girl gets lonely now and then," she told them. "We got so many insensitive men in the world. I tell you one thing, I ain't cooking dinner for those drunken fools, tomorrow. Half of them have guns that'll only make the bear mad. I got a shotgun in the pick-up."

Recognizing an absurd pattern, Byron started to laugh.

"Well, Judson, old pal, at least we got away from romance and women folk. Thought you were safe, didn't you? Who knows? Mary might come with an FBI swat team to join in the fun."

"It's becoming a spectator sport," Maureen agreed. "Anyone might show up."

That night, Byron stayed in the sheep camp while Judson slept outside. Byron wondered what a sheep drive was like, remembering cattle drives from old movies.

In the morning, groups of men had gathered in the yard, and Byron smelled the cooking food and heard muted conversations. Smoke drifted in the cold air. He and Judson drank coffee around a fire, watching as more hunters, some deathly ill from drinking, staggered into the camp. Byron stared at the array of rifles and bear guns, unfamiliar with any of them. Sterling wasn't there, but he saw Leo, hung over but armed. Maureen and Gus argued in the distance; Gus walked away to saddle one of the horses. Then a pack of bear dogs came into camp, growling and snapping. Byron had never seen such big, ugly dogs, barking and snarling, eager to hunt. They glared around at the men with mad, almost evil eyes, showing their teeth, straining against the leashes. Sterling arrived, pale and sick, refusing any food. Leo took out a bottle and passed it around.

"Stirrup cup," he bellowed.

Judson passed the bottle on without drinking. Byron took a sip of the cheap whiskey.

"Let's hunt," Gus shouted. "Mount up, boys."

The hunters mounted and followed a fat man holding the bear dogs. Byron rode in a pick-up with Maureen. "Why aren't you riding on horseback?"

"That fat slob is gonna ride Buckskin. I told him he's very skittish. I know how to ride him. Course, the men don't allow us girls to ride or hunt. We get to stay in camp, cook, and maybe fuck the lucky hunter afterwards. Meanwhile, they might ruin a good horse and lose a few dogs."

The dogs charged ahead up into the mountains and Caribou forest, followed by men on horseback, including the fat man riding Buckskin.

"I think Mr. Sterling thinks he's in England. We don't ride side saddle, here."

They saw Sterling posting on his mount in an elegant fashion. Judson rode straight up, with little bounce. The pick-up bounced on the mountain road.

"I hate men," said Maureen. "I mean, I love them, but I hate them, as well."

"I could think of a few women I'd like to drown," Byron said.

Up ahead, the fat man suddenly disappeared from the saddle, the horse leaping to one side, the fat man cart wheeling into a ditch. Maureen got out of the truck and approached the rider, now getting up, bruised and covered with dust. Byron watched their argument from a distance, and Gus dismounted to join the discussion. They could not drive much further in the truck.

Sterling was pale and sickly.

"You look the way I did on that river trip, last year."

"I'll be fine," he insisted, his forehead moist.

They moved on, Maureen driving, glaring through the window.

"Fatso insists he can ride Buckskin, and he tied the dogs to the saddle horn. What a stupid move. The horse will bolt and run over his goddamn stupid, *ugly* dogs!"

At that moment, the dogs took up a fierce hysterical baying. They bolted forward. Byron saw the hunters spurring their horses. Buckskin began to gallop, running down the dogs, then pulling ahead, tangling hooves in the many leashes.

"Oh shit," Maureen said, pressing the accelerator.

She cursed again as the horse went down and the fat man, still pulling the reins, rolled from the saddle. Maureen bolted from the truck and ran ahead, kicking her way through the dogs, reaching for a knife to cut the tangled leashes as the bear dogs howled and bayed and snapped at the kicking horse and each other; then she was up on Buckskin and rode down the trail, the hunters reining in, shouting to her. The fat man crawled out of the ditch as the dogs rushed ahead on the fresh scent of the renegade bear. Mounted hunters disappeared up the trail after the dogs. The whole woods seemed to ring with the resonant baying of the hounds. Byron suddenly found himself alone in the truck.

He got out and stood in the road. He could hear the dogs growing more and more faint as they plunged into the woods. Then he saw the bear on a distant ridge, standing up, roaring, slashing once with a huge paw, striking a bear dog in mid-leap, killing it. The bear plunged into the woods followed by the shouting men on horseback.

After a moment, it was quiet. Byron wondered what happened to the fat rider thrown from Buckskin. No one had thought to stay with Byron or the pick-up truck. The CB radio cackled, and Byron picked it up. He heard first Spanish, then another language he didn't recognize, then English.

"Señor, can you drive the truck back to camp?"

"Maureen has the keys, sir. I guess she'll have to drive it back."

The radio transmission stopped. Byron left the truck and walked up the trail, taking the shotgun. It was a beautiful walk, the colors much brighter in the woods. He followed the path when there was a path, following the horse droppings, listening for distant sounds of running dogs. In California, he had walked once through a grove of redwoods that felt like a living, breathing cathedral. Byron climbed to a high ridge, looking over the forest for any distant road. The forest seemed to be unusually quiet, except for a single woodpecker knocking on an old tree. Then he came upon a clearing with hoof prints and empty whiskey bottles. Byron could imagine the scene, the men reining in and tying the horses, passing around the whiskey bottles, the dogs tugging at the leashes. They must think I went back with Maureen, he realized.

He walked on.

I have to find them soon, he thought. The shotgun felt strange under his arm, but he was glad to have it and the two extra shells in his jacket pocket. It was getting warmer with the sun and the long climb. By the time he realized he was lost, Byron felt his first taste of fear. He didn't want to spend the night in the woods. He found a small stream and knelt to drink, his reflection broken over the waved and whorled sandy bottom. Somewhere in the woods, a bird called. He saw the reflection of an eagle in the water, and looking up, saw the majestic bird. For a moment, Byron was no longer afraid, but actually happy and touched by the forest.

It can't be far to a road, he thought.

Byron wondered if he should follow the stream downhill toward a main road. Then he saw another ridge, knowing it might give him a vantage point. How could so many men, dogs and horses vanish without a trace or sound? He clutched the gun, feeling invisible eyes in the brush. The birds stopped singing and it was quiet, still.

I have to keep moving, he thought.

"I've been in the woods before," he said aloud, his voice sounding unnatural.

Byron heard the sinister rattling and quickly stopped. A huge rattlesnake slithered back and forth on a fallen log. Slowly, the snake backed away and slid down into a gully. Byron watched the retreating diamondback and gripped the shotgun. He felt calm, though he could feel his heart thudding with a deep hollow sound in his throat. For a moment, he wondered if shooting off a round would alert the others. Byron looked at the sun, assuming it was noon. He didn't have a compass.

But what direction is home? he thought.

He heard the helicopter. It soared overhead, flying over the trees, gone before he could wave or call out. Byron crashed through the brush, and then heard something else besides the distant blades of the chopper. He listened in the silence that seemed to engulf him.

It was the sound of running, baying hounds, but there was an excitement different from the early morning. Gunshots echoed through the forest. Human voices shouted in the distance.

They were coming his way, and fast.

Byron stared at the wall of trees, the white slender aspens, the thin tall pines, and many taller, thicker trees he couldn't identify. He held the gun that seemed too small to stop a running bear, and as the sounds of the pack came closer, Byron searched for a tree that he might climb. The woods were full of dogs and gunshots and men and horses, and then he heard the crashing in the brush and saw the bear emerging from the forest, running almost in slow motion, though closing the gap quickly. Byron lifted the double-barreled shotgun as the bear charged; he fired both barrels at close range as the bear swiped at him, knocking the shotgun into the brush. The bear clawed again at Byron as he went down, then ran into the forest. Two hounds appeared and chased the bear in a furious dash. The hunters rode their lathered mounts into the clearing, one drunken rider brushed from his horse by a branch. Byron croaked at Leo struggling with his panicked horse.

"Leo, wait!"

"Jesus, where the hell did you come from? I thought we had him treed."

"Give me a ride."

"I'll send someone back."

Leo howled and kicked his tired mount toward the fading sound of running dogs. The drunk got up and stumbled after his horse. Byron picked up his gun and stared at the forest, cursing. He could hear shouts coming from other parts of the woods. A terrified foaming horse galloped past him into the brush. Byron recognized the animal as Sterling's. He followed and found the horse lying on its side, bleeding and exhausted; Byron laid his hands on the horse.

"Take it easy, boy."

The horse groaned, stretched out and died. The sounds of the hunt died away in the forest. Byron looked down at the trickle of blood welling up under his torn boot. Trembling, he reloaded the gun. Then Maureen rode toward him, the buckskin calm. She glanced at the dead horse and pulled Byron up behind her.

"I knew this would happen. I see you drew blood and got hurt yourself. Watch the gun, Byron. We already mighta lost a man."

They rode along a narrow game trail. "Who got hurt?"

"I don't know for sure. The helicopter got him. Had a hard time landing in this brush. Where's that Sterling fella?"

"I don't know."

They rode into a clearing, and Maureen got down and treated Byron's bleeding leg with antiseptic. They heard a helicopter land, and Byron saw a tall forest ranger walking toward them.

"Just what the hell you people think you're doing?"

"Oh, some dumb rangers left a nasty bear in the area. We thought we'd give it a little run before it ate all our sheep," Maureen said.

A shorter ranger was getting out of the helicopter.

"We're conducting an investigation. I just may have to arrest *all* of you."

"On what grounds?" demanded Byron.

He followed the ranger's eyes, and then touched the imprint of bear claws on his lower leg and ankle. They were not deep, but he suddenly fainted.

THAT NIGHT, the hunters cooked their own food and told stories of what happened and what was lost, including at least five dogs and one horse. One hunter had been shot.

Gus sat by the fire, drinking.

"Where's your wife?" someone said. "She's supposed to cook. I can't eat my own cookin'."

"She won't cook since Fatso damn near lost Buckskin."

The fat man, one eye black, took a swig.

"Hell, that damn buckskin had no sense. I lost three hounds, today."

Leo held up the boar gun. "I couldn't shoot—my horse spooked."

They regarded Byron. "I guess you got a taste, yourself."

"That's right. I'd be still out there except for Maureen. Thanks for stopping, gents."

"You know how it gets when the hunt's on."

They were silent when Maureen walked into the firelight. She didn't look at the fat man or her husband. "I don't want to hear a word. Not one *word*."

"Johnny's in the hospital," said Gus.

"I know," said Maureen. "He might lose an arm. Byron, I'm sorry you got lost, but they coulda shot you, too!"

"He hit the bear, point blank," observed Gus. "Got close enough to get clawed up, a bit."

"We drew some blood, at least," another hunter said.

"That's *great*—and now he's wounded, still alive, and *really* mean," Maureen said. "You all make me sick!" She walked away from the campfire. "Cook your own muck, tomorrow."

"Shall we go to the tavern?" suggested Judson.

Sterling had gone to his motel after getting his ribs taped. Leo pulled out another pint of whiskey. None of them wanted to think of tracking a wounded bear. They were drinking at the bar when the tall ranger entered and warned them that anyone caught bear hunting without a license would be arrested and fined for poaching. There were no permits allowed. After the ranger left, Gus ranted about all the sheep and cattle the locals had lost. Leo bought a round and helped Darlene to a chair, shouting that she was an Isolde for any potential Tristan; no one knew the Wagner opera so Leo sang a few bars in high German.

Judson and Byron sat in the corner, quiet. Maureen walked down the bar toward them.

"I admire someone who doesn't panic in the woods."

"But I fainted."

"Dead away," Maureen said. "It happens."

"Tomorrow, I'm staying right here. I have no plans for hunting or hiking," said Byron. "I'll sit in a motel and read about the death of Keats in Rome."

"Stay in the sheep camp," said Maureen, sitting down. "I feel sick about Johnny, getting shot by one of his own hunters. He needs that arm to farm."

Then Darlene cried again, hugging Judson who gently disengaged himself. He turned into her distorted, crying face. "Just leave me alone, okay?"

Darlene pushed him away and took another drink. Moments

later, she and Leo were dancing a dirty boogie.

"I'd like to go home tonight," said Judson. "The karma is a little sick around here."

"Stick around one more night," said Maureen. "I like your company. We can have breakfast, tomorrow. I got no one to talk to in this joint."

Gus stood behind the bar, pouring out free drinks. A number of hunters, very drunk, were swearing vengeance on the bear. He had gone too far. This was war. Byron saw the line of sweat on Gus's fat upper lip as he poured raw whiskey into paper cups.

"Tomorrow, Mr. Bear, he is gonna *die.*"

Judson smiled weakly, an anxious look in his eyes. The labeled bottles glowed behind the bar. "I may have to join the hunt, tomorrow."

"Why?"

"I had the cleanest shot at the bear, since my horse didn't spook, and failed to kill him. We *have* to exterminate the brute." He glared at Byron, his voice slipping into a lower rasp. "And those shotgun shells will *really* enflame him. No hiker will be safe."

Byron was silent. Maureen got up to answer the phone. Darlene had joined in the singing, and Byron felt some pity, even as she danced with Gus, now very drunk.

"You don't want to stay here for a lot of reasons, Judson."

"I know," he said, holding his iced tea.

Maureen hung up the phone with something in her eyes that Byron didn't recognize. Then she laughed and took a shot of whiskey, slapping Judson once on the shoulder and gently touching Byron's cheek.

"I like you lugs, but I knew I wouldn't get through this week without complications. At least, Buckskin is ten miles away, safe in a corral." She smiled at Byron. "Cheers. The offer is still good if you and your girlfriend want to sack out at the sheep camp and tell stories and make love. Don't pay us no mind. Don't let the smell of sheep stop you. Of course, a motel might be more romantic, but she sounds like she wants a taste of the action. Hell, she oughta join the hunters, herself, even if they don't let girlfriends or wives on the run."

"Maureen," Byron asked. "What the hell are you talking

about?"

"Someone on the phone was just asking directions, and she's on her way over. Sounds like maybe she's in love with both of you bozos. Hell, I understand. I'm a liberal."

Maureen poured another shot. Judson and Byron were running through the possibilities, when they heard a resonant female voice. Judson barked a laugh and embraced Mary who laughed through tears. Her hair had been cut shorter; she was wearing jeans and boots and a heavy coat, and while Mary and Judson embraced, Byron sat in silence. He did not see Maureen watching him intently. Then Mary wiped her eyes and stood before him.

"Jesus, I missed you guys, and when I heard about the bear hunt, *damn*." Mary waved at Darlene still dancing. "Byron, hold me, please."

They embraced.

"Where's our little friend, Agent Dalton?"

"Our little friend's in Pocatello." Mary cupped Byron's face in her strong hands. "I told him I wanted time alone with you two clowns. Let's not talk about him, or the FBI or *any* of that crap."

Mary became aware of the bar growing briefly silent at the mention of the FBI. Maureen bought a round of drinks. As she was introduced, Byron felt Mary's eyes on his face. The day's adventures were repeated.

"*You* got in a shot? Byron, you're becoming a macho man of the woods."

"That's right."

Maureen leaned across the bar.

"Before this place becomes a madhouse, why don't we adjourn to the quieter bar down the street? Yawl can all catch up."

"Sure. Where's Sterling?"

"Nursing his wounds. He fell off his horse, today." Mary laughed. "Killing the horse," Maureen added, in a dry voice.

They went to a bar called The Crossroads with country music on the jukebox. Byron could feel the sense of a vast forest outside the small tavern that had been built by trappers and hunters. They sat and talked until closing time.

"How come no one named the sheepherder's place?"

"We didn't think it needed a name. Just 'The Tavern'," Maureen said. "We keep things simple, here."

Sitting next to Byron, Mary occasionally touched his thigh, his shoulder, or stroked his face.

"I love this country," she said.

"So do I," said Maureen. "The old Idaho."

Mary reached over and kissed Judson. "And you've dried out."

"I don't want to talk about it," said Judson.

"How long are you here for?" Maureen asked.

"I have to leave tomorrow evening."

Then it was late, and Mary and Byron walked along a country road within sight of the ranch and the sheep camp where they could spend a night together. A soft light covered the landscape. They saw Leo carrying a passed-out Darlene. In the morning, the field would be filled with amateur and professional hunters, and more dogs and horses. Byron still remembered the frightening sight of the bear so close, the huge jaws and teeth, the powerful slashing claws.

"Your letters are frustrating, Mary."

"I know. I'm terrible."

"Are we supposed to make love, and then call it a night until next time?"

"Does that bother you?"

"Of course."

"I want you to *want* me, not *need* me."

Byron stopped, staring at her, the night air cold. "What the hell does *that* mean?"

"I want you in my life, Byron, but I also want some distance."

"What about Dalton?"

"He's part of my training, but he won't be living with me. I have so many things to work out."

"What is there to work out?" Byron felt his anger and couldn't stop. "When you want to be serviced, I can just come on over? *Want* you but not *need* you?"

"You make it sound awful, Byron."

"Does Dalton want to marry you?"

Mary dried her suddenly wet eyes, and then grinned at him. "Yes. He does. I don't want *that*, either."

"What *do* you want?"

162

Mary blinked at the bright full moon, and for a moment, seemed lost in the stillness of the chill but clear night. A silver glow covered the trees.

"I honestly don't know, Byron. Maybe I *am* a little sick. They could put a hit on me at any time—if they find me. That would settle it, forever."

"I am sick of your FBI Melodramas."

"So am I. And they may come after you."

It was a dramatic moment and Byron savored it. "Let them. They'll eat my lead."

Mary's eyes and mouth opened. "You have a gun?"

"That's right. A Walther PPK."

Mary laughed. "Like James Bond? Byron—this isn't a game for amateur spies."

Byron cocked one eyebrow. "I know," he said. "I've been practicing at the range. I can shoot that sucker pretty good and it fits nicely down the crack of my ass."

"Always start off with a .22. You got the gun here?"

"In Judson's truck," Byron told her.

"Which will do you a lot of good if hitmen try to take you down." Mary shook her head. "They don't want you. They want me." She touched his arm, and he felt the strong slender fingers. "The good news is that major terrorists usually can't be bothered killing one person. They like to take out whole buildings, cities. I'm not even a blip on their screen."

"That's comforting."

Mary stopped and he was struck by the strength and resolve in her eyes. "Byron, we're still at war."

Judson sat on the porch with Maureen as they walked toward the sheep camp. Maureen called out: "It's real comfortable, don't worry. See you in the morning."

Then Mary slipped off her clothes and lay naked on the blankets, a single lamp illuminating the interior that felt like an old pioneer wagon, throwing Byron's shadow on the canvas walls. Byron slipped off his boots and jeans, kneeling then. Mary was silent. He felt excitement and fear running though his body, the light soft on her breasts and eyes.

"You want to make love to me, Byron?"

"Of course."

A 1911 .45 pistol lay next to the bed on the floor.

"Is that sucker loaded?"

"Of course. I can't shoot an unloaded gun. Get in bed, Byron."

He felt a sadness remembering happier times. There was a scar from the bullet she took in the abdomen. Points of light glowed in her eyes and hair. Then she slipped under the covers, waiting for him.

"Don't think about it, Byron. Just *do* it."

"Do you need me?"

"I *want* you."

He slipped into bed next to her, slipping off his underwear. He reached out to touch her.

"I guess I want you too," he said.

She kissed him. For the magical moment, Byron lived in the moment, touching the naked body of the woman he loved. They never completed their lovemaking.

Perhaps the bear had wanted revenge, and still felt the slugs in him even as he devoured part of Sterling's dead horse. No one, including wildlife experts, would ever explain why the bear came onto the actual grounds, or whether it had enough intelligence and memory to take the offensive. The bear had terrorized campsites in Yellowstone, but for the bear to find the sheep camp and attack the man who had blasted him with shotgun slugs seemed unnaturally vengeful and cunning, even for this animal.

Byron was holding and kissing Mary when he heard the distant barking of many sheep dogs; there was a note of hysteria that warned him. Mary screamed as the bear roared and stuck his paw into the camp, the large head thrusting itself into the small wagon that rocked with the bear's weight. Byron sat up, naked, staring at the enraged bear. He screamed: "Get the hell out of here, you son-of-a-bitch!"

He pushed Mary behind him as the bear tried to force its bulk into the sheep camp, swiping again with a massive paw, scattering cooking utensils. Byron could smell the bear's fetid breath. He saw the wound in the shoulder, raw and already infected. Outside they heard a furious barking. Byron grabbed the pistol from Mary, now frozen, and aimed at the gaping red mouth, the light from the lamp casting a surreal glow on the animal as it began to rip up the heavy mattress, lunging at them. Byron fired rounds into the open jaws before the bear could squeeze into the wagon. The lamp fell and went out, throwing them in darkness. Mary pulled him as the wagon toppled, the enraged bear finally inside. Byron lost the pistol. Scrambling outside, he felt the sudden cold air. Mary was beside him, clutching a blanket when they saw the bear, his jaw broken, coming up out of the overturned wagon. Blood poured from his mouth, and one eye was gone.

"Mary, run!"

She didn't run, and Byron felt himself frozen to the spot, as in a bad dream. The bear stood up on its hind feet. Two sheep dogs circled the wounded animal, barking but staying beyond the bear's range, the bear roaring and tramping toward Byron and Mary. Then they heard the deafening roar of a heavy gun. Byron saw the explosion of blood from the bear's chest in the moonlight. The animal took a few steps and collapsed, the dogs rushing in to bite, then withdrawing, trembling and barking. Maureen stood in her bedclothes, holding a .470 Rigby elephant rifle.

The dead body of the bear seemed to fill the yard.

"You better get some clothes on," said Maureen, and looking down, Byron realized he was still naked.

In the morning, the sky was pink along the horizon and many herders, farmers and hunters came to see the bear and drink coffee, talking in low, awed tones.

"We had to kill him," Gus said, "but I never heard of no bear taking the hunt to us."

"It was the monster in *Beowulf* coming in for revenge," explained Sterling.

"Beo- who? What kinda wolf is that?"

"He was in pain," Maureen said. "He was crazy. Good thing I had that there old big game bazooka"

Maureen could feel and see a new respect in the eyes of the other hunters. Judson and Byron drank coffee, sitting on the steps, Mary staring at the distant body of the bear in the yard. Someone had righted the wagon.

"One way or another, you want to get me killed, Byron," Mary observed. "I don't need hitmen, I got you."

"You're lucky," Judson said. "His jaw and face were destroyed, but he could've mauled you both pretty bad."

Mary confronted Byron. "Don't *ever* take my gun outta my hands again, Byron. I was about to shoot. You could've shot *me*!"

"Sorry," Byron said. "But you paused."

"A good marksman *does* pause," said Judson. "But don't forget, Maureen saved your lives."

They sat, drinking coffee as a crowd gathered around the dead bear.

Later that afternoon, they had lunch at the tavern, but they did little talking. Byron showed Mary the Walther PPK, and she held and examined the small semi-auto. Then Byron walked Mary to her car; she gave Byron a nervous smile.

"See you soon, Byron. It will all work out, one fine day."

"We'll always have Pocatello," joked Byron.

"We'll have Pocatello *again*."

They stood by her car, like two actors in a romantic film. Mary started to cry freely, without sobbing, then wiped her eyes. They kissed, and moments later, Byron watched her drive away.

Maureen and Judson sat in the tavern, drinking iced tea, discussing the bear while Gus worked the lunch grill. Byron walked into the bar, feeling the approving glances of the men. He drank coffee but tasted nothing. Leo and Sterling were gone. There was nothing left to do but ride home with Judson. He would not miss Mary but feel her absence, like a void he had almost filled in the woods. Their brief meeting aggravated everything.

And we didn't even make love, he thought. *Thou still unravished bride but not immune to silence and slow time.*

Byron did not want to think about the fact they might never make love again. Maureen smiled at him across the smooth table, her light-colored hair combed back.

"The bear was carted off to a lab for an autopsy. If you guys are in the area, do drop in."

Judson lit a cigarette. "I think I've had enough adventure for a while."

They said goodbye outside. Maureen shook Judson's hand, hesitated, and then kissed Byron.

"I owe you one, Maureen."

"All in a day's work," said Maureen. "See yawl."

"*Adios*," Judson said.

They drove in Judson's car back to Pocatello. Byron gazed at the fall colors, thinking of how close he had twice come to death in this open country—on the Salmon River rafting trip and hunting in the Caribou Woods. Then there was the incident with the militiamen at the Fort Hall river bottoms. The Walther was tucked down behind his belt, which Byron knew was illegal. He remembered Mary's face and eyes and lovely hair and naked thighs, and felt something sad and strong stirring inside him. Sentimental country songs played on the radio; someone was losing his girl. They drove past houses, an occasional barn, past brown fields and groves of aspens, white birch and pine, basking in the glow of a Keatsian autumn, forlorn and sad, the fields warm-looking with the somnolent stillness of Indian summer.

"Damn," Byron exploded. "I'm soon pushing forty. I think we survived for something, but *what*?"

Judson didn't answer. They drove on.

DYSFUNCTION

DR. LUCY, A SEX THERAPIST, had brown eyes and long blonde hair, and though attractive, had a blunt professional manner. The walls of the examination room were bare except for illustrations of naked men and women, a cabinet for medical supplies, and a long drawer. The doctor wore a standard white coat—open—and the top buttons of her blouse were loose, revealing the gentle swell of her breasts. She looked up from Byron's chart. He sat on the raised bed, wearing black jeans and holding a black leather jacket.

"I'm puzzled, Mr. Duffy. You seem more confident that this chart suggests."

"It's just an illusion."

"So many of my referrals have symptoms of chronic failure in everything. I find this intriguing since I suspect you have a high self esteem, yet this woman is giving you some serious anxiety with erectile dysfunction." She crossed her arms. "What's going on?"

"You tell me."

"If you were in a wheelchair, I might assume you had serious physical problems."

"No, I just hate the bitch."

"Then why not walk away?"

"I also love the bitch."

"I see. You like that term—'bitch'?"

Byron avoided the doctor's objective stare. "No."

Dr. Lucy read her notes. "This Mary has another partner?"

"Of course. Mr. Bad-Ass FBI agent."

"And she values him more as an individual of action and

courage?"

Byron nodded in the affirmative.

"From what I've heard, you're a man of action yourself. I read the newspaper account. You've been through a serious trauma."

"I guess I have."

"Stress can be detrimental to performance."

"I still have nightmares about drowning."

"Another therapist can address that. How's your general health?" She asked the usual questions and he answered them: diet, use of tobacco, alcohol and drugs, past medical history. "Have you had a prostate exam, recently? Checked your balls for masses?"

Byron stared at her and blinked. "Excuse me?"

"Testicular cancer kills young men, and prostate cancer kills older men. You're in between. Drop your pants."

"Hold on. I'm a good Catholic."

"This is a routine procedure. How is it the doctor failed to check?"

"I never let another man touch my ass *or* balls."

"Well then, allow me. Drop them."

He slowly pulled down his pants and she slipped on a latex glove.

"You'll be gentle?"

"Turn around and lean your elbows on the table."

"I prefer a dildo to fingers."

"Elbows on the table!"

Byron complied and suddenly felt the probing finger. It was unpleasant. Then she roughly turned him around and cupped his testicles, staring into his face. She ripped off the glove and dropped it into a basket for waste. "No masses. Prostate okay. I have another question."

Byron pulled up his jeans. "Shoot."

"Could you be deliberately refusing intercourse as a revenge tactic? In other words—are you pouting with your penis?"

"I hate that word."

"We can say 'pee-pee' if you like. Is that a possibility?"

"That I'm pouting? I don't know."

"Because then she gets angry and hurts you, and that terrible cycle begins again. I suspect the first new woman you meet who is receptive will get a vigorous response."

"Really?"

"How does your partner respond to rejection?"

Bryon told her and the doctor took more notes. He enjoyed telling the story, and saw a pattern of cruel behavior as he spoke.

"You both should see me. If she consults a different therapist, she won't be part of the cure and it may cause more problems. You indicated she can't... can't reach a climax without a vibrator?"

"Correct."

"How does that make you feel?"

"Shitty, but it wasn't always that way," he said, remembering a brief vacation in San Francisco and their hot lovemaking in a hotel. Dr. Lucy leaned against the cabinet, observing him. Byron returned the stare.

"You enjoy manhandling men?

"Yes," she said, smiling for the first time. "Nothing indicates you have any physical problem but rather an emotional one from rejection. I can write a prescription for viagra. There has to be to be intimate physical manipulation for it to work, however."

"Then it won't work."

"Why not?"

"There's no touching. She just lies there, waiting to be serviced. I'm the warm-up for the vibrator."

"And that causes more resentment. Perhaps we can break the pattern if you *both* see me." She dropped the professional mask. "Byron? All men have occasional difficulty. You just need to relax. Maybe rent a sexy movie, and watch it together."

"You mean porn?"

"I find it degrading to women but if it works—"

"All porn is boring," Byron said, "unless it involves a nun and a donkey."

Dr. Lucy didn't smile. "I'm glad you have a sense of humor. To conclude, Mr. Duffy, this will pass. I suspect you'll find yourself responding to a receptive partner."

Byron slipped on his jacket. "Doc, you're right. I'll fuck the first woman I see. Bring her home in a wheelbarrow."

"I hope it's your current partner who responds."

Byron stopped at the door and held her eyes. "How about you, Dr. Lucy? You saw my equipment. Want a date?"

She didn't flinch.

"Mr. Duffy. You disappoint me with that cliché response."

"Maybe you don't like men?"

"I can't respond to that." After a pause, she said, "Do *you* like men?"

"I'm not wired, that way."

"I see." She ran her hands through the thick blonde hair. "We need to discuss my fee." He drove to Buddy's to meet Mary. Inside the pizza bar, he saw her sitting at a table, looking drawn; Byron also saw the darkness and faded dreams. The owner had renovated the bar but the classier decor only drained some of Buddy's unique color.

"What a day," Mary said over her beer. "So how was therapy?"

"Great. Dr. Lucy told me to get fucked as soon as possible."

"By her? She come on to you?"

"No." Finally, he said, "Mary? Maybe we should both see her."

Mary's hard bright queer eyes regarded him across the table. "Therapy? This I don't need, therapy."

"She thinks you do."

"Byron, when you're healthy, come by. Until then, we need a rest. This is wearing me out. I think you hate me, and it's killing me—not to mention recent death threats. That small Walther of yours won't do the job."

"I will ignore the symbolism of that statement."

"Don't be so sensitive."

Byron suddenly got up.

"Please don't go, Byron."

"I'm outta here," he said. "Wake me up when the shooting starts."

"Byron—let's talk this over."

Mary sat at the table, tears filling her eyes.

"Come on, Mary, stop it. I'll call you later."

He left and drove home, knowing that Mary would continue crying, her public tears becoming too frequent. As he drove,

Dalton's car passed him on the way to Buddy's, the two men staring at each other through the windshields as they passed. Byron could see the grim resolve in Dalton's eyes, as though he and not Dalton was the intruder. Byron entered his apartment and lay on the bed. He knew it was important that he sever all ties with Mary Goldstein. For a moment, this seemed logical, even easy, and he could think about leaving town for another job. Then he felt the tears, and something choking him. Too many images crowded his memory, destroying those good moments from the past: Mary lying naked on the bed, begging him to make love to her, and nothing happening, as though Byron had become a ghost with little desire, or Byron in the bathtub and Mary roughly trying to arouse him with her hands and Byron only waiting to hear a simple, "I Love you." Mary would suddenly declare, "This is not working for me," leaving him stranded. Mary always stopped at critical moments. It was her skill.

But he got revenge, thought Byron, remembering Mary lying on the bed naked, waiting for him to ravish her after all, and Byron tossing her the small, battery-powered, pocket vibrator that he had purchased in a porno shop at a bargain price. "Here. Get yourself off with this."

Byron wanted to talk to Michael Wells, a proclaimed misogynist, but his number had been disconnected and the Los Angeles Times no longer listed him among their writers. For some reason, Judson had become distant, self absorbed. Byron finally lay down and went to sleep. In a dream, a crocodile was pulling him under black waters. Struggling, he woke to find a living weight pressed on his chest. It was Suzi, smiling, hovering over him, knees across his shoulders. It was cold in the house, and dark outside.

"You were having a nightmare," Suzi said, releasing him.

Byron sat up and rubbed his eyes. "Good evening."

Suzi seemed mature after a year of modeling, her hair stylish, her body still beautiful though a little heavier, her movements graceful. Her youth shone through the painted makeup, her eyes still playful as Byron described his therapy session.

"Let me take you to Harris' Bar-Be-Cue," Suzi said. "I have to leave for LA, soon, so let's catch up."

"Nothing else to catch up. I discovered I can only hump dogs."

Suzi's laugh was that of a drunken sensuous concubine.

"I don't believe that. Frankly, this Mary sounds like a dog. Who needs a disapproving cop as a lover, for Christ's sake?"

"Another cop," said Byron. "Which seems to be the case."

She stroked his cheek. "Byron, some of the finest loving I ever had was right here in this old moldy, sagging bed."

Byron felt a genuine affection. "Great. How about a rerun?"

"We're friends, now. It'd be like incest."

Suzi pulled him off the creaking bed.

"Incest is best," he said.

As Byron stood and buttoned his shirt, Suzi insisted—"No, it isn't."

On the refrigerator, Suzi found Judson's note about going to see an animated children's movie with his daughter. "He hates those kids' movies," she said.

"But little Joan *loves* them."

Byron pulled on a heavy coat.

"Too bad we never had a kid," said Suzi.

She stopped as Byron tightened a scarf. "I guess you took that out of our hands."

"I have a career, Byron. Maybe we'd better not discuss children."

They went to a Bar-Be-Cue joint run by an old black man named Harris who photographed all his customers and hung pictures in his home just behind the small restaurant, one room dominated by shots of Martin Luther King, Jr., and the Kennedys. Suzi and Byron took a seat.

"I have to lose about three pounds or my career is in the drink," said Suzi. "The modeling business is ferocious. It's a kind of licensed vanity, and there's nothing glamorous about it. I often feel weird parading in front of all those shallow people. The men who aren't gay are wolves and dismiss women as just pussies with legs." She dipped a spoon into the soup. "I love LA so I might try acting."

Wearing an incredibly filthy apron, Harris cooked up the next big batch of greasy ribs. Out the window, they saw a few tables left on the patio, now covered with snow.

"Do you have a passion for acting? Do you *have* to do it?"

"I don't know, Byron."

"I believe it has to be a driving passion."

Harris finally brought them a plate of ribs and they ate.

"Maybe I shouldn't use the word, 'passion'," said Byron. "I have so little of it."

Suzi wiped her mouth, then noticed the sauce on Byron's lower lip and laughed softly.

"Byron, there is nothing wrong with you. Remember all them...all those nights, including that old hotel with cats prowling the hallway? You gave me a good poundin', honey. Maybe you just don't want to bang her because she's pissing you off. Fuck her!"

"I'd like to," Byron said. "I just *can't*."

Byron took in the ribs, wondering if he would ever find a graceful, clean way to eat them. Harris hovered over them, one gold tooth gleaming in his black face.

"Them's good ribs," he said.

"You're sure right," Suzi agreed. "Cholesterol city!"

Harris took out his Polaroid camera and shot some pictures for his photo gallery. His photos over the years caught fading images of people from another time.

"I'll never be lonely," he said. "I got all my customers up here on the wall with King and the Kennedys. I just *know* they was a conspiracy with the Kennedy brothers. King, too."

"Well, you got a conspiracy right here, Harris," said Byron. "People want to eat your ribs until they drop."

Harris looked at them with dark, glittering eyes. The gold tooth flashed.

"That ain't no conspiracy, that's common sense."

"And I'm supposed to lose weight," said Suzi.

After eating, they drove to the Green Triangle, a country tavern with many bars inside. Male customers hunted available women while a country band played and couples danced on the wide dance floor. Suzi and Byron sat at a small table. A number of men in Stetsons stood at the bar and stared at her. She slipped her arm around Byron.

"Welcome to the testicle festival. Byron? Come dance with me."

"Sure."

They danced to a slow tune on the jukebox while the band took a break.

"I guess I should go home and call Mary. I know she's called me, by now."

"Forget her, Byron."

"It's not that easy."

Suzi held him closely. He liked the wonderful feel of her moving, swaying body.

"Mobsters and feds. It's all too creepy for me," she said. "I'd stay away from her."

They sat down.

"You know, I like that chapbook by your friend, Becky, that 'Behind the Barn' book. She's right, you know. The only currency in America *is* a blowjob."

"You an expert?"

"You become an expert or die."

"How bleak," Byron said. "Becky's getting known as an acerbic critic."

When Byron left for the bathroom, Suzi sat at the table, touching up her makeup, aware of men watching her. She liked the attention, but realized the bar held little excitement. A black man wearing jeans and dreadlocks drank at one of the bars. He smiled, though his eyes were cold. Suzi didn't respond, thinking of New York clubs and Broadway. She was thinking about Times Square when Byron walked past wandering customers and sat next to her. A woman with long hair and a slight hump in her back made brief eye contact with Byron.

"You know, Suzi, maybe Dr. Lucy was right."

"About what?"

"That Mary needs therapy, not me."

Suzi yawned. "We all need therapy. Let's go."

Outside the bar, a young man in jeans, boots and a weathered Stetson appeared out of the dark parking lot. He stared at Byron, something flat and dead in his eyes.

"I remember you. You was out at that Meridell Park place when it caught fire. After the Posse and Aryan Nation boys took it over."

"It's nothing but a crater now," Byron said. He nodded and tried to pass but the young man blocked him. "Excuse me."

"Them liberals are taking over the Aryan Nation compound up

north," he said. "Making it into a human rights center. I think that's gonna upset a lot of people."

Suzi confronted the wiry man in the Stetson. "Upset who? Other cracker rednecks?"

"Craig's the name." He smiled and tipped his hat, his eyes on her face; then he glanced at Byron. "Have a safe night, folks."

Before Byron could respond, Craig walked away. They drove to the house, the heater humming in the car, a light snow falling. Byron always felt cold, no matter how well he dressed. They parked and entered the house. Judson was still gone with his daughter. Suzi began taking off her clothes.

"Byron, I have to be out of here at four in the morning. Talk to me in the shower, okay?"

They carried on their conversation while Suzi washed herself in the shower, her body beautiful in the steam with water running down her breasts and arms and thighs. It seemed natural, and Byron felt no sexual stirrings, not unlike another evening at the Louvre admiring naked female statues of Greek goddesses. Then she stepped from the shower and grabbed a towel; Byron rubbed the towel over her body, feeling like a father drying his child. Suzi put on a bathrobe and finished a cigarette, the inside of her thighs visible. She followed his eyes.

"Okay," Suzi told him, "you can sleep with me if you like."

"Why? Don't you have a lot of boyfriends on the road?"

"A few. Nothing serious. Course, now we got AIDS to worry about. It took some of my gay photographers, but it's knocking off straights, too."

"I lost an actor friend from the old days."

"No need to change the subject. Byron—you don't have to make love to me, but if it happens, it's okay. If not, *that's* okay, too."

Byron considered this, eyeball to eyeball. "Do you *want* to make love, after all this time? It won't be the same."

Suzi nodded. "You're right. It won't be the same."

Byron gently tucked her in and kissed her.

"You're a beautiful woman, Suzi Johnson. It's lovely having you as a friend."

"I feel the same way about you. The night's still early. Go out and live a little."

He could see her face in the partial darkness. Suzi smiled and closed her eyes, suddenly moist with beginning tears. When she had gone to sleep, Byron stared at the phone, wondering if he should call Mary. He had a sudden destructive desire to get drunk. Byron knew that Judson had thrown out all his bottles, so he walked to his car to find another bar. He stopped at a pay phone and dialed Mary's number. She answered, sounding tired.

"Hello, Byron. Where are you?"

"In a pay phone. It's snowing, and I've decided to go out, get drunk and get *laid.*"

He could hear Mary sucking in her breath.

"Don't get drunk, Byron. Come over here if you want to get laid. Even if you *don't* want to get laid. I need a truce, okay?"

"Maybe tomorrow."

"Byron?" There was a pause. "Come over. I love you," she whispered.

Byron felt the cold cutting into him, and he watched as a car slid across the slick road.

"I love you too, kiddo, but I need to have my own adventure, tonight. I'm freezing. Talk to you later."

"Byron, let's talk, now. No arguments, I promise."

"Tomorrow," he said, watching the snow falling.

Byron felt good hanging up. Perhaps it was a bitterness that kept him from cutting the cord; he had to be stronger. He drove to the Owl Club on the edge of town, the bar scheduled to close down. There was a small rock band and a few patrons inside. Up the road remained nothing but a charred scattering of timbers. Sitting at the bar, Byron felt a sense of daring, and saw three men watching him, looking away when he glanced in their direction. He thought briefly of Ted now in Hollywood. A tall woman in her mid twenties, with long hair and a slender body, sat near him, nursing a beer. She looked familiar, and when she turned toward the window, he saw nice breasts and the small hump in her back.

Ah, he thought. A tragic flaw. *Perfect.*

He drank whiskey with beer, knowing about his father's alcoholism and the history of Judson. There was something sweet and intoxicating in deliberately putting himself into a dangerous situation. The band played some bluesy rock and roll and Byron drank, feeling the sweet fire from the whisky burning inside him. The tall woman with the hump returned his stare. With her long hair and dark eyes, she might have been a refugee from the sixties. The blond tattooed band broke into a Stones' medley, and Byron asked the tall woman to dance. She complied, and he liked the feel of her body. His hand led her in turns and swirling motions around the floor, and then they played a slow tune and he slipped his hand up her back, gently sliding over the small hump.

"It will get bigger as I get older," she said. "But for now, it's not too bad." She pulled away and studied him, her lips full and sensuous. "I like to be up front, you know? I worry about my posture in ten years. What's your name?"

He told her.

"Byron? A romantic!"

"Yeah, I'm Byron from Brooklyn."

"I saw you at the Green T. My name is Janet. I'm from Montana."

"Beautiful country," said Byron. They walked to the bar. He bought her a round, and had another drink, himself. Janet reached over and gently touched his wrist.

"You don't need to get drunk," she said. "It can't last."

"Is it that obvious?"

Janet suddenly grinned. "Woman problems?"

"You got it," said Byron. "But I *am* recovering."

"I understand," she said. "I've had problems with men all my life. I'm leaving tomorrow," she suddenly added.

"For Montana?"

"Yes. I don't know when I'll be coming back again."

They danced, and when the band took a break, they found a quiet booth. Briefly, Byron told her about his romance, but Janet gently pressed her hand against his mouth.

"I don't need details. They all sound the same after a while. Boy meets girl stories have a certain sameness, don't you think?"

Byron agreed. "I won't give you certain details, anyway."

"Good, not that I wouldn't listen."

Her back was pressed against the booth and in the bar light, the gentle slope of her shoulders appeared normal.

"Is there no back operation? Nothing they can do?"

"Not yet. I don't have much time, so I hope they find something. I'm not anxious to be a female hunchback of Notre Dame."

She sipped her beer, her gaze bold and direct. "The   alcohol seems to make you more nervous."

"I'll settle down." Feeling tipsy, Byron smiled at her. "What's in Montana?"

"An abusive, asshole biker husband," Janet said. "I'm going back to divorce his ass. If I'm lucky, I'll escape without a beating."

"Stay here. Me'n my roommate will protect you."

Janet leaned forward. "From now on, I take care of my problems," she said. "*I* take control."

The band was starting another set. He noticed Janet had slightly crooked teeth.

"Listen," she said. "From what I'm hearing, your crazy girlfriend may bust in here looking for you."

"She would never come in here."

"She might if she saw your car. We could take my van somewhere else. I have two big dogs. Is that a problem?"

"I'm allergic to dogs."

"Love me, love my dogs," Janet said. She glanced at the couples now dancing on the small floor. "I just feel like being with someone, tonight. You have a nice energy, even if it is a bit scattered."

Byron picked up the shot glass from the table; he knew he had to stop.

"I got a place," he said, finally.

"No. If we boogie, tonight, it's on *my* terms. And I think you better order coffee."

"Janet—you'll only have a wide awake drunk."

They left the bar and drove to Lava hot Springs and the Wagon Wheel, where they danced and Byron drank some coffee, giving his drunk a sharper edge. A chubby man with an English accent asked the bartender questions about the Arco Desert. A few bikers called the Outlaws had come to the Wagon Wheel; Janet danced with two of them, but quickly pulled away, coming over and taking Byron by the arm. He could see the bikers smirking with an arrogant contempt. Byron glared at a biker with a snake tattoo. Another man in a suit wearing an old-fashioned ducktail haircut eyed him without smiling. Somehow, Byron knew he packed a gun. He had left the Walther in his car trunk. The cowboy named Craig entered the bar and stared at Byron.

"Don't even think about it, Byron. We are here to dance and have fun, and you wouldn't last ten seconds."

"I have a pink belt in karate," said Byron.

Janet threw back her head, laughing. She had gotten a little tipsy herself. "You're funny, Byron. I envy your girlfriends."

"Don't. I'm impotent."

Before she could respond, Byron leaned over, kissing her gently. He felt a thrill touching her full wet lips; then they danced again. The portly Englishman watched them. Later, they parked near a river and watched the two dogs playing in the snow, one of them a small terrier with a high-pitched yelp, and the other, an incredibly old German shepherd named Warthog. Byron had never seen a more crippled ancient dog, its skin dry and flaky, its whiskers white. With the cold biting into his lungs and the dogs, he anticipated an asthma attack. Janet threw a stick, and the terrier fetched it while Warthog barked feebly, his sides heaving. A single streetlamp glowed on the white snow. Preparing to throw the stick again, Janet saw Byron breathing from an inhaler.

"My dogs bother you?"

"Dogs wipe me out," he said. "And I can't make love if I can't breathe."

Janet lifted her eyebrows. "Really? Aren't you assuming a lot?"

"That's true. I can't do it anyway."

Janet reached out to pet the old dog. "You really are impotent?"

He gave her a general sketch of his story.

"Aside from those famous available blue pills, why don't I believe you, Byron?"

"Actually, I got hurt in the war."

"I read *The Sun Also Rises*, professor." Janet opened the door to the van and the dogs jumped inside. She had to help the ailing Warthog. "I also felt your cock stirring when we were dancing."

"Really? I missed my own hard on?"

"You just need to stay in the moment. Why don't we get a cheap motel, and the dogs can sleep in the van?"

No residents stirred in the empty snowy streets of Lava Hot Springs; they had started a theatre one summer but now it was torn down and only rubble remained. A few hippy head shops and stores had appeared, and a new elegant looking motel. Off the street was the River View Hotel where he had spent time with Suzi the year before; up the street were the public baths. For a moment, Byron felt as though they were the last people on earth.

"Sounds good," he said.

Then they were in the motel near the river, and Janet slipped out of her long dress and boots; she wore no bra, but kept her panties, the long hair falling over shoulders and breasts, and down her small hump. A package of rubbers had appeared on the small table. She stood by the window, her back to him, then sat on an overstuffed chair and rolled a joint. He didn't like marijuana or the acrid smell, sharp in his nostrils.

"That's right. You like to drink. I think we ran out of booze."

"It's okay."

She pulled up her legs under her, calm and uninhibited, watching him. He sat on another chair facing the bed.

"I haven't made love in a long time, either," she said. "If my husband tries to touch me, I'll kill him."

"Stay in Idaho."

"I have to settle with the bastard."

She stood up, hair falling across her hard nipples in the glow from the lamp.

"I'm going to crash. You can sleep in the bed, on the couch—whatever." She reached over and kissed him, and again, he felt the full sweet lips and probing tongue. "A joint makes me horny," she said, followed by a quiet laugh.

Her eyes followed his as he gently touched her breast. Janet moaned softly, then reached inside his shirt and rubbed him, sitting on his lap. They kissed. Byron slid his other hand up over her shoulder blades, feeling the hump again, though it now seemed a natural part of her curves. Janet knelt in front of him and unbuckled his belt, pulling off his pants, and he felt the cool air on his thighs. Janet placed the pants neatly on the floor. She pressed her mouth against the rise in his underwear, running her fingers over his chest and stomach while her breasts filled his cupped hands. Then, she paused; Byron was about to speak when she gently pressed a finger to his lips, shaking her head. Janet slipped down his underpants and stood.

"Take mine off," she urged. "Take your time."

He slipped down her panties and holding her thighs, gently ran his tongue up into the wet labia, searching; Janet closed her eyes, gasping once, and then straddled his lap, holding his face, kissing him, hips moving. He felt her softly probing fingers.

"It feels hard. Nice."

He felt the blood rushing through him, so that he was unaware of the slight chill in the room, Janet skillfully rolling on a condom, then posting on his lap, her arms around his neck, the long hair falling over her shoulders and brushing against his face. He felt a rush of sweet carnal power being inside her and his eyes filled with tears.

"Jesus Christ!"

"Slow down," she said. "Yes, yes!"

He came, suddenly. Janet rocked him, making little gasps. Then she came, breathing rapidly against his neck. "You made me catch up, real fast."

"Sorry."

"Don't be."

She got up and walked over to the bed. "Come to bed."

Byron felt an exhilarating sense of joy walking across the rug to the double bed. He slipped under the covers; Janet curled up next to him, kissing, searching, exploring.

In the morning, without protection, he made love to her in the shower, Byron taking her from behind, hot water washing over them, Janet's hands and breasts pressed against the wall as she uttered little cries. Before breakfast, they walked the dogs, Warthog stiffly moving. Breakfast was excellent. Janet smiled across the table, drinking coffee.

"That was real fine, Byron, but I won't see you again."

"Why not?"

"It's fate."

"I think you're right."

Janet drove him in silence back to his car. The highway ran along fields now covered with snow. It had been a wonderful

182

evening, and Byron felt a sudden Whitmanesque joy at everything, the nacreous landscape of snowy fields, mountains and pearl-colored sky, then the sun on wet bright streets. He remembered Janet's naked body, sensuous, floating above him. He would carry the memory of a wonderful one-night stand, and not the vision of the older woman, stooped over with an ugly hump. When they stopped, he leaned over and kissed her, and for a moment, considered riding to Montana. He searched her face, staring into the dark brown eyes, memorizing the fine upturned nose above the wide sensuous mouth. There was a mysterious smile on her lips. It was like a farewell scene out of Chekhov, two lovers who would never meet again, saying good-bye on a wintry day.

"If I pass through, we'll find each other."

"I hope so, Janet."

He got out and she drove away. He came within ten feet of his car when Agent Dalton rushed him, as though it were some kind of arrest. Byron was startled to see Dalton so panicked. Dalton screamed: "Just what the *fuck* do you think you're doin'?"

"I beg your pardon?"

"Where've you been, all night?

"Why do you care?"

"I don't, but Mary found your car and freaked out."

"I was out having a little fun. Get out of my face, Dalton."

"Call her—now!"

Byron drove away and napped the rest of the morning. When he woke up, Mary was sitting on the bed. She wore ski pants and a down jacket, a thick scarf around her throat. She held a wool cap, and smiled at him. "We're skiing. Me. Judson. Come with?"

"Are you sure this is a good idea?"

"Absolutely," Mary said.

Byron had never mastered skiing. That afternoon, he started with Joan on the bunny hill while Mary and Judson skied down the slopes in Z patterns, twisting over the broken undulations of snow. The agile Joan learned quickly, and soon abandoned Byron on the small hill, many young children on tiny skis racing around him as he went into a snowplow, only to dump. He used a rope tow to bring him to the top, and once collapsed, too tired and aching to lift himself. Snow stopped his ears, and the cold burned inside his lungs. His arms and shoulders were sore as Byron half skied, half walked, to the lodge. It was cold inside the lodge, even by the fire. A number of skiers in their thick monster boots tramped in and out. Byron leaned his rented skis against the wall and sat, nursing coffee, waiting for Mary who had not questioned him about the night before. Once, he saw her through the window soaring and turning down the bright slope, followed by Judson, remarkably graceful for such a big, lumbering man.

Mary came into the lodge and ordered a drink, sitting across from Byron. Her face was bright from the cold and skiing.

"Thomas says you were dropped off by a woman. You get laid?"

"I'm impotent," Byron said. "You know that."

"Sorry. I guess it's none of my business."

"Correct."

"I want to talk."

"So talk."

Mary's eyes began to mist up, again. She stared into the fire.

"This summer, they're sending me into the desert for special training. It could be dangerous but I'll need it. We'll work with explosives and live rounds."

A log suddenly popped and flared in the fire.

"All this is FBI business—right?"

Mary's eyes narrowed. "My life should be *our* business."

"I am not *in* your life, Mary."

Byron ignored her accusing glance, knowing it was a disturbing pattern of their relationship. They would fight. They would part. They would meet to talk and reconcile and then fight, again. She would cry and he'd withdraw.

"Byron?"

"Yes?"

"I'm taking your advice and going into therapy."

"Good." Byron reached over and touched her. "I'm glad to hear that. I really am."

"Let's have a quiet dinner, tonight."

He hesitated. "Perhaps."

Joan, laughing and tugging at her father's jacket, came into the lodge; they sat down at the table. Joan's face was red and her whole body shivered. "I am hot *and* cold," she shrieked. "My nose is an icicle." Judson looked like a giant snowman, white snow on his cap and in his beard. He wore a thermal jumpsuit. "I'd rather freeze here than be warm in Southern California."

"I don't know if I agree," said Byron, "but you and Mary sure can ski."

Mary shot him a guarded smile. "Thanks."

"There was another suicide bombing in Iraq today," Judson said.

Byron decided not to comment on a war he opposed when he saw Mary's expression freeze, and when they looked out the window, they saw the square hard body of Thomas Dalton in a red jumpsuit rushing down the nearest slope.

"Jeepers, your boyfriend can *also* ski," observed Byron.

"He's *not* my boyfriend."

"Why not? You're two peas in a pod."

Byron stood up and backed against the fire. His legs trembled.

"I think I better go. I'm cold and sore. Mary? Give me a call, later." Byron gave Joan a hug. "Adios."

He dropped off the skis and left the lodge, walking slowly to his car. The cold wind was blowing into his face, and his arms felt dead and aching. He became aware of Mary behind him as he reached for the car door.

"Byron?"

He turned. "What?"

Mary seized him by the collar. "Byron? Let's give it a shot. Come by, tonight, and let's make a fresh start, and if it falls apart, okay—it wasn't meant to be. I can accept that. I can't go on with this horrible *negative* energy."

Byron felt something breaking inside him; he held her, kissing her only to gently push her away. Her face had been a series of masks that changed so often.

"You're right, it *is* time for a truce."

"I won't ask you about last night."

"She wasn't nothin'," he said, slipping into street grammar. "Some hippy anarchist who hates authority figures. Nice tits, though."

Mouth suddenly tight, Mary closed her eyes; when she opened

them, they seemed to bore into his face. "I won't bite, Byron. I *am* jealous, but a truce—remember?"

He got into the car and rolled down the window. "I'll see you tonight."

That evening, they sat at the dinner table eating a nice meal by candlelight with Mozart on the stereo. He was searching Mary's handsome face for a clue. Despite exhaustion, Byron realized something had endured and he felt a surge of love, though he knew it was over. The sweet music of Mozart provided an excellent score.

"We could meet secretly," she said.

"That might be exciting. An *intrigue*."

For a moment, Byron imagined Mary and himself in a thriller novel. Would readers find them exciting or boring?

"Tom Dalton says that one of the men fished from the quicksand that night has a lot of relatives who may blame you for his death. Be careful."

"I get stares now and then. I can take care of myself."

"With that little dick gun?"

"It's good enough for James Bond."

Mary leaned forward, smiling. "We might be good lovers if we could meet and fantasize being other people."

"Only if you dress up as a nun."

"Will you wear jack boots?"

"Absolutely."

Mary laughed sharply. "I discovered recently that I have always been suspicious of other people—of adults. I don't know why." After a moment, she asked, "What did Lucy cost you?"

"With lab work, after insurance, I owe about a grand."

"Too expensive. I found someone else."

"Then I'll lose you, for sure," Byron said. Mary didn't seem to hear him. "She insisted we had to have the same therapist."

"Nonsense. Let's dance."

They danced to country music, Mary a little drunk; then they were both drunk and dancing naked in her bedroom to Dylan's *Like a Rolling Stone*, though Mary hated the song, the angry voice and building piano crashing over them. Later, they seemed to discover new lovemaking techniques as they spent the rest of the night in bed, loving and spending themselves with an animal surge that excluded the world. Mary came without the vibrator.

Feeling like a voyeur, Byron watched Mary apply make-up standing nude before the full length mirror, curving buttocks tight, morning light softly diffused like a Vermeer painting. A Star of David gleamed between her breasts. He marveled at the precision of her lipstick. Mary made a face, pouting; her mirror double glanced at Byron in the bed. She turned and smiled, gently squeezing a nipple, then ran a tongue over her moistened lips. Mary put one leg up on the bed and he gazed between her smooth thighs.

"I like it when you look at me naked, Byron."

Suddenly yanking back the sheets, she climbed on his body, straddling his thighs, rocking him into arousal, hands cupping his face.

"Come on, baby. You brute! Give it to me—*again*."

She slipped him inside her. Their lovemaking revived all the old times when they were happy and in love and the romance would never end, and they would grow old together and one day watch their children graduate from college. After they had dressed and stood by the door, Mary cried softly, though they were not separating in anger.

"Mary. It's all right."

"I know," she said. "We're silly people, aren't we?"

"Maybe tomorrow?"

"I have more training. Call me."

"Okay."

"Maybe we could do lunch."

"That would be fine," Byron said. "When?"

"I'm not sure. We can't see each other for a while."

"I know. I understand."

"Do you? Really?"

"Yes. You need secrecy in your world."

"I do."

Mary embraced him, and he saw something sad and lost in her gleaming eyes. Perhaps they wouldn't grow old together. Feeling empty and drained of energy, he drove away. At a stoplight, he felt something in his coat pocket. It was a check from Mary for a thousand dollars.

THE PARTY

BYRON AND MARY HAD THEIR FINAL MEETING at a party thrown by Debbi Blackstone, a local Marxist social worker. Debbi was celebrating a grant for a wayward girls' home, the occasion marred by Pocatello's first drive-by shooting involving gang members. Agent Dalton's warnings about LA gangs had been right after all. Two young men, deaf and speaking in American Sign Language, took shotgun fire from a gang thinking they were using rival gang language.

Debbi's house was south of town, and train tracks ran along the highway. Her parties had become famous for the variety of guests: students—white and black—Indians, anarchists, lawyers, atheists, local farmers, and the inevitable artists. Mary arrived with Dalton; she was well dressed and professional and Byron wondered if she secretly entertained having Byron on the tossed coats of guests, risking Dalton's discovery since any element of danger had transformed their relationship. Dalton wore a tailored suit, and stared at the mixture of guests, suspicious, amused—even appalled. When he caught Byron's eyes, Byron recognized the hurt and envy. Perhaps they defined each other with a mutual shock that Mary found them both attractive.

"My, my," said Debbi, her blonde hair combed out, thick and curly, "we got *everybody* represented, tonight. How democratic. FBI super Agent Dalton, how *are* you?"

Dalton smiled. "I'm just fine, Comrade Blackstone. How are *you*?"

"Happy as a clam," said Debbi.

Debbi wore a black dress and Indian jewelry, her body firm and attractive for a woman in her early forties, her face always possessing something mischievous, like a malevolent clown. She

188

bore two children, and had adopted three, two blacks—a boy and girl—and one Indian boy named Joshua. Dalton had a grudging admiration for any white who adopted non whites.

"I guess we are just the United Nations, here," said Debbi, pouring some wine. Guests were everywhere, and rock music filled the two-story house in the country. Joan Judson played with the Blackstone children outside. Judson sat on the couch, drinking iced tea. Byron roamed the party, pretending to ignore Mary even when she cornered Joe Ragsdale, a reporter.

"Freedom of press is one thing, my friend. Putting my life in danger is another. Your article almost smoked my ass."

The reporter smiled, clutching a drink.

"News is news," he explained, a small man with thin red hair and pale blue eyes; he wore a wrinkled suit. "The public has a right to know."

Mary pushed him against the wall. "Ragsdale, you blew my cover! You went too far."

"You had *left* Idaho, and it seemed like a viable story."

"You want to see the scar from the bullet I took?"

Dalton pulled at her arm, and Mary released the harried reporter. Then she was being pushed toward Byron who leaned against the sink discussing the mob and toxic dumps with Teton. Another Indian named Edmo reached in the refrigerator for a beer.

"Indian reservations are perfect mob targets," Teton said, looming over Byron who suddenly felt Dalton's presence. "We always need sovereign control."

"Mr. Duffy? Mary has something to say before we go," Dalton said.

"Don't *go*," implored Debbi. "I *like* the FBI. I even know a few by first name."

"I like you, myself," Dalton said, being charming. "You're the nicest Communist I ever met."

"Now Dalton, you darn homosexual agents always confuse Marxists for Communists. There *is* a difference."

Dalton ignored a few snickering guests. "I bet there is," he said.

"Byron, let's go for a walk," Mary said.

They walked along the gleaming railroad tracks. The night was cool, not winter, not yet spring, but something of both. A stream ran near the two-lane road.

"My psychiatrist and Tom both believe my immature behavior must end."

"How mature of you to recognize that," agreed Byron. "Okay."

"Okay what?"

"Maybe they're right."

Mary seemed disappointed. "I mean our secret little trysts."

"I know. I said 'Okay.'"

"Put up *some* fight," she said.

"They're right, Mary. My own Dr. Lucy would agree."

They walked on. Shadows covered the road and a train roared by them into the night. They heard a whistle blast receding into the darkness.

"The Swat Team and the Terrorist Division will take all my time. They consider you a liability."

"I *am* a liability."

"I could get fired."

"You mustn't allow that," Byron argued.

"Be serious with me."

"I *am* serious. Mary, can you love Dalton *and* me?"

"It's hard for you to understand it but—yes, I can."

They turned on the road and began walking toward the house. Voices from inside rang and echoed through the trees. A helicopter flew through the night sky.

"It can't go on," Byron said. "Be realistic."

"Byron? I can't have kids. I'll never be a housewife. You represent something...different." She searched for the right phrase. "And I just love you...differently."

Byron could hear live fiddle and guitar music coming from Debbi's house.

"I'm an academic saddle tramp. Dalton's an Eliot Ness throwback. *That's* who you need."

"Maybe—but he's not as intellectually exciting as you."

"I never wanted to be just *intellectually* exciting."

They stopped. "Since our past problem, you've become very virile."

Byron shook her hand.

"What's this for?"

"Good-bye. Good luck. God speed."

She began to cry, at last, and Byron felt his own tears. He had vowed that this would not happen, that the break would remain clean, logical, without emotion.

"We'll always have Pocatello," he told her, adding, "Lighten up!"

"I know," Mary agreed, her voice flat. "I know, I know! We're adults! We *have* to be big people." Then in a small voice: "Byron, what the hell are we gonna do?"

"I don't know. Move on?"

"I bet that asshole reporter is writing another article about my new assignment and training," said Mary. "They'll find me for sure."

"They've forgotten you," Byron said.

"What if they *haven't* forgotten, Byron? What then?"

For a moment, Byron realized Mary could still be in danger. Perhaps they had lived with it too long. It had become a story, a myth with no reality.

"If they nail me, scatter my ashes out on the reservation. I'll always remember that wonderful moment we had there."

"No one will nail you," Byron insisted.

Mary met his eyes and held them for a long time.

"Let me see your gun," she said.

He handed her the Walther from his back pocket. She pulled back the slide and checked the compact weapon, then handed him the semi auto.

"You must feel some danger to be packing." She looked across the road to the tracks and the distant stream "Byron, the weapons I have seen. What terrorists can do, and not just with hijacked airplanes but with nerve gas and deadly biological weapons. Something colorless and odorless thrown into the air from a hill could poison New York City and then infect the entire state. Debbi's amusing but she's old fashioned. A hippy Marxist is about as dated as a Whig. We have real enemies, Byron, and you *need* us."

"I believe that, Mary."

They heard an alarm clock ringing and a shuffling gait on the road. Mary tensed. Byron turned to see an old white face and blond hair appearing against the darkness. Mary reached for her gun. The lonely figure wore a shabby greatcoat; he shuffled five steps forward, two back, and then ten more down the road. He grinned at them and stopped the clock.

"Hello, Austin," Byron said.

"Hello, Duffy."

"Selling tee shirts?"

"Sold out," Austin said.

Austin was a town legend who reminded Byron of a Beckett tramp. Many stories attempted to explain the vagrant who shuffled about town at any hour. The tee shirts showed a photo of Austin's wrinkled grinning face and the line: *Shufflin' with Austin.* His hair seemed unnaturally blond and bright for the old face and gaunt body.

"What are you doing here?" Byron asked.

"Came for the party," Austin said. "I *love* parties. He nodded at Mary. "Hello Goldstein."

Mary slipped her weapon back into its shoulder holster. "How do you know my name?"

"I know everybody. I'm the town tramp."

"Why the alarm clock, Austin?"

"It's a wake up call."

"For what?"

"The world's ending."

Austin laughed and turned toward the house, shuffling forward, stopping, retreating, then rushing forward to gain some ground. He would stop, pause, then shuffle forward again, repeating the process.

"We better go back," Byron said, realizing he still held his gun. "God, Austin walked a long way from town."

"He scared me." Mary touched Byron's face. "Friends," she said, taking his hand.

Inside the house, Dalton and Debbi were dancing to John Lee Hooker's "Boogie Chillen."

"You're the nicest racist I ever met," said Debbi.

"I ain't no racist," argued Dalton. "But I warned you about big city gangs coming to rural areas. Precious, you will admit, the guys in that drive-by car weren't wearing burnt cork."

"There were whites too," Debbi said.

"Hippies ain't white." Dalton eyeballed Mary. "Ready to go, my precious?"

"I guess you got a lot of training in the morning," said Debbi. "Target practice—surveillance of misfits, fruits and niggers."

"Such language," Dalton said. "Of course, who can get federal money without fruits and niggers on the payroll? And we *have* to train to keep America green."

"For whom? White imperialist pig dogs?"

"Why I declare, Miz Blackstone, if you don't sound like a throw back yourself. Who's prejudice, me or you?"

Once again, a small group had gathered to watch the Debbi—Dalton sparing match.

Mary turned away. "Byron? Come upstairs with me." Byron followed her upstairs and into a room where she found her coat. They went into the bathroom with an old fashioned bathtub from the 19th century. The ornately framed mirror was large with designs carved into the glass.

"We will always be special friends."

"I hope so," he said.

"Mature."

She glanced at his reflection while drawing a thin line of lipstick on her mouth. She licked her lips with a curled, darting tongue. Then she slammed home the bolt. Turning, she pushed him down on the toilet seat.

"How about a quick one?"

He didn't answer, even as she was kissing him, pulling at his belt, Byron quickly dropping his pants, feeling a sudden rush of excitement as Mary, wearing no panties, pulled up her skirt, then sat on him, pressing his face into her breasts as the music continued downstairs and people talked in the hallway.

It was over quickly.

They heard knocking as Mary wiped her mouth, reapplying lipstick; Byron zipped his pants. When the door opened, Dalton stood in the hall, his eyes cold and malignant.

"Good evening," Byron said.

"Well—time to go," Mary said cheerfully.

"You whore!"

Dalton slapped her, the sound echoing in the hall. Then Byron was on him, seizing Dalton's throat, feeling a rapid succession of hard blows to his stomach and rib cage. Byron went down, gasping, Mary shrieking profanely in the hallway as others rushed to contain Dalton. He disappeared beneath a crush of bodies.

Later, Byron sat on the couch; his ribs were sore and his breath came in harsh rapid pants. Judson gave him a drink and the alcohol tasted sharp, burning in his throat.

"You just can't let feds into your house," Debbi explained with a dreamy fury. "They just don't know how to behave. Drunk. Shooting at neighborhood cats. It's awful. Imagine feds moving in next door. There goes *that* neighborhood!"

"Where the hell are they?"

"They left, Byron. *Together*. They *deserve* each other."

"You better learn how to box," Judson said.

"Did I draw *any* blood?"

"No. I *do* think Dalton felt bad."

"The Bureau *ruined* that woman," Debbi insisted. "She needs a new man. Or maybe a new woman to *really* love her."

Silent, Byron finished the drink. Joe Ragsdale sat down.

"Just what was all *that* about?"

"Whatever you want to know, I'm not talking."

Ragsdale smirked. "Why not? News is my job."

"Gossip is your job," said Byron. "Bed habits. Or high security assignments. I don't know who you work for, but if anything happens to Mary, I'll have you killed."

The reporter reacted with a mock shock when Edmo seized him by the collar. "He won't have to kill you. I'll put a curse on you, Tybo reporter. Your dick will fall off."

Furious, Ragsdale pushed away the heavy-set Indian. "Don't touch me you filthy savage!"

Ragsdale felt the sudden silence and saw people staring at him. He turned and rushed from the room. Edmo saluted, chuckling. "Me savage," he said.

Byron stepped outside. Joan was playing with Debbi's son, Joshua. Many dogs guarded the yard, though most of the guests had left. Listening to the rock and roll inside, and gazing up at the black sky, filled with stars, Byron relaxed; the fight had washed him clean. Judson came out onto the porch and they sat, Judson still drinking only sodas and iced tea. It was nice to watch the children playing, acting out childish fantasies. One of the cars pulling up contained Darlene, now almost gaunt from a crash diet. Her cropped hair was bleached blonde and she regarded Judson with a smile and a sense of reconciliation. Her eyes drifted to Byron and she nodded.

"Hello, boys," she said.

And then they saw the other woman, also slender with bleached blonde hair cut short and tight jeans with a thick shirt, a mirror double of Darlene, and as she reached out to take Darlene's hand, introductions were made.

"This is Carol," Darlene told them, "my wonderful partner."

They all shook hands.

"You're not a liberal Democrat, I hope," said Byron.

Carol grinned at him. "God no, a Log Cabin Republican—even if they don't acknowledge us."

The two women walked into the house.

"You have to admit, everything is more basic and wild in Idaho," said Judson, nodding to Darlene as she walked inside. "It's only my perspective, but if you're hungry, you just kill something and eat it. If you love a woman, you just reach out and grab her, and if another buck doesn't kick in your stall, you're home free—unless she plugs you. I suppose that makes us into rutting reindeer but forces a kind of honesty."

They sat as the dogs and children ran in a circle.

"I don't blame Dalton," Byron said. "I've been there."

Byron wondered, *Did he know I had a gun?* Teton walked past them with Edmo who stopped and nodded to Byron. Ragsdale watched silently from a doorway.

"Mr. Byron, you come out to the reservation. We'll sit up and wait for the Water Babies. Hayball says they be walkin', soon."

"Too scary for me, Edmo."

Edmo didn't move, and Byron couldn't see his eyes in the shadows. Teton started the jeep, waiting. After a moment, Edmo spoke.

"Mary is a warrior, but she needs help. They could take her out."

"They?"

Edmo nodded his large head. "If they come out to Fort Hall, we'll eat *them*."

"Eat who?"

"Away from the bottoms, whites got stronger magic than Indian. Fire in the sky. Understand? Only on the rez—Injuns rule."

"I see."

Teton called out; Edmo waved to Byron and staggered toward the jeep. He looked like a trained shuffling bear. They drove off and Byron stood up.

"Was that a warning?"

"I think he's worried about Mary," Judson said.

"She can take care of herself. I have to go."

"It *is* puzzling."

"What?"

"That the FBI sent Mary back here. She's very visible. Her enemies could find her, even without any article by Ragsdale. Are they *that* inefficient?"

"You have a point," Byron said. "But maybe she's old news."

"Let's hope so."

At the crossing, Byron watched the last train heading toward Pocatello. Trains always made him think of hoboes riding the rails, American isolation and loneliness celebrated by folk singers singing of poverty and lost love. It was a world of unrequited love, revenge, murder and characters with names like Stagalee and Pretty Polly. The train passed, light bringing up the brief images of trees and houses, the whistle coming back at him like a ghostly voice out of the darkness. Byron thought he saw a lone figure standing in the trees, but then the train was gone and the landscape vanished into darkness.

He drove home.

THE END

AFTER INTENSE TRAINING WITH LIVE ROUNDS on the volcanic desert, Dalton and Mary took a motel room in the small town of Arco. It had many stucco cottages with an open courtyard, and the rooms had an anonymous look they both recognized. The motel was deserted.

After vigorous lovemaking, Mary stood naked by the window looking out at a dark sky full of thunder and rain, streaked with the occasional lightning bolt that would illuminate the deserted town and her nude body in the window. Though it was a furious thunderstorm with lightning striking close, followed by the clap of thunder, Mary felt somehow calm. A lot had changed in the late spring. She had walked into Buddy's Pizza with Dalton and spied Byron with another woman, and they had waved to one another with no jealousy.

She glanced once at Dalton, lying asleep on the twisted sheets. They were compatible and would need each other when enemies attacked, foreign or domestic. Dalton had a movie star face, a rock hard body and knew weapons; recently, his jealously had subsided. He no longer insisted she not shower after spending a sweaty afternoon or night in bed, his mind always suspecting Mary would exchange secret notes with Byron and meet him somewhere else. He had been right, actually, and once Dalton shocked her with his oddly homoerotic fantasy.

"Don't shower. When he grabs you and kisses your mouth, he'll be tasting me. He'll smell my scent on your body."

"Listen to yourself," Mary had said. "Maybe you two guys should spend a night together."

Dalton had laughed, and it disturbed her. Now she was

seeing only him and she showered and left without Dalton's disapproval or endless questions. Perhaps he had been tailing her and finally realized that things had changed, that Mary was now truly his, her old love gone. In the past, walking through her day reeking of sex had thrilled her, and she often waited for Byron to react to another dog possessing his bitch.

Mary watched the black sky, listening to the steady rain on the roof and waited for another flash of pure white light. She had experienced an unnerving moment at the morgue the previous day, looking at naked corpses on tables, some opened up, others sewn back together, when she saw a young woman dead from a car accident. The broken body on the table resembled her. Mary looked again and realized her mistake, unsettled until the overweight female technician who sliced open skulls discovered and read aloud a tattooed message on a corpse's penis.

When Mary lay down next to the sleeping, partially nude Dalton, she remembered the technician's harsh voice. The tattoo read: "If you can read this, I love you."

———————

DALTON had agreed there was no need for the governor to have so much security around the state capitol, and the added guards at the ball seemed overkill. Dalton and Mary joined a force of other FBI agents and state police to roam the ballroom while many couples in black tie and gowns waltzed around the spacious room. The reason for the ball was to congratulate donors.

Mary wore a man's suit and carried a 10mm. She wore a wrist watch radio, but she and Dalton met briefly while couples glided around them, no streamers or balloons, just the heat of many inebriated people inside a closed room. All of the faces were different yet somehow similar with the same expression.

"The governor is a showboat," Dalton said. "He's a cotton candy Republican. Who would shoot him?"

Mary was amused to hear Dalton turning against a fellow conservative. The governor did have a handsome lined face with thick wavy wind-blown hair and a photo that changed on his web site every day. He spoke well in a honeyed baritone, but the speeches held little substance, and often people on both sides of the aisle fell asleep.

"Think of it as overtime pay," Mary said, smiling.

Toward midnight, something disturbing happened. A long-haired young man wearing jeans and a tee shirt appeared and stopped. He grinned. She watched him, waiting.

"I got some stuff if you need it," he said, pointing suggestively.

Mary felt for her gun.

"What did you say?"

"A little taste," he said.

The out-of-place young man winked and disappeared. Mary followed him with her eyes until he vanished into the well dressed crowd. Why had no guards stopped him? The governor danced with his trophy wife while police lined the perimeter of the dance floor. Mary looked around for Dalton, feeling the heat of so many people. She saw a child approaching her and scanned the crowd for an assassin; suddenly, the little girl with golden curls held up a balloon and popped it in her face. For just a moment, Mary felt panic and nearly displayed her weapon. The waltz continued.

That night, driving back to Pocatello, Dalton handed Mary the newspaper. There was a shot of her in full combat gear about to scale a cliff.

"That son of a bitch!"

"We'll ask for a transfer," Dalton said.

———

THEN IT WAS LATE AUGUST. It was the hottest summer ever recorded. Mars, closer than it had been since the Neanderthals, burned in the southeastern sky. Byron played in the back yard with Joan, spraying cold water on her and a neighborhood child as they splashed in a small inflatable pool. The two girls squealed in delight.

"Don't get burned out here," he said.

"We won't."

Judson came out into the back yard, and Byron put down the

hose. Joan wiped the water from her eyes and blinked.

"Byron, come inside for a minute."

"What's wrong, daddy?"

"Nothing, dear. I'll be right out."

Then they were standing in the kitchen where Judson and Byron could still see the children playing outside. Judson seemed out of breath, his eyes averted.

"Judson, what the hell happened?"

"The Swat Team was running some survival mission in the Arco Desert," he said. "One of their helicopters went down."

Byron felt something churn in his guts. Judson's voice sounded strange.

"It may have been hers. I saw it on the news. They have search planes out."

"That's a hard area to find anything in," said Byron, shaking.

"They might have a radio transmission."

Byron looked out the window at the playing children, remembering a recent article published about Mary's new life and Mary's new training after Mary's former work as a narcotics officer and a shoot-out in Montana. He remembered her angry voice on the phone:

"Jesus, Ragsdale gave away *everything* about me."

"You got plenty of guards," Byron had insisted.

"You don't understand," explained Mary. "In the witness protection program, people get new names, new identities. I haven't got that far, and this reporter practically gave them a map to my door!"

The girls were laughing. Byron turned to Judson.

"Was it an accident? Sabotage?"

"No one seems to know. Maybe it wasn't her chopper, and maybe she survived if it was."

"I better go."

Judson stopped him. "Go where? What are you going to do?"

"Help them look."

"Don't get in their way, Byron. There's nothing you can do they haven't already done, or tried to do."

Byron left the house and drove to Blackfoot, listening to the radio that was running bulletins on the search by police and FBI officials. A few citizens with small planes had volunteered to join in the desert surveillance. Byron drove to a small air field. Inside the hot office sat a fat man with long, dirty hair and a beard. He was reading a racing form.

"What can I do for you?"

"I want to rent a helicopter for the day."

"All of ours are out," he said. "They're looking for that narc who went down."

Byron blinked once; he stared at the fat man. "What narc?"

"They don't say, but one of them was a woman, so I guess it was that narc in the paper." He sat up. "You wanna join the search party, mister?"

"Yes."

"I could get Jason, out back, but he's probably afraid the feds will nab him."

The fat man laughed. Byron reached for his wallet.

"Tell Jason I got plenty of money."

Then they were flying over the Arco Desert, passing a sign from the fifties about the new "Nuclear Age" and Atomic City, now nearly a ghost town. They turned toward open volcanic plains with black rock formations, and a shotgun two-lane highway running through it. The pilot had snorted some cocaine before taking off, and wore a small spoon suspended from a necklace.

"I need a little lift," he barked. "I don't want to talk to no cops, that's for sure."

Byron sat by the open door. It was hard to hear once they got into the air. He saw the thin, unhealthy-looking pilot take a sniff from a bottle. He had bad teeth.

"What's that?"

"Amyl Nitrate," Jason said. "Gets you off real good. A short high." Jason spoke into his headset, then listened. "Looks like they found her," he said. "But the feds don't want no one flying close. That suits me just fine."

"Fly by them," Byron shouted. "Please."

Jason shook his head. "Okay, but they'll shoo us away," he said, taking the helicopter into a sudden turn.

Even from a distance, Byron could see the downed chopper had broken apart, its tail section one hundred yards from the burned cockpit. The police and federal agents had taped off the isolated area, and it looked alien in the middle of the desert. A police chopper flew close to them, and Jason began flying back.

"They're madder'n hell. We better git before they shoot our asses down."

"Tell them I knew Mary Goldstein, if that's who it is."

"Mary? I did some coke with a girl named Mary. Maybe *she* was a narc."

Jason spoke into his radio, and then took the chopper toward Blackfoot. Byron searched the forbidding desert below, trying to remember where the chopper had crashed. If it was Mary's chopper, no one could have survived. Then he heard Jason cursing.

"I'm glad you paid real good. They wanna see your ass at the airport. I gots to throw some of my drugs overboard, buddy. I ain't too happy about that."

"Sorry," Byron said.

The pilot dropped a small container out the window. They seemed to be floating in toward the small airport that didn't have a flight control tower. "Bad crash," shouted Jason. "What was you doin' hanging with a narc?"

"Old friends," said Byron. "Drugs have become a real problem, these days. We *need* narcotics agents."

He could see the disbelief and tension in Jason's face and gaunt body as they went into a hover pattern. As Byron stepped from the helicopter, he saw two men standing by a small airplane. One of the men wore a suit and a turtleneck tee-shirt; his hair was combed into a duck-tail. The other man was black with dreadlocks. Byron ran toward them.

"Hey, you! Stop!" Both men turned to face him. "What are you doin' here?"

Duck-tail said nothing, his eyes in shadow.

"Hey Mon," the black man said. "What is dis? You lost, Whitey?"

Byron cornered Duck-tail. "Mafia, right? You and him been dogging her, you pricks!"

Duck-tail smiled. "Listen to him. Mafia? See ya, my man."

He got on the idling plane; Byron took a step but Dreadlocks blocked him.

"Stay where you are, Motherfucker."

His accent had gone. When Byron tried to push past him, he saw the pistol.

"Stick that gun up your ass."

"Bro? This .45 will open yo ass right up. Turn around!"

Byron turned around. He felt the man's strong hands frisking him, and seconds later, he held the Walther PPK.

"You got a permit to carry this, Whitey?"

Byron didn't answer. He saw an unmarked car racing across the tarmac. The driver directed him inside the car.

"Who are you?"

"FBI," the driver said. "We'll need to ask some questions." The black man pushed him in the car, then slid in beside him

"Ask *me* questions?"

"That's right," the driver said.

"Whatever happened, this punk right here was part of it. I saw him snooping around."

The driver, wearing sunglasses, looked in the rear view mirror. "Hey, Rastus, you done been snoopin' around white folks?"

"No Mon," he drawled, exaggerating his Jamaican accent. "Me no like white folks. Me just get high all de time. Dig Bob Marley and good weed, Mon." The black man glared into Byron's eyes. "You nearly blew my cover, you fuck."

They drove to a small air conditioned office in Blackfoot, and walking inside, Byron felt a cold sweat coming over his face and body. An agent wiped Byron's hands with a thin wet cloth. A gaunt man in a tight suit motioned that he sit down; he examined what looked like a dossier.

"You say you knew our operative, Goldstein?"

"Of course. I knew Dalton, too."

"You *knew* Agent Dalton?"

"Yes. Don't you have my dossier?"

"*How* did you know Agent Dalton?"

"Because he knew Mary."

"How did *you* know *her*?"

"How do you *think* I knew her?"

An unseen man stood behind Byron. The black man's face was only inches from his. He didn't speak but grinned. The director asked another question: "Who do you work for?"

"The university."

"Who else?"

"No one else. What were you testing my hands for?"

"Why were you sleep—spending time with Agent Goldstein?"

"Because I loved her."

The director's eyes went dead suddenly. "I bet you did."

The black agent laughed. "Mon," he said, slipping into his fake accent. "I think de white boy was jealous and killed her. They'll luv him in da joint. He be fine punk ass, Mon."

"Better than your momma, Rastus?"

Before Rastus could respond, the gaunt man cut him off. The man with the towel left the room. "Your hands are negative for explosives, Mr. Duffy."

He glanced through a file. The bony man met his eyes for the first time and took out a recent photo of Mary and Dalton, both smiling at the camera. It looked like a snapshot taken in a restaurant. They seemed happy, together, and Byron felt a brief moment of jealousy.

"Can you identify those people in the photograph?"

"Of course."

"Tell us."

He told them. "Look, I worked with Mary."

"Okay. She *did* work undercover as an English instructor."

"What happened?"

The director looked past him and the room was silent.

"I'm sorry to report they were killed on a training mission," he said. "If you can tell us of anything strange or unusual…maybe an argument, a strange car. Anything."

Byron felt a constriction in his guts, a dryness in his mouth.

"They're both…dead?"

"Yes."

The director's voice had a softer tone. Byron took a deep breath, holding his sides.

"Foul play?"

"We cannot divulge that information."

"Do you need me for…for identification?"

"That won't be necessary. Tell us what *you* know."

"Why didn't you move her immediately when the article came out? This happened once before."

"Tell us what you know," the director repeated, his voice flat and cold.

When Byron had finished telling what little he knew, it all seemed so formal—distant, even, like details from a newspaper article. "Maybe you didn't take the Jamaican Connection seriously. Is that it? Huh?"

An agent grabbed him. "What do *you* know about the Jamaican Connection?"

"It was common knowledge in Montana. Why don't you ask Mr. Dreadlocks, here, and his girlfriend—the greaser with the duck-tail?"

"You're very impolite, Mon," Dreadlocks crooned, eyes closed. He puckered his lips obscenely. "Ouch."

The thin man motioned for the black agent to leave. "He's one of ours," he explained. "Now—do you know someone connected with the Jamaican gangs?"

"I only heard about Carl."

"*What* did you hear about Carl?"

"That he was a terrorist." Byron repeated the story of Mary's shoot-out. "But this is published news. What do you feds know about *them*?"

"I ask the questions! What did Agent Goldstein tell you?"

"She was afraid."

The bony director regarded him as though he were in a line up.

"I see. Afraid. She was also sloppy...*and* Dalton who should've known better."

For a long time, the emaciated man behind the desk said nothing.

"Don't you people want revenge? I do!"

"Mr. Duffy, don't leave the area for a while. We will question you again." He turned a page of another dossier and stopped. "You were involved in an altercation with some survivalists on the Fort Hall Reservation, weren't you?"

"Yes. An Indian ghost saved my ass."

"I heard it was an Indian ghost with a big gun." Byron felt the man's cold objective stare. "How's your protest novel coming?"

"I'm not writing a protest novel."

"Really? I thought you people were *always* writing a novel about how fucked up the government is."

"Who was the guy in the suit and duck-tail haircut?"

"No one to concern you. Tell me—do you know this man?"

Byron looked at a black and white photo of a fleshy man with a spotted complexion and thick dark hair.

"I think I saw him—yes—once at a bar in Lava Hot Springs."

"And the other time?"

"He had an English accent, and I was sitting outside at a bar listening to some live music. I spotted my psychiatrist—"

"And who is that?"

Byron gave him Dr. Lucy's name.

"—and she was crying and getting drunk. I guess she and her husband were separating. We were discussing divorce when this pudgy Englishman with a red nose came up to us and asked if we wanted some cocaine. I told him to bugger off."

"Did he ask questions about Mary Goldstein?"

Byron stared at the bony man now watching him intently.

"No. Why? Did they know each other? I know Mary had a problem with drugs but—"

The director took back the photo. "We had him under surveillance for drug trafficking, and then he fell off our radar."

"Was Mary his customer?"

The director folded his slender fingers. "Mary Goldstein was clean," he finally said.

"But they knew each other? Where did you shoot that photo?"

The director slipped the photo into his desk on top of another thick envelope. "Let's say, we tracked him to this area. That will be all, Mr. Duffy."

"Was he looking for Mary? Did he know *we* were connected?"

"Mr. Duffy—I ask the questions."

Byron leaned across the desk. "That Englishman was connected to the Jamaican terrorists, wasn't he? Is that why you brought Mary back here—as bait? You wanted to lure him back, and get his information?" The eyes remained opaque.

"Are you writing a spy-thriller, Mr. Duffy?"

"No." Byron stood up. "I know an excellent gym," he added.

For the first time, the bony director smiled.

"You know, we're not too fond of white supremacists and militia, either." He handed him the Walther. "Keep this in your trunk. Carrying a concealed weapon without a permit is a felony. Good-bye."

"Are you gonna arrest this creep?"

"Eventually. Take care, Mr. Duffy."

Later, Byron sat in his used Dodge at the Blackfoot airport, staring at the small airplanes landing and taking off. He did not want to believe they had found Mary through him. Then he drove to the Arco Desert, stopped at a point where he felt the chopper went down, and parked his car. Suddenly, he began to cry, hot air baking the car. When he recovered, he stepped out into the fierce late afternoon sun and walked into the desert, carrying a jug of water. He traveled a hundred yards and stopped. He could feel the throbbing heat on his face and head, his throat dry, the thermal waves wavering on the desert floor. Byron took a swallow of water, warm but refreshing.

Jesus Christ, he thought. *What am I doing here in this heat?*

He walked into a small canyon, feeling the oven effect from the black lava rocks, remembering a troupe of young people who got lost and died on a survival mission. Byron walked to a ridge, expecting to see the broken helicopter and investigating officers, but it was only the Arco Desert and black, jagged formations. The sun was going down, casting long shadows from the majestic but fierce rocks, still radiating heat. Byron took a long swallow from the plastic jug and shouted Mary's name into the shimmering desert.

"Mary! Mar-ry!"

His voice echoed along the black rocks and died in the desert. He called out again.

"Mar-ry!"

His eyes and nose and throat were dry. For a moment, he imagined Dalton holding her as the chopper blew apart and they went down. Perhaps it was a bomb that brought them out of the sky, and they had no chance to return fire. He turned toward the highway, knowing it would be dark, soon. Byron looked south, or what he thought was south, and didn't see the highway or the old white Dodge with its extra gallon of water in the trunk. He looked east and west, not really knowing direction until he remembered that the sun set in the west, but each time he looked, the long dark shadows only revealed a monotonous lunar landscape, with no white Dodge in the distance. He felt dizzy.

The car is south, he thought.

Byron began walking south, judging his direction from the last growth of sun, knowing the sharp cold would replace the now throbbing heat. He still carried the jug, and took another drink, realizing how foolish this might seem to an observer. Even if he found the wreckage, what was he trying to accomplish?

So their affair had truly ended, with all conversation stopped, all bridges smashed. He had never said a final pleasant good-bye. It was finished and he was trying to remember survival manuals and familiar names from the Arco: Cox's Well, Crystal Ice Caves, the buried treasure of a Minedoka bank robbery in another century.

"Congratulations," an inner voice was saying, "you have the honor of dying in a beautiful desert."

The blackness of night arrived quickly, so that the rocks resembled strange desert monsters; Byron marveled at the desert in the silver sheen of the moonlight. He felt the falling temperature along his bare arms. He should have reached the highway and car, by now. Byron had to control the same rising panic he felt the day of the bear hunt when he was lost.

If I am going in the wrong direction, I'll have farther to walk, tomorrow, he thought. *If I spend the night, I could freeze. If I am walking in the wrong direction with no water, tomorrow, I will die. The search party won't have much time, if they know I am even lost.*

Byron walked on, fearing he had begun walking in circles. He drank more of the water, realizing it was low. Then he stopped and listened for distant highway sounds, and searched the horizon for car lights. The crescent moon had risen in a black sky. He couldn't have walked that far from his car, yet he didn't see the highway and sign with President Eisenhower's quote about nuclear energy. Dark shapes loomed around him, and the rocky floor of the desert cut into his shoes. He found a huge rock with a small cave and sat down, staring at the scattered dark shapes in the moonlight. His mind was clear but he felt weak, and the cold cut into him. Shaking the jug, he had only a few swallows left.

Tomorrow, I will have to find shade and stay immobile, he thought. *Last it out. I don't dare move in the heat.*

With a grim sense of irony, Byron waited for his life to parade before him. Was it possible they took someone else from the fallen chopper?

"Mary was too alive to die!" he shouted into the dark silence of the desert. His voice echoed back at him. For an absurd moment, Byron imagined himself wrestling with Death, fighting to pull Mary from his black cold maw. He sat, staring at the surreal landscape, dead and still.

Then something moved.

Byron heard a lizard scurrying across the sand and over a rock. Then he saw the coyote watching him, the moonlight catching a highlight in its blond fur. The animal pulled back its ears and retreated. Byron felt sudden cold slide through his blood and along his skin. He had left the Walther in the car trunk.

Coyotes don't travel in packs and attack humans, he reasoned. *They are not like wolves.*

The coyote stood on a distant rock.

"Go ahead, you bastard, howl."

The coyote disappeared.

Byron walked on. He didn't care which way was south, he just wanted to walk all night and not think of death, walk until he crossed the highway, walk before the fatal heat of the day, when the temperature rose to 120 degrees. Once, he turned and looked back, but the coyote was not visible. Byron stopped and saw a dark patch on the side of his foot where he had cut himself. He had also lost the jug. The black sky was clear and bright with stars, and the moon cast faint light on the rugged terrain. After what seemed a long time, he found a smooth patch of sand and sat down, feeling sleepy. Byron thought he heard an ocean sound coming across the desert; maybe it was the highway. He stretched out on the desert floor and fell asleep. In a dream, he was flying above the gleaming golden towers of the Golden Gate Bridge, soaring high and dizzy above a shining San Francisco Bay.

Byron woke up, shivering with the cold, and a cloud covered the moon. He heard the scrape of animal feet, and looking up, saw the coyote. Byron sat up and screamed; the coyote bolted. He wanted to believe it was the same coyote, but turning, he saw two more watching him from a jagged rock. Byron took a few steps and stumbled. He heard music. Someone was singing Dylan's "Mr. Tambourine Man." He followed the strummed guitar and voice and saw Michael Wells standing on a black rock, singing as he did in the old days:

> *"Take me disappearing*
> *through the smoke rings of my mind*
> *down the foggy ruins of time*
> *far past the frozen leaves*
> *the haunted frightened trees*
> *out to the windy beach*
> *far from the twisted reach of crazy sorrow...*
>
> *Hey Mr. Tambourine Man, play a song for me...."*

Burning eyes bored into his and then the guitarist disappeared.

Oh God, he thought. There were no tears, only a dry retching and gagging.

Byron rolled over on his back, staring into the sky's black eternity winking with stars. The clouds had drifted on, the dead moon bright on his face. He felt small rocks digging into his back; Byron sat up, searching the shadowy desert landscape before him with a forced calm.

Who could wish me harm? he asked no one.

"You'd be surprised," whispered a soft female voice.

Byron should have been frightened, since he recognized Mary's voice, but he was not. He looked around. "Where are you?"

"Over here...beneath the red planet."

He saw a shape—faint—like a silver image in a twilight room. Her face glowed with a light breeze lifting her thick, curly hair, and she wore a jumpsuit, the kind used for training. Mars blazed above.

"Why did you come out here? Morbid curiosity?"

"Yes. I guess I refused to believe it."

"Silly boy. You're delirious, walking in circles. You've passed the highway twice and walked back out into the desert. By the time they search for you, you'll join us. Byron—it's not your time, yet."

"Was it *your* time?"

The apparition wavered in front of him, going in and out of focus. "No. But we chose dangerous professions."

"The last moment. What was it like?"

"Strange. I heard a kind of pop, saw we were going down and held Tom. He was silent. I was scared, then calm, even accepting. There was this sudden explosion of white light, and then nothingness. But I *did* think of you and here we are. It *is* kind of galling. I mean, years of life, left— and now *this*."

Though it was empty space, he felt her presence, still.

"This? What is *this*?"

After a moment, he heard the voice. "Death? I can't tell you. They may let me come back."

"*They*? Whom do you mean by 'They'?"

There was a long pause.

"We have to get you back to the highway. Follow me. Don't ask questions."

"I could die and join you, Mary."

There was another moment of silence, and then a gentle fluttering wind over the desert.

"Don't be ridiculous."

He started walking, following the light from her fading image. Somehow he could hear the Goldstein voice, always a little petulant even when happy.

"I loved life. Champagne brunch with bagels and lox. Sex in the morning. That first cup of coffee. I feel so free, now, but I miss being physical."

Byron asked what he considered an absurd question: "Is there a God?"

"I'm an agnostic, remember?"

He suddenly stumbled across the hard surface of something different: asphalt. In the morning light, a road sign advertised the country's first nuclear reactors and an atomic powered city that symbolized the future. Red light was spreading across the sky; desert plants and scrubs appeared. Byron looked for Mary in the harsh desert.

"Mary, if they found you through me, I'm sorry."

"Forget that. You're safe, now."

"Don't go."

His voice sounded off-key, and his throat and mouth felt dry and cracked.

"It's no good to stay. I *did* love you, Byron. I *will* miss you, but I'm fading. Good-bye, old friend. You'll know where to find me."

He could feel a breeze on his suddenly warm face. Her light dwindled as the sun rose, and the morning was hot when Byron saw the white Dodge and the parked Indian police car on the black road. Teton got out; another man, Officer Hayball, sat inside looking out the back window. Byron peered at the dark Indian face, and the white desert light suddenly engulfed him.

"They took her out," Byron murmured, then slid to his knees.

———————

HE WOKE UP, hearing many voices speaking from a distance. He was in a bright, too white room, lying on a hospital bed. A nurse watched him, her face pretty, her expression passive, professional.

"What happened?"

"After your little walk in the desert, Mr. Duffy? A little dehydration, some exposure, but you'll be all right. You were lucky you didn't get lost early in the day. It doesn't take long out there to die."

She brought him a tray of food, but he wasn't hungry. "Looking for the Minedoka treasure?"

"No."

He tried to explain to her about Mary. The nurse listened in silence, and when she had left, Byron lay back on the pillow. He looked around the room that resembled so many sterile hospital rooms. The phone rang and when he picked it up, it was the familiar voice of Ashley Roland.

"My God, how did you find me?"

"I called the English Department, and they knew about your little adventure. Boy, maybe I should write a screenplay about you, eh? Welcome back to the world, old friend."

"Thank you."

"The BBC rejected your short story for adaptation. It was too American."

"Of course—I'm a Yank."

"But they want to see more of your writing. Come visit," she said. "You'll like London."

"I saw Michael Wells playing his guitar in the desert." There was a long pause. "Ashley? You still there?"

"I contacted the last place he worked, the Washington Post. Byron—he died."

"Of what?"

"The obit said Hepatitis C. It can sit there undetected for a long time before it kills you."

"My God."

For just a moment, Byron saw Michael Wells staring at him across the table with a smug arrogance before pulling out another manuscript. Empty bottles filled the table. Old songs lingered in the air. They had heard the chimes at midnight and as artists, they would change the world before closing time.

"Sorry to tell you this, Byron, but I'm happy you're still alive."

"So am I."

"I have to go. Maybe we can work together. Keep in touch."

"I will."

Byron realized how glad he was to hear Ashley's voice, again. The nurse brought him the morning paper and he read of a shoot-out between the FBI and an Englishman named Neal Jones, a former FBI agent and suspected drug dealer funding terrorists. The stand-off ended when Jones shot himself; the FBI had recovered his laptop computer yielding vital information. Byron came to a brief passage and stopped. He read the passage a second time.

> *"Sources confirmed Neal Jones was present at the slaying of a Jamaican drug dealer by FBI agent, Mary Goldstein, recently killed through sabotage. Montana police subsequently released Jones who was wanted by the FBI until yesterday's confrontation in Arco."*

Byron tried to imagine the scene, the unstable drug-addicted Neal Jones, paranoid from cocaine but confronting the real enemy at last, tear gas filling the room, the pistol pressed to his temple. Did he have any last thoughts about Mary revealed as the enemy?

Byron tried to recall the brief conversation at the outdoor café, a rock band playing, his psychiatrist wiping her tears, the sickly bloated Neal Jones leaning close, offering cocaine. Byron had pushed him away.

"No cocaine, today—okay?"

"I say, it's a bloody good lift. Why not?"

"Bugger off."

The blobby face suddenly invaded his space. "Is this your new girlfriend?"

"No. She's not even an old girlfriend."

Neal had walked off, grinning. Had he been stalking Byron for information on Mary? Byron was still considering the possibilities when Judson entered the room, bringing Maureen.

"Boy, you inspire admiration," Maureen said. "What were you trying to do?"

"I can only imagine," Judson said when Byron said nothing.

"You won't believe me," Byron said.

Later, they walked on the grounds. The weather had cooled off, and there was a pleasant breeze through the trees.

"It was a plastic bomb," Judson explained. "Someone got on the training base and fixed it to her chopper. Who had *that* kind of intelligence is what I want to know?"

"There was that article by Ragsdale," said Maureen.

"They still had to break security."

"It was a set-up," Byron said. "Someone was paid off."

"And you know that how?"

"It doesn't matter. I think I saw her."

They stopped and listened as he told the story of the ghost in the desert.

"It might have been a hallucination. You *are* alive, that's all that matters."

Maureen was dressed in a conservative gray suit, her hair recently cut, and there was something hard and direct in her eyes.

"Maureen? You came just to see me?"

"No, Byron. I'm also in town to see about divorce proceedings."

Byron remained silent.

"We know all about divorce," Judson said.

BON VOYAGE

A WEEK LATER, BYRON SAT IN A CHURCH converted into a temporary synagogue. A lion of Judah was embroidered on a carpet laid out. Though he had never seriously thought of Mary as Jewish, Byron listened to the sonorous Hebrew of the rabbi's prayer. He stared at the flag draped coffin, trying to remember the living, vibrant woman he knew, and the spirit that had led him out of the desert when he was walking in circles.

The rabbi stood at the lectern:

"Jewish history tells the story of Masada, and the brave Israeli warriors who either died fighting or committed suicide rather than give up to the Romans. An old expression suggests that 'He who saves one life saves the world.'" He started to speak again but coughed. Then, after looking at the casket for reassurance, he continued his speech.

"Mary Goldstein was a warrior who instructed us how to live, and how to fight, like the ancient Israelis who fought the Romans. In those days, you died, people mourned. Nowadays, they can't *wait* to shovel you under and leave. You're forgotten. Well, we all know that Mary Goldstein will *not* be forgotten, because she saved lives. Not forgotten by you, not by me—not by us."

As the rabbi continued, Byron thought of his father's funeral and how he sat in the church, staring at the flag draped coffin, his ex wife by his side. It would be their last public appearance. Byron had never been close to his mother who had left him at an early age, and it was brutal to accept that he would never see his father again—a man who smoked and drank too much, lived not enough, and never realized his dreams. The Catholic ritual his father loved had been empty, and outside the church, Byron felt as though his life existed in a vacuum. *To what base measures we return*, he thought.

The rabbi's words brought him back: "We have with us, a fellow agent of the Bureau who has a few words of remembrance."

Ramon walked up to the lectern. "I remember Mary and I won't forget her," Ramon began in a strained off-key voice. "She died with her fellow officer…they died on the job."

Byron felt himself drifting away as Ramon spoke of courage and bravery under fire and protecting lives and falling victim to evil violence. He sat up when Ramon suddenly couldn't speak anymore and the rabbi helped him, sobbing now, to his seat. Byron should have noticed the older couple sitting across from him, the ruggedly build man in his late sixties with a white mustache and wearing a black suit. He was staring at the coffin, and at some signal, four men wearing yarmulkes walked to the front of the church, walking up the aisle toward the coffin. Byron realized they were Mary's brothers as the four men took up the casket and walked up the aisle, the man with the white mustache and slightly bagged eyes and the attractive older woman falling in behind the pall bearers, staring ahead, walking out of the church past the turning faces.

Ramon, other agents and mourners followed, passing through the door and disappearing outside. Elegant sad music broke over them as Byron moved down the aisle toward the bright patch of the open door, his face rigid as he walked, Judson falling beside him at some point. They walked out onto the steps. The red-haired reporter stood outside. Byron approached him, the small man backing away.

"Touch me, Mr. Duffy, I'll sue!"

"I am going to do *more* than touch you," Byron hissed. "Ragsdale, you son of a bitch! I'll blow your kneecaps off!"

He felt Ramon seize his arms, even as the small man from the local paper bolted down the stairs. "Freedom of the press," the reporter said.

"*Calmate, Señor.* Calm down. *Ese!*"

A moment later, Judson held him. "It won't do any good, Byron. She's gone."

He felt the blinding sun on his face, and saw Maureen, her eyes filled with compassion and concern. Dr. Lucy, beautiful in a new suit, found his eyes and nodded. Ragsdale adjusted his tie and observed from a distance.

"Her folks are here," declared Judson.

Byron saw the older woman, wearing an old-fashioned hat, veil and black dress, approaching him. The four men slid the coffin into the hearse, and the older man with the mustache turned to face Byron.

"Mary told us about you, Mr. Duffy," the woman said. "I'm Alice, her mother. My husband is Alfred. We are having a special service and want you and Mary's close friends to attend."

Byron tried to smile. "Of course."

Then they were sitting in a semi-circle, watching old home movies and recent police training videos. Byron felt he was reviewing someone else's history. Judson sat next to him, with Ramon to his left as the four brothers sat drinking spiked coffee; Mary's retired police father was respectful but didn't speak.

"You were her favorite, Mr. Duffy," whispered Alice. "She wanted to be cremated, and have some ashes turned over to a special friend."

Byron nodded politely. "I see."

"She never loved Detroit. She *did* love Idaho."

"I believe that," said Byron.

Ramon began talking about the Bureau and the Bureau's right to get even, discussing Mary and Dalton as though they were his sister and brother. Alfred Goldstein showed his old police revolver as he and Ramon drank and compared guns. It was only a matter of time before they would find a list on Neal Jones's computer and destroy them all, their drunken fantasies becoming incontrovertible realities as the afternoon progressed. Judson read a letter addressed to Mary's spirit:

"Goldstein, how can you do this to us? You promised me a date at Passover. It ain't fair!"

The rich humor of Judson's letter to the deceased only made Byron more aware of her absence, as did the Bureau training videos showing a vibrant woman going through dangerous exercises, crawling across smoky fields under live fire, only to be blown out of the sky by a person or persons unknown who broke Bureau security. She was gone, and with the fading dead afternoon, all of them felt her silent voice screaming out of a void.

"She was a federal agent," boasted her father, now drunk. "And a damn fine one. It took terrorists!"

"Right," said Ramon. "We will be revenged!"

Alice touched Byron with her old woman's soft hands.

"We will bury some ashes, and some will be given to you. It is something she wanted, if it happened. She said you would know the proper resting place."

"I don't know if I am capable of this," Byron said.

"I am sure you are, young man," insisted Alice. "It was you she trusted to carry out this sad task." Mary's mother smiled. "You'll always know where to find her."

Byron remembered the words uttered by Mary's spirit. Judson drank iced tea.

"We can do it together," he said.

Later that night, Byron and Judson sat in Buddy's, watching the many drinking and eating patrons who were unaware that something had irrevocably changed their lives. The sameness and lack of surprise at Buddy's suddenly became oppressive.

"Judson?

"Yeah?"

Byron took a sip of his beer.

"I just can't imagine holding an urn of Mary's ashes, knowing what the living, breathing person was like. We fought a lot, and God knows, we were so different, but I *did* love her, and why am I chosen to dispose of her remains?"

Judson finished a soft drink; his face reflected a personal understanding.

"The final place itself could be sacred ground, if you will. Mary knew that, and her mother, Alice, knows that. It's part of the healing process."

"Healing process?"

"Correct."

"Please don't use that awful word—'closure'."

"I won't."

"America has made a lot of enemies," a female voice said. Byron felt light fingers touching his wrist. He turned and saw Debbi Blackstone. "You're suffering, but I think we *all* have to suffer," she continued. When he made no response, Debbi said, "Everyone in the world hates us! Maybe we *deserve* to get blown out of the sky."

Byron met her eyes, holding something mischievous and cunning.

"We?"

"Some of us."

"Are you saying they deserved to die?"

"Dalton chose that life."

"I see. And Mary? *She* deserved to die?"

"I didn't say that."

"Just what *are* you saying, then?"

"America is guilty of a lot of crimes—particularly against Muslims."

"Maybe so. Are we sure Muslims did this?"

"No."

"If the Islamic terrorists take over, you'll be the first one they shoot."

"Oh my, the old bourgeois party line. Byron—I thought you were a little more visionary than that. Don't tell me *you're* a reactionary."

Byron broke eye contact, finding himself unable to answer without throwing a punch. Two men argued at the bar. Debbi was about to speak again but Judson gently shook his head.

"Condolences on your loss," Debbi finally said.

Byron heard her walk away. On a television screen, a muscular ballplayer hit a home run. No one cheered. For the first time, Byron noticed the new paintings on Buddy's dining room wall. It was a crude depiction of 19th century Italy with soldiers and patrons drinking wine at outdoor cafes. Another drawing showed what seemed to be the Spanish Stairs in Rome. Judson had followed his gaze.

"Local art. Next will be the Sistine Chapel by Seers."

Byron began laughing and Judson joined him; other patrons turned to stare. The laughter was a good release.

"Actually, I *do* like the Spanish Stairs," Byron said. "Some day I have to visit the Keats-Shelley House."

They finished the meal. While walking toward his car, Byron saw Dr. Lucy pulling into a parking space. Smiling, she got out and shook his hand.

"You're okay?"

"I think so."

"If things get a bit rough, see me or I can make a referral."

"I'll let you know." Dr. Lucy looked more relaxed and informal, a warmth unlocked in her eyes. "How are *you* doing?"

"We have both agreed to an amicable separation. I'm amazed how often I discover that one can be in love with a person you may not even like. We have no children." The street light caught highlights in her porcelain skin and blonde hair. "The judge gave him the dog, however."

"This seems to be the season of divorce," Byron said.

"I'm meeting a friend for some girl talk, something you macho men never understand—emotional connections—but let's stay in touch, Byron."

"I will."

Byron had lost touch with a number of friends; others might fade. Ashley Roland was in London. Michael Wells had died young. Suzi remained silent though Becky had sent an article attacking the Royal Shakespeare Company as retrograde and old fashioned. It had made her the focus of a hot artistic debate in Los Angeles. There was no mention of Ted. Had he failed pursuing his artistic dreams; had therapy failed him?

It was a late afternoon two days later when Maureen came by and they rode her jeep to the Fort Hall river bottoms. She was planning to start a new life with a job in the city. "You hear about Ragsdale?"

"No. He's writing another expose?"

"Not for a while. Seems he woke up with some weird disease they haven't diagnosed yet."

"God, did Edmo's curse actually work? His dick fell off?"

"Ragsdale's paralyzed, and went deaf and blind."

"Close but no cigar," Byron said.

They drove on until they found a meadow near the Fort Hall Monument. Beyond the meadow was the now fenced pool of quicksand surrounded by gnarled stunted trees. Buffalo grazed in the distance. An old smoking truck passed them on the road. They walked along a white narrow path through tall grass, heading toward the river; on a distant small hill, Byron saw three Indians on horseback, Teton and his two deputies, Hayball and Edmo. Teton lifted his rifle as a salute and rode off, followed by Hayball. Edmo sat on his horse, watching them. It was too far way to read his expression, but there was something sad and forlorn about the image of the lone Indian horseman. Byron thought of ancient hunters enacting a timeless ritual long before he existed, and for a moment, he could see mounted Indians chasing galloping herds of buffalo across a summer prairie, still lush and green. Spirits of the Indian dead still haunted the reservation, and listening, they heard the voice of the Snake River running through valleys and meadows. Would the grass and wild flowers and river contain Mary's spirit?

Then Byron held the canister that looked nothing like the brass urns he remembered from films, and prepared to scatter the remaining ashes. Judson met him at this same meadow where Byron and Mary had made love, one lost day. Byron and Judson would soon go their separate ways, Judson married and working in a bank, a new wife challenging old drinking friends who still navigated the river and came by to visit. One afternoon, he would visit Judson as he reviewed a client's loan, looking up to nod at Byron standing by the desk, and Byron would see the professional loan officer in a three-piece suit and remember the rugged man thrusting an oar toward him while the river God fought to claim another victim.

Today, they had this final chore.

Darlene and Carol drove up to attend the ceremony; they both glowed with happiness and love. Opening the tin container, Byron scattered white ashes over the new grass while Judson read from Keats's *Ode to a Nightingale*, his rich voice resonating with the melodic vowels:

> *"'Adieu! Adieu! thy plaintive anthem fades*
> *Past the near meadows, over the still stream*
> *Up the hill-side; and now 'tis buried deep*
> *In the next valley glades:*
> *Was it a vision, or a waking dream?*
> *Fled is that music: - Do I wake or sleep?'"*

It felt complete to scatter all that remained of Mary Goldstein over a field that once held magic. Hidden birds sang and called in the trees and brush. In his imagination, Byron conjured her spirit. Then he walked across the near meadow to the bank of the Snake River and tossed out the urn; the silver-colored canister bobbed for a moment, gleaming on the moving current, then sank beneath the bright surface and was gone.

Acknowledgements:

This is a work of fiction. Any resemblance to persons living or dead is purely coincidental.

I have to point out that Edmo and Hayball are very common names on the Fort Hall Reservation, like Smith and Jones for Caucasians.

I must thank James R. Dean for a day at the shooting range, learning about firearms.

In addition to the lines quoted from Beckett, Rilke and Keats, other writers have indirectly inspired scenes in this book. I recommend the late Bruce Embree's book of poems, *All Mine*, and Greg Keeler's book about Richard Brautigan in Montana called *Waltzing with the Captain*.

Laurel Johnson was enthusiastic about revising and finishing this book.

Any major mistakes are mine

Printed in the United States
40968LVS00006B/27

9 781589 397637